PRIVATEER!

BUILDING A BUSINESS · REFORMING GOVERNMENT

MAXIMUS Revenues

$600 Million

$500 Million

$400 Million

$300 Million

$200 Million

$100 Million

DAVID V. MASTRAN

Founder, MAXIMUS, Inc.

Dedication

I am dedicating this book to my father, Col. Joseph
L. Mastran, and to my uncle, John L. Mastran, for the
inspiration and guidance given to me throughout my life.
Without them, the events described herein could
never have happened.

*To Emily
Keep Going
Dan Mastran*

ACKNOWLEDGMENTS

Now I know why the Acknowledgments section of a book is always so long. I have many, many people to thank.

Fred Laughlin, my good friend and West Point classmate, kept telling me to keep going. He reviewed the drafts and gave many excellent suggestions. My cousin-in-law, Dick Paterson, a former government executive in the Forest Service, also read the entire draft and made comments that were very helpful. Steve Gilreath who works for me at QuaverMusic.com gave some very thoughtful and helpful comments, which I have tried to incorporate. And Dan and Arleen Cox, our friends in Idaho, provided needed encouragement.

Larry Wright, another friend from Great Falls, was kind to review several chapters for me. He helped me see the forest for the trees. Rachael Rowland, former head of Public Relations at MAXIMUS, helped me cast the right tone for the book. Jack Svahn gave valuable comments and reminded me of some things I had forgotten. And Jack Tidwell, my friend since the ninth grade, also helped with great comments and continued support. Peter McCann, my cowriter on many songs in Nashville, was also encouraging.

Kristin Clark Taylor, a former White House speechwriter in the Bush Administration, accomplished author, and friend of Donna helped me immensely. She told me to reveal more of myself in the book, and I have done so. She gave very specific advice that I followed.

I also have to mention Graham Hepburn, otherwise known as Quaver, my young partner in Quaver's Marvelous World of Music. In trying to develop Graham into a better manager, I continually told him about the management lessons I learned at MAXIMUS. He loved the stories and always encouraged me to tell him more. He was the impetus for the book. I finally told him I was going to write down these lessons so I would not have to keep interrupting our work to tell him another story. He and Jeremy Ruff, also at Quaver's Marvelous World of Music, can still learn about management when I'm away.

Last but not least, I have to thank my family for encouraging me. My wife, Donna Mastran, was indefatigable in her support. She was the heart of MAXIMUS and helped me remember many of the incidents related in the book. My brother, Joe Mastran, loved the book so much he said I should charge $20,000 a copy. How could I not keep working on it? My son, David B. Mastran, said he thought the book was really good and kept making me answer the question why was it being written. Praise from him is the greatest praise of all.

In closing, I have tried my best to be accurate in recalling the events in this book. If there are any errors, they are solely my fault.

PROLOGUE

Sitting there in the hearing room at the State Capitol in Sacramento, California, I remembered my plebe year at West Point when I had three upper classmen surrounding me. One was screaming instructions in my left ear, while another was screaming in my right. The third was in my face barking out questions I had to answer. I felt like the world was in chaos. But the experience repeated many times over taught me how to focus in a crisis.

The situation wasn't as bad this time—twenty-seven years later—but the stakes were much higher. The purpose of the hearing was to cancel a major, ground-breaking contract awarded to MAXIMUS, the company I founded. We had won the first contract in the United States to privatize a social welfare program, the Los Angeles County, Greater Avenues for Independence (GAIN) Program. As a result, some 175 jobs that otherwise would have gone to unionized county employees were going, instead, to the private sector.

There were two California state senators sitting at a table in the front of the hearing room, and two very serious uniformed officers sitting on either side of me in the witness chair. They thought I was a flight risk. I had been subpoenaed to appear before the Senate Committee on Budget and Fiscal Review. I was told I was the first person subpoenaed by the Senate in over ten years. What did I do? They didn't have to subpoena me. I would have gladly come of my own free will.

I guessed there were about three hundred people already seated in the gallery behind me, all paying full attention. I was really scared, but calm and focused. This would come to be the highlight of one the first major battles in the war on privatization of social welfare programs—a war I had just begun to sense I was in.

Senator Bill Greene and Senator John Garamendi (later to become California Insurance Commissioner) were present. I understood that the Los Angeles County Board of Supervisors and the Head of the Department of Public Social Services were all listening on a squawk box from Los Angeles. This was a very big deal! I was to be the star at a public execution—in the spirit of *A Tale of Two Cities* and Madame DeFarge knitting with the guillotine nearby.

Senator Greene questioned me angrily about the Los Angeles GAIN program, our qualifications, how we won the contract, and anything and everything that he could muster. He challenged me on everything I said, no matter how trivial. Again, memories of West Point. He wanted to discredit the procurement process, MAXIMUS, and me. He kept digging for anything he could find.

He bellowed in his deep, African-American baritone voice, "Why do you call yourself California MAXIMUS here in California and MAXIMUS everywhere else?" I explained that the name MAXIMUS was already taken in California, and the clerk at the Secretary of State's Office suggested we use the name California MAXIMUS. She said that we could still use our regular name and normal letterhead. Senator Greene then said, "I cannot understand how you could let a lowly clerk in the Secretary of State's Office name your company. I would never do that." I knew better than to respond, and we moved on.

Later, I found out Senator Greene had a notorious reputation for intimidating witnesses. Many witnesses had broken down and cried before him. He was brutal and highly energetic. He was also alleged to have had an addiction, but he was clear-headed that day and had extensive notes from which he interrogated me.

The hearing went on—just he and I—hour after hour—with no breaks. Senator Garamendi had excused himself after about an hour. Senator Greene asked how much time I spent in Virginia, which was our corporate headquarters. I said I was in Los Angeles to see the project through, but that I was still based in Virginia. Then in his booming voice, he commented that Machiavelli had said, "A prince cannot rule from afar. How can you?" I bit my tongue rather than tell him about telephones and FedEx—no Internet then. It was so tempting. Thank you, West Point upperclassmen.

One interchange worth noting happened when I was establishing the credentials of MAXIMUS to perform the Los Angeles GAIN contract. I explained that MAXIMUS had developed the National Integrated Quality Control System for Welfare, Medicaid, and Food Stamps. This was a nationwide system involving coordination by three federal agencies to reduce fraud and abuse. I said that California was using our system to manage fraud and abuse in its programs. Senator Greene interrupted me, saying he had never heard of the system. He stated that he was in charge of approving all such systems in California, and he had never heard of MAXIMUS. He reminded me that I was still under oath.

Suddenly, without invitation, this fellow, Dennis Boyle, comes out of the gallery, walks up to the front of the hearing room, and hands Senator Greene his business card. He said he was head of the California Department of Quality Control and that no such MAXIMUS system was being used. The gallery murmured. Is he finally cornered? Is he perjuring himself?

I was very surprised, but didn't panic. Why? Federal regulations mandated that every state use our system. If California didn't use it, they were out of compliance with federal regulations. Having to respond, I said, "Senator, Mr. Boyle is wrong, and I am willing to bet you on the side that he is." Senator Greene paused for about a minute not knowing what to do, and then went on to the next subject.

I wish I had said, "Senator, please put Mr. Boyle under oath and ask him the same question you just asked me." Later, I would prove to be right.

California was using our system but as an interface to its system. In fact, Dennis Boyle later apologized to me in writing for being wrong.

After four nonstop hours, everyone in the gallery was restless and tired, and they could all see the hearing was coming to a close, with no head rolling on the ground that day. I told the Senator I had no hard feelings about his tough questions—he was just doing his job. Then he gaveled the hearing closed.

Because there had been no breaks, I had to relieve myself urgently. When I was dismissed, I raced to the men's room down the hall and stood in front of the urinal. When I looked up, who should be standing next to me but Senator Greene. So I said to him, "I guess this is our second pissing contest of the day—eh, Senator?" He laughed.

When we went outside, we exchanged pleasantries, and he promised to come to Los Angeles to visit the project. Within a month, he was in our Figueroa office and became one of our ardent supporters, much to the dismay of the unions and his liberal colleagues.

TABLE OF CONTENTS

PART I: INTRODUCTION AND OVERVIEW

PART II: BUILDING THE FOUNDATION

PART III: CORE COMPETENCIES

PART IV: SOCIAL WELFARE PROGRAMS

PART V: MANAGING RAPID GROWTH

PART VI: COMPLICATIONS

PART VII: CONCLUSIONS

PREFACE

A *privateer* is traditionally defined as a mercenary commissioned by the government to attack enemy shipping. In this book, privateer is redefined as a person who privatizes government programs, replacing government employees with private-sector employees. I was called a privateer by the government employee unions as a slur. As Chief Executive Officer of MAXIMUS, a firm specializing in privatization, I came to regard the name positively—someone who helps government do a better job for the people.

Nonprofit organizations have traditionally provided a wide range of social welfare services under contract to the government, as have for-profit companies. These private sector organizations were contracting for services, not privatizing government programs. MAXIMUS was the first company in the United States to privatize a social welfare program. This happened in 1988 in Los Angeles County, California, with the GAIN Program, a state-funded, welfare-to-work program.

Today, MAXIMUS has evolved into the largest social welfare privatization firm in the United States, and possibly the world. How did it happen? I was a person with no business experience, no influence, no partners, and only $12,000 in capital. The journey on which you are about to embark seems impossible.

The story begins in 1973, when I was appointed Director of R&D programs in the Social and Rehabilitation Service (SRS) in the Department of Health, Education, and Welfare. I was filling a GS-17 position, equivalent to a major general in the military. SRS oversaw the major poverty programs of the United States, to include welfare cash grants, health care, social services, and rehabilitation services for the disabled. These social welfare programs consume hundreds of billions of dollars in the federal budget and are the largest line items in state budgets. Medicaid alone costs over $350 billion per year!

During my tenure, I observed huge inefficiencies in how poverty programs were being administered by the government. Over time, I became more and more resolved to do something about it. Since I faced huge obstacles trying to reform these programs inside government, I left government to try to reform these programs in the private sector. I didn't have the qualifications or resources, but I was determined to try.

This book is about my experience as the first person from the private sector to privatize these social welfare programs—the first Privateer. Under me as CEO, MAXIMUS broke the barrier on programs traditionally managed exclusively by government employees. The result was far more efficient and compassionate services to the program recipients and far greater job satisfaction for staff providing the services.

Specifically, MAXIMUS was the first company to privatize the administration of welfare-to-work programs in 1988. We privatized the Child Support Enforcement Program in 1992 and the Welfare (or TANF) program in 1997. MAXIMUS was among the first companies to privatize the administration of Medicaid Managed Care programs in 1995 and the State Child Health Insurance Program in 2000. We eventually managed far more of these programs than any other company. Federal law, for political reasons, still prohibits privatization of eligibility determination in Medicaid and Food Stamps, two key poverty programs. But we pretty much privatized everything else.

For twenty-nine years while I was CEO, MAXIMUS revenues grew at the astonishing average rate of 36.5 percent per year. *This growth was achieved without ever going into debt. MAXIMUS was profitable every year for twenty-nine years—never a loss.* I was the only employee in the beginning; when I retired, there were over 5,500. Today there are almost 9,000.

MAXIMUS achieved stellar success against "impossible odds," both as an agent of government reform and as a for-profit public corporation. Government unions fought MAXIMUS ferociously to stop privatization. Ironically, we became a major financial success because we were obsessively focused on helping government, not on making money.

MAXIMUS was listed on the New York Stock Exchange (Symbol: MMS) on June 13, 1997. In the subsequent seven years until my retirement, Forbes and Business Week magazines repeatedly recognized MAXIMUS as one of the top one hundred growth companies in the United States. MAXIMUS market capitalization reached $1 billion during my tenure and more recently stood at $1.9 billion

Privateer! is the untold story of MAXIMUS. It is not the entire story of the company or its people, nor the complete history of privatization of social welfare programs in the United States. The book is about what I learned and experienced during my tenure that should be useful to others building a company or reforming government.

The book is replete with nontextbook solutions to many problems encountered in managing a growing business. It describes the extreme difficulties of challenging the status quo as a change agent in government and what to expect on the journey. I hope that it also sets the record straight on what really happened in the privatization of government entitlement programs in the United States. The record needs to be straightened.

In the chapters that follow, you will experience how a small company, MAXIMUS, grew to become a very large company. You will understand the flexibility I had as CEO in building MAXIMUS, as opposed to what I would have been able to do in government. You will see how MAXIMUS helped government in areas where government could not really help itself.

Hard evidence is presented that proves the private sector can truly help government overcome its inherent limitations in managing entitlement programs. You will see why government becomes much more responsive and more compassionate to people in need when the private sector is employed.

The lessons in the book apply to audiences with a wide variety of interests and perspectives. At a minimum, the following should find it very helpful:

- **Citizens Concerned about Government** – Citizens from all walks of life, both Republicans and Democrats, can learn about social welfare entitlement programs—how they work, what the program recipients are like, and what can be done to improve the programs. All can appreciate the extreme difficulties and barriers to changing these programs and the effort required to be successful.

- **Government Officials and Legislators** – The book explains in detail many of the inherent limitations of government and how to use the private sector to make government more efficient and effective. Proven guidelines are provided to help government make better contract decisions and ensure successful privatization efforts in social welfare programs.

- **Executives Managing a Business** – The book also provides a step-by-step blueprint for developing and managing a successful, growing company. The lessons begin before the company is even formed and continue all the way to being listed on the New York Stock Exchange and beyond.

- **Business Schools and Schools of Public Administration** – The story of MAXIMUS represents a major case study with real-life business problems and real-life solutions that worked. No theory here. Students can learn how to "think outside of the box," solve problems in managing people, develop winning business strategies, overcome stall points on the growth curve, and work within a hostile, competitive environment.

- **MAXIMUS Employees and Competitors** – Last but not least, the employees of MAXIMUS and its competitors can learn about the history and traditions of MAXIMUS. They will see, again, what made the company successful, so they can carry on those traditions with conviction and pride.

So what are we waiting for? Let's get started.

PART I:
INTRODUCTION AND OVERVIEW

The raison d'être for MAXIMUS is helping government do a better job. The first three chapters set the tone for the book by explaining why government needs help. The next three explain how I became involved in social welfare programs and the role MAXIMUS ultimately played.

CHAPTER 1

GOVERNMENT DECISION-MAKING

There are many very smart and very dedicated people in government. They exist at all levels of state, county, and city government as well as the federal government. The government doesn't need help because its people aren't smart or dedicated. The government needs help because of the constraints under which these people operate.

MAXIMUS staff never claimed to be smarter or more dedicated than those in government. Most of us came from government. Because we had far fewer constraints, we could do a better job serving the public.

This chapter provides examples of the inherent limitations of government in managing social welfare entitlement programs as well as the inherent flexibility the private sector adds to manage these programs more efficiently and effectively. *When government and the private sector work together, government is better.*

Purpose of Government

Let's go back to the beginning. The Framers of the Constitution summarized the purpose of government in the Preamble:

> We the People of the United States, in Order to form a more perfect Union, establish Justice, insure domestic Tranquility, provide for the common defense, *promote the general Welfare* [emphasis added], and secure the Blessings of Liberty to ourselves and our Posterity, do ordain and establish this Constitution for the United States of America.

Promote the general Welfare! That clause turned out to be much more significant than the Framers originally envisioned. General welfare, to be sure, encompasses social welfare, which is now a pervasive function in government. A major aim of this book is to examine this purpose of government and the limitations government faces in achieving that purpose.

Nothing polarizes politics like social welfare entitlement programs. Nothing in government costs more than these entitlement programs. Medicare and Social Security alone accounted for $1.24 trillion of the US Budget in 2010. Some 43.8 million people received Old Age and Survivors Insurance benefits, 10.2 million received Disability Insurance benefits, and 47.5 million were covered under Medicare, the health care program for the aged.

Programs for the poor and disadvantaged are even more controversial. Medicaid and the State Child Health Insurance Program, both health care programs for the poor, cost another $350 billion! The Food Stamp Program, with 40 million recipients, costs $60 billion. And then there are the core welfare and social services programs. These include TANF (Temporary Assistance to Needy Families), the Child Support Enforcement Program, Foster Care, Adult Protective Services, and many more. And don't forget Section 8 Housing Assistance and Unemployment Insurance.

I suspect most readers have not yet been on the receiving end of these government entitlement programs. You likely haven't applied for

Unemployment Insurance or even received food stamps. So you probably don't know fully what people in these programs experience.

But you must have been involved with the federal, state, and local governments for other reasons—driver's license, passport, building permit, post office, Amtrak? Was the government efficient? Were you a happy customer? Would you have changed anything? Whatever you experienced with the services you received, those unfortunates relying on programs for the poor and disadvantaged experienced far worse.

The key question addressed in this book is whether the government is the best choice for providing public services—specifically, for social welfare entitlement programs. Can the private sector do a better job and help government become more responsive to people in need and also be less costly? I know it can, and I promise to explain why and how.

Politically-Correct Decisions

The political decision-making process differs from the decision-making process found in the private sector. Political decisions need not follow economic principles, but instead must follow "politically-correct" principles. These decisions appeal to voters. Politicians do what's required to be reelected, even if it's building a bridge to nowhere. Politics is largely about discretionary power and the use of influence to enrich one segment of the population at the expense of another—subject, of course, to the law. Private sector decision-making is about keeping revenues and costs in proper balance.

Adding to the controversy and complexity of entitlement programs is that federal and state legislation grant elected officials the power to change the eligibility requirements and benefits of these programs. The officials can decide who receives the benefits and how these programs are administered, including whether or not they are privatized. So the whole process is politicized.

The big problem we are facing in this country is the struggle between cutting the deficit and continuing to fund these entitlement programs at their current levels, or even adding more entitlement programs. At the very least, these programs can be far more efficiently managed.

In the private sector, a company has to do what is economically sound to survive. Creative destruction is a basic tenet of capitalism—if a company doesn't make economically sound decisions, it is "destroyed," or goes bankrupt. If it can't operate efficiently at a competitive cost, it will go out of business. To be efficient like the private sector, the government needs to make decisions based on economic principles—which it cannot always do.

A Turning Point in My Life

The following story from my personal experience shows one example of how government makes politically-correct decisions rather than economically-sound decisions. I relate the incident since it was the prime reason I chose to transfer to the Social and Rehabilitative Service from the Department of Defense. The story affirms something you already suspected—that noneconomic decision-making in government is not limited to social welfare entitlement programs.

Before MAXIMUS, I worked in the Pentagon in the old Whiz Kids group, created by Robert McNamara. My boss at the time asked me to conduct a detailed analysis of the costs and benefits of procuring a heavy-lift helicopter for the US Marine Corps. I was tasked with comparing the proposed CH-53E Super Stallion against alternative existing helicopter choices. Despite my repeated attempts, I could find no way to justify the procurement of the heavy-lift helicopters, even if they were lifting pure gold! Other choices were far more cost effective.

My boss briefed William P. Clements, Jr.—the number two person in the Pentagon and a political appointee—on the study methodology and its conclusions. Basically, there was no way to justify the procurement on economic principles since other options existed at far less cost to satisfy the Marines' mission requirement. It was clear, however, the Deputy Secretary of Defense intended to approve the procurement anyway.

After the briefing, he said to my boss, "Son, the only thing you have on your side are the facts." He was right. That's all we had, and all I would ever have. The Marines bought the helicopter anyway because they wanted it. The decision was the trigger that started me looking for another job outside the Department of Defense. Little did I know, I would be jumping from the frying pan into the fire. Decision-making in entitlement programs was even more politically driven.

I observed state and local politicians, under threat by government unions, take action to deprivatize well-run programs. This happened even though the agency secretaries and financial analysts strongly recommended that privatization continue. The private firm had proven to be far more cost effective than government employees doing the job. But the politics weren't right, and so the recommendation to continue privatization was turned down—economically unsound, perhaps, but politically correct.

Politically-correct decisions help make government both inefficient and ineffective. These decisions are not made just at higher levels of government, but also at lower levels. Well-meaning bureaucrats make politically-correct decisions up and down the line. To the extent lower level decisions are outsourced to the private sector, the decisions are made on economic terms, and the government is more efficient.

For example, the private sector can hire the number of employees it really needs for a job. This assumes the unions haven't gotten a stranglehold on a company, like they did with the automakers in Detroit. In response to fluctuating demand for government services, the private sector can hire and lay off employees more quickly than the government. The private sector can also implement systems to improve efficiency more quickly. The private firm does not have to go through a lengthy and burdensome procurement process to upgrade an old system or acquire a new one.

The private sector can also invest millions of dollars to make a program more efficient without waiting years for a budget to be approved by the legislature. In short, the private sector has much more flexibility than the government and has the primary goal of being efficient and effective in serving its customers. *So being efficient and effective in the private sector is the means to survival, just as making politically-correct decisions is the means to survival in the public sector.*

Therefore, when a program is outsourced or privatized, the private sector will be making economic decisions as opposed to politically-correct decisions. This may not make the totality of government more efficient and effective, but it will have a significant impact, especially if the privatization occurs at the service delivery level.

The paradox is even if government could make economically-sound decisions at the service delivery level, it would still need the private sector to operate more efficiently. In the next chapter, I explain why.

CHAPTER 2

INHERENT INEFFICIENCY OF GOVERNMENT

Making politically-correct decisions instead of economically-sound decisions is not the only problem with government. There are also inherent limitations in government that are necessary to govern properly. In this chapter, I explain why government is necessarily, inherently inefficient.

Deliberative Decision-Making

Our government abhors a single decision maker like nature abhors a vacuum. (This likely stems from the king's absolute power in prerevolutionary times.) There is just too much power to wield in government, so decision-making is slow and deliberative. Few in government can take unilateral action, except perhaps for judges and chief executives. All the rest are constrained—especially mid-level managers and front-line employees.

I would frequently tell MAXIMUS staff that most bureaucrats can say "No," but very few can say, "Yes." Most bureaucrats don't have the authority to say "Yes," and are encouraged not to take chances. "The answer is No; what's the question?" Significant "Yes" decisions, or decisions that commit the government to action, have to be reviewed and often re-reviewed. Like Diogenes looking for an honest man with lamp in hand, MAXIMUS staff were always searching for the bureaucrat who could say, "Yes."

Committees make decisions; votes are taken to choose a course of action; and legislative oversight is imposed to guide and then second-guess the Executive Branch. All state legislatures except Nebraska's are bicameral, further clogging the legislative process. Consensus is required. The result is red tape and slow decision-making. No one said democracy was efficient.

Because of accountability to the public, government has to be careful. A well-advertised ninety-day comment period is required before issuing a federal regulation. Anyone interested can make a comment, and the government has to respond. *So government is slow and deliberative because it has to be.* But with that requirement, comes the cost of inefficiency.

Government Pay Scales

Noncompetitive pay scales are another drag on government efficiency. From my experience, government compensation policies suffer from two problems. First, government cannot pay enough to attract and retain the very best managers. Pay scales are fairly rigid in government and capped. Even the President of the United States makes only $400,000 per year, far less than many private CEOs. There are very good managers in government, but they don't stay very long.

Recently, more options became available in government for advancing a person in pay grade for outstanding performance. However, the pay increments are small and the rate of advancement limited. For this reason, exceptional performers tend to migrate toward the private sector. I hired many government superstars myself and gladly doubled their government salaries because they were worth it.

On a seemingly contradictory note, the average mid- and lower-level government employees are well-compensated relative to their peers in the private sector. Survey after survey shows this to be true. One reason for the higher compensation is the overly generous fringe benefit and pension plans. These plans are creating huge liabilities far into the future and promise to bankrupt many state and local governments. The recent actions by Scott Walker, Governor of Wisconsin, highlight the problem of overpaying public employees.

Although the private sector pays more for higher-level employees, it pays proportionately less for mid- and lower-level employees, and less overall.

Difficulty in Terminating Poor Performers

More important than any other reason, the government is less efficient because it's very difficult to take an "Adverse Action" against a nonperforming government employee. This is not the case in the private sector.

An Adverse Action in government is an action that disciplines or actually terminates an employee. Unfortunately, in many agencies providing public services, significant numbers of government employees are not performing. This problem is critical in social welfare programs because there are large numbers of lower paid workers in these programs. At last count, for example, the Social Security Administration had 62,000 employees administering its retirement and disability programs.

The personnel system in government has been bureaucratized to the ultimate degree. To demonstrate the extent, let's review the process of taking an Adverse Action against a federal government employee. Many state, county, and city personnel practices mirror federal practices, so the process is often similar in design.

The Civil Service Reform Act of 1978 created three independent federal agencies to oversee personnel practices in the federal government. The

Office of Personnel Management manages the federal work force; the Federal Labor Relations Authority oversees federal labor-management relations; and the Merit System Protection Board protects the merit systems and the rights of individuals within those systems. In addition, the Equal Employment Opportunity Commission protects employees against discrimination of any kind.

Most federal agencies are authorized under civil service regulations "to suspend, demote, furlough (place on unpaid leave), or remove employees" for "such cause as will promote the efficiency of the service." This is very good, since employees can be disciplined or terminated.

Adverse Actions can be taken for "misconduct, unacceptable performance, or a combination of both." Adverse Actions can also be based upon nondisciplinary reasons, such as medical inability to perform. So far so good—there is a way to terminate nonperformers in government!

OK—let's say we want to terminate an employee, Edgar Smith, because he is a malcontent and should never have been hired in the first place. He has retired on the job and does substandard work because he doesn't have the skills to do his job. He has been warned repeatedly about his attitude and the quality of his work. He occasionally is insubordinate because of his frustrations. Several attempts to transfer him to another department have failed. Training has not helped him.

Regulations clearly state that the government has the burden of proof when taking an Adverse Action to terminate Edgar Smith. This means that we must address the following:

- **Proof of Charges** – We must prove by a "preponderance of the evidence" the factual basis of the misconduct we relied on in taking the Adverse Action. In proving the charges, we may also be required to establish a number of subelements. So a detailed report is required enumerating Edgar's behavior and proof of his ineptitude.

- **Nexus** – Nexus is the connection in an Adverse Action between the act of misconduct and the efficiency of the service. We must prove that the misconduct had a negative impact on the agency mission. We have to show how Edgar's behavior degraded the agency's performance.

- **Appropriateness of Penalty** – We must also establish that the penalty selected, termination in this case, is within the tolerable limits of reasonableness. We have to show we tried everything else.

OK, again none of this seems out of line, though it is burdensome.

In the process of taking an Adverse Action, Edgar Smith has certain "entitlements" as well. These include

- Thirty days' advance, written notice, stating the specific reasons for the proposed action

- The right to be represented by an attorney or other representative

- The right to review the evidence relied upon to support the proposed action

- A reasonable amount of time for reviewing the evidence relied upon to support the proposed action and for preparing and making a written and oral reply

- A written decision and the specific reasons for the action at the earliest practicable date

- The right to appeal the decision to the Merit System Protection Board

- Or the right to appeal the decision through the negotiated, union appeals grievance procedure, if the employee is a member of a bargaining unit

- And the right to file a discrimination complaint in those instances in which the employee has raised an allegation of discrimination during the advance-notice period of the Adverse Action.

Now all this taken together seems like the right thing for government to do. Government needs to set the example. *But the net effect is that no government manager wants to go through this process to take an Adverse Action against an employee.* That is, a manager won't do it unless the employee's behavior is so egregious as to be intolerable. I know, because I was once a government manager with forty-six people reporting to me. So, in this case, Edgar Smith will not be terminated, and instead, a new person will be hired to take up the work.

And the more nonperforming employees there are in the agency, the more difficult it is to isolate and terminate any single employee for non-performance. The problem compounds itself.

To compensate for the nonperformers, the government has to hire more employees who do perform. This causes the bureaucracy to be bloated and the cost of government services to be excessive. Thus, there are often more people in government required to do a particular job than required in the private sector. The primary reason is the difficulty of taking Adverse Actions against nonperformers, making it necessary to hire others to compensate.

If government does not hire additional employees to compensate for the nonperformers, then the overall effectiveness of government is compromised.

This is not all. There are even more reasons why the government is inherently inefficient, as explained in the next chapter.

CHAPTER 3

IF YOU STILL DON'T BELIEVE IT

If you still don't believe government is inherently inefficient, I'll explain how government suffers from even more severe problems in terms of providing cost-efficient and effective services.

Employee Unions In Government

My grandfather was an Italian immigrant who came to this country in 1902. He was a member of a union in Peekskill, New York, working as a laborer for Fleishman's Yeast. Thankfully, the union protected him during the days when capitalism was running rampant; he was able to support his family—barely. So unions did my grandfather and this country a great service many years ago. *But what good are they doing now?*

I believe government unions diminish overall government efficiency and effectiveness. The American Federation of State, County, and Municipal Employees (AFSCME) and the Service Employees International Union (SEIU) have very strong footholds in state and local governments. There are many unions in the federal government as well, too many to mention.

Few people disagree that unions negatively impact worker productivity, whether in government or in the private sector. Unions can shut down government services altogether. Legally or illegally, unions have struck vital government services such as fire and police protection. Teachers and mass-transit workers have gone on strike. President Ronald Reagan had to end the Air Traffic Controllers Union strike by hiring replacements. I believe unions should not be allowed to strike government at all.

Government employee unions make privatization almost impossible for a government agency. The unions fight viciously, using their political influence to stop privatization to retain their membership. The only social welfare programs privatized to date—at any meaningful level—are those where new government programs were created, and there were no existing union employees.

Despite gains for privatization, unions are still growing in government, if nowhere else. After being voted in, unions are almost impossible to dislodge. There is no provision in labor law for employees to vote periodically on whether or not they want to retain the union. Once in, the union is there to stay.

Unions hurt government's ability to be responsive to the people. They impose work rules that are out of date, inefficient, and difficult to change. You can see this in your personal reliance on government services. *Why are there unions in government at all, given all the protections provided government employees?*

Lack of Competition in Government

Another reason for inherent inefficiency is the government doesn't have to compete with anyone. There are a few counties, by the way, that have programs to compare government worker performance to private companies. Los Angeles County and San Diego County do this now. The practice is making the government workers more efficient. But it is rare.

16

A private firm working for the government has to compete with other private firms to win contracts. Because the government does not compete with itself, there is no driving, survival force for efficiency. The private sector works hard to become efficient, to be the low-cost provider, to survive and earn a profit. The government does not have to do this, and as a result, can stagnate.

As Thomas Jefferson said, "It is better for the public to procure at the common market whatever the market can supply: because it is by competition kept up in quality, and reduced to its minimum price."

More Innovation in Private Sector

The private sector is also the great innovator. Private firms have to innovate to remain competitive and be successful. At MAXIMUS, we were continually trying to develop new ways to do our job more efficiently. We often automated processes the states and counties did not. State and local governments couldn't build their own systems. They had to procure their systems following cumbersome procurement regulations and, therefore, were usually operating the last—not the latest—technology.

MAXIMUS and our competitors were the principal forces advancing the state-of-the-art in managing social welfare entitlement programs. That's not to say there weren't ardent innovators in government, but they had no life-or-death stake in the outcome. If we weren't successful, we would go out of business. *The government never goes out of business.*

In fact, like entropy in the universe, the natural tendency for government is to expand constantly.

Relative Lack of Accountability

Another reason for inherent inefficiency in government is the relative lack of accountability compared to the private sector. Of course, an agency is accountable to its legislative committee and to the governor, county supervisors, or mayor. They, in turn, are accountable to the voters. But this accountability is considerably diffused, compared to the private sector.

How many government agencies have been held to specific performance standards? How many agency secretaries have been fired because their agency did not meet the standards? How many government managers have been fired because their staff was not productive? How many government employees have been fired for not doing their jobs? The answer to each question is—none or not enough.

I remember in the 1980s and 1990s when the federal government announced it would sanction states for having welfare error rates higher than 4 percent. The feds continually threatened to reduce federal matching funds in proportion to the amount of money wasted in erroneous eligibility determinations. While most states had error rates well above 4 percent, not one was ever sanctioned, as far as I know. The irony is that the public focuses on specific anecdotal cases. Having an error rate over 4 percent was not something the voters could relate to, so the government ultimately accepted it—politically correct.

The fact is that government is not accountable in the way a private firm is accountable. And for those ongoing tasks that can be well defined with clear performance measures, a private firm will do a better job than government 100 percent of the time, assuming the private firm is qualified and fairly paid.

Advantages of the Private Sector

The private sector, then, can bring significant advantages to the table in helping government better manage social welfare entitlement programs. The private sector can make up for the inherent, but apparently necessary, inefficiencies in government since it has few of the disadvantages of the public sector. The private sector is more responsive, more decisive, more flexible, and more accountable. It can provide high levels of expertise and can be used temporarily without committing to long-term costs. The private sector is more efficient, especially when workloads or caseloads are fluctuating.

As you will see, the private sector can also be more compassionate than government toward recipients. Performance standards can be set for both profit or nonprofit contractors on minimum acceptable levels of recipient satisfaction, maximum waiting times, maximum validated complaint rates, and a host of other standards. These standards ensure recipients are treated with care and dignity, since failure to meet the standards would result in financial penalties for the private firm.

Moreover, those government employees who are converted to private sector employees will enjoy greater job satisfaction. At MAXIMUS, former government employees were better trained, better managed, had better office space, and a greater sense of accomplishment.

Incidentally, the federal government has a process to compare the costs and benefits of hiring private contractors to the costs and benefits of retaining the function within government. OMB (Office of Management and Budget) Circular A-76, first issued in 1966, defines federal policy for determining whether recurring commercial activities should be performed by the private sector or by federal employees.

Social welfare entitlement programs to aid the poor and disabled, however, are almost exclusively administered by state and local governments. Hence, OMB Circular A-76 specifically does not apply. The presence of unions in state and local governments deters A-76-like comparisons, although these comparisons sometimes do occur.

One problem in the early days of privatization was the difficulty of designing well-constructed contracts and then monitoring the contractors.

Privatization contracts were fairly loose, without the specificity they have today. As government contracting officers gained familiarity with privatization, they became increasingly adept at creating better contract vehicles and more effective contract performance standards.

The government also had to learn how to monitor contractors. Monitoring costs may offset some of the savings achieved, but monitoring is essential to keep everyone on his or her toes. As those skills were learned, privatization became much more attractive to government decision-makers.

Streamlined Government

Government can be streamlined and made more efficient by changing its organization and staffing. All ministerial duties should be contracted out. Ministerial duties are those duties for which policies and procedures can be clearly defined so that anyone can follow them—no discretion is required. Clerical-type tasks represent one example of ministerial duties. Serving the public through a service desk or call hotline is another.

In state and local government agencies serving the public, staffing should be limited to program administrators, policy makers, contract officers, and contract monitors. Government employees should not be doing ministerial tasks the private sector can do. The agency organization and staffing should be designed to perform all discretionary tasks internally and outsource or privatize all nondiscretionary or ministerial tasks. Appendix A: Government of the Future provides more detail on these ideas.

There is a natural symbiosis between government and the private sector. Each brings different strengths to the partnership, and together they do a better job for the people.

With this background on inherent government inefficiency, then, you can understand why I wanted to help state and local governments manage social welfare entitlement programs from the private sector. As the next chapter shows, I was at the right place, at the right time, with the right motivation. As is often the case, luck played a huge role in determining the success of MAXIMUS—but so did hard work. I liked to say if you compressed all the energy I put into MAXIMUS into one second, you'd probably have an atomic bomb!

CHAPTER 4

WHY ME?

This chapter explains how I became involved in improving government social welfare entitlement programs from inside government and then why I left government to form MAXIMUS.

Before the Social and Rehabilitation Service

I grew up in a military family. My father was a graduate of West Point, Class of 1940. His father, as I mentioned earlier, was an Italian immigrant and could not read or write English. Through sheer determination, my father rose from the clutches of poverty and into the elite ranks of the US Army. And he was forever a patriot and deeply grateful to West Point for the opportunity he was given. He ingrained in me as a young child, the Academy motto: "Duty, Honor, Country." And throughout my early life, he repeated the cadet honor code: "A cadet will not lie, cheat, steal, or tolerate those who do." These were powerful messages that shaped me, and as you will discover, MAXIMUS, as well.

In 1965, I graduated from West Point "007" in my class. However, I joined the Air Force instead of the Army. At that time, the Air Force Academy was not at full capacity, and 15 percent of the West Point graduates could elect to go Air Force.

The Air Force sent me immediately to Stanford University, where I earned a Masters Degree in Industrial Engineering/Operations Research. My first assignment was at Kelley Air Force Base, Texas, where I worked on assessing the reliability of ICBM nuclear warheads. Because of my work there, I came to the attention of the Vice Chief of Staff of the Air Force, who selected me to join a special evaluation team reporting to the Commander of the 7th Air Force in Vietnam.

I spent all of 1968 in Vietnam and Thailand working on computer analyses of McNamara's Wall and Air Orders of Battle against the Ho Chi Minh Trail. McNamara's Wall was a series of sonic and seismic sensors airdropped over the road network the North Vietnamese Army used to resupply its forces in the south. The idea came from the Whiz Kids! That year was, without a doubt, the most exciting year of my life, juxtaposing imminent mortal danger with a highly responsible and fascinating job.

The third day I was in Vietnam, the Vietcong tossed three hand grenades into the bus I was riding to Tan Son Nhut Air Base. Fortunately, I was in the back of the bus and escaped unharmed. Later that day, my friend Captain Bob Appleton, who was not on the bus, said to me, "Dave, do you want to be scared the whole time you're here and hide or have a good time?" After some thought, I said, "Let's have a good time," and we did. I ultimately was awarded five campaign ribbons and the Bronze Star, and that shaped me, as well.

In Vietnam I learned to deal with real fear while continuing to focus on my job, something that would also serve me well later at MAXIMUS. And as my father always used to remind me, "If there aren't bullets flying around, things can't be that bad."

I returned to work in the Pentagon in 1969 in the Air Force Operations Analysis Office. After resigning from the Air Force in 1972, I continued to work in the Pentagon, but as a civilian in the Office of the Assistant Secretary of Defense for Systems Analysis—the old Whiz Kids group I mentioned earlier. I earned a Doctor of Science Degree in 1973 from The George Washington University while working at the Pentagon.

After a year as a civilian, I was asked if I wanted to transfer to the Social and Rehabilitation Service within the Department of Health Education and Welfare (now the Department of Health and Human Services). The request was timely, since I had just finished the Marine helicopter study and was disillusioned with the Department of Defense. The purpose of the transfer was to bring more analytical and technical thinking to the management of social welfare entitlement programs. That sounded worthwhile.

As you can surmise, I had a strong sense of duty instilled by my father to serve my country, but I no longer wanted to serve my country in the Defense Department. I thought the Social and Rehabilitation Service would be a far better place, so I said yes.

Social and Rehabilitation Service

From 1973 to 1975, I was Director of Research and Demonstrations in the agency. At that time, SRS administered the major social welfare programs for the poor, except for Food Stamps and Housing. I was responsible for directing the Section 1115(a) and (b) Grant Program. This section of the Social Security Act allowed the government to waive any provision of the Act for purposes of trying out new ideas to improve its programs. *This was perfect for me.*

While at SRS, I found very few private companies that knew anything about social welfare. There was no place to turn for help in improving these programs except within government. Medicaid and AFDC (now TANF) were hardly efficiently administered and were costing the nation more than anyone had projected. There was a genuine need for welfare reform, and the Joint Economic Committee in Congress had been holding many hearings on the subject.

In the spirit of the times, I decided to reform the R&D program to focus on administrative efficiency and effectiveness, including the reduction of fraud and abuse. I chose this direction rather than investigating such issues as the adequacy of benefit levels, the "notch effect" for income earners, the impact of poverty on social behavior and crime, and similar subjects of interest to social workers. This had been the previous focus of the grant program. I wanted to reform how social welfare entitlement programs were managed, so they met their intended purpose and better served the people in need.

I oversaw an R&D budget of $16 million and some four hundred grants to states and nonprofit organizations. As old projects were completed, I would replace them with new projects, focused on improving program administration and accountability. My staff was not the least bit quantitatively oriented—they were social workers and academics. There was no graph paper, for example, to plot any statistics or performance measures. There were no computers in our offices. The differences between SRS and the Department of Defense were striking.

I spent considerable time studying the poverty programs and reading the Joint Economic Committee reports. I developed and presented new R&D plans for reforming Welfare, Medicaid, and Social Services to the Agency Administrator, Jim Dwight. He gave me the go-ahead to change the R&D Program the way I wanted. My government staff was eager to help—the challenge excited them—we had a new mission.

I immediately initiated projects to determine if eligibility determination in the entitlement programs could be automated. Computers were just coming into their own for health-care claims processing. Automation could streamline the eligibility determination process and make it more consistent and more accurate. We found that eligibility determination, despite its complexities and what the skeptics thought, could be automated.

Although it took many years before the government fully adopted automation, now automated eligibility determination is everywhere. We also looked for ways other than automation to reduce the administrative costs of the programs. We did this by identifying best practices in the states and by developing new, more effective model policies and procedures.

My staff also focused on projects to reduce fraud and abuse. We developed programs for helping states reduce their error rates in eligibility determination. We did this by helping redesign and upgrade the quality control system for measuring error rates and by developing statistical tools for identifying fraudulent recipients, much like a credit score identifies poor credit risks.

In Medicaid, we worked with the Social Security Administration on Cost by Case Type demonstrations that later turned out to be Diagnostic Related Groups (DRGs). The government uses these codes to reimburse health-care providers.

My office also funded a pilot Early Periodic Screening, Diagnosis, and Treatment Program (EPSDT) for young children in Texas so they could be medically screened at very early ages. We showed that it was far more cost effective to treat children when they were young through vaccinations and periodic health exams than to let medical problems grow in severity and cost as the children grew older. Now all states are required to have an EPSDT program.

We also funded a study to determine how long a recipient would need to remain eligible in Medicaid to make it cost effective for health plans to provide preventive care. Health plans had to be responsible for the recipient long enough to make the cost of preventive care worthwhile. At that time, there were hardly any recipients in managed care programs. Now, most Medicaid recipients are in managed-care programs.

I initiated studies on Medicaid Utilization Review, which involved reviewing physician claims for health-care services. We had a project in Ohio where we analyzed paid claims tapes and calculated for each physician how many injections were given per office visit, how many drugs were prescribed per office visit, how many office visits per month were billed per patient, and the like.

We then rank-ordered the physicians from high to low on each indicator. I took the computer listing to the Deputy SRS Administrator, who at that time was John A. (Jack) Svahn, later to become Commissioner of the Social Security Administration. He wanted to go after the apparently fraudulent physicians immediately. I calmed him down, saying we were still in the research mode and had not verified the data. It turned out later the data was accurate. The project soon became an integral part of the Medicaid Management Information System in use in every state today.

I commissioned the first cost-effectiveness study for collecting child support from fathers who had abandoned their families to welfare. We wanted these "deadbeat dads" to reimburse the government for supporting their families. Data from the study was used two years later, in part, to help justify enactment of the Child Support Enforcement Program, known as Title IV-D of the Social Security Act.

In those days, there were no R&D projects to test privatization. Privatization had been relied upon only for computerized tasks, such as processing Medicaid claims. Incidentally, this is what made H. Ross Perot rich and famous with Electronic Data Systems. He processed the claims that physicians and hospitals submitted to the Medicaid program; his first contract was in Texas.

Throughout the grant administration process, we issued Requests for Proposals (RFPs) to have companies bid on the work to help the non-profit organizations and states that received the grants. As I mentioned above, amazingly, we could find few responsible companies to bid. They just weren't interested or didn't know enough to submit proposals. Therefore, we got by without them.

In late 1974, I met with the federal Office of Management and Budget (OMB) to ask for an increase in funding for the SRS R&D program from $16 million to $24 million. I explained that the programs we were reforming through R&D—those programs helping the poor—were in complete disarray and in dire need of change. I explained that we were funding projects with higher than a one hundred to one benefit-to-cost ratio for the government. Or, for every dollar we spent on an R&D project, the government would get at least $100 back—likely much, much more.

To dramatize my point, I explained that if the amount of federal money then being spent on these poverty programs was equated to the height of the Washington Monument (555 feet), we had less than 4 inches of money to find ways to improve them. Could OMB make that 6 inches and give us $24 million? The answer was *No*—a resounding *No*! I was uncomprehending again. How could this be? This would never have happened in the private sector, where decisions are more economically based. Projects with a ten to one benefit-to-cost ratio receive funding as quickly as possible.

So, now, I couldn't get the right decision at SRS either. Politics reigned supreme—decisions based on economic principles were out. The facts didn't matter. Government wasn't the place where I could get any traction. I had committed all the money in the R&D program over the next three years, and there was not much else I could do.

Therefore, I decided to leave government and try to change these programs from the outside, rather than from the inside. I would start a company that became expert in social welfare entitlement programs and operate on an economically rational basis. The company would grow by helping government do a better job for the disadvantaged. The major stumbling block, though, was that I didn't know a thing about running a business. I had to learn—and learn quickly.

Arthur Young & Company

Fortuitously, Arthur Young & Company (a Big Eight firm at the time) offered me a consulting position in its Washington DC office. I embraced this as an opportunity to learn the consulting business, so I resigned my position in the government and went to work for Arthur Young.

While at Arthur Young, I naturally declined to work on SRS business because of potential conflicts of interest. The firm's management assigned me initially to work on energy business with the Federal Energy Administration when gasoline rationing was being explored. I also worked on projects for other federal agencies, and quickly gained a broad view of the civilian agencies in the federal government. I learned exponentially.

After a seven-month stint at Arthur Young, I decided I was approaching the time when I could start my own consulting business. Little did I know! Arthur Young sped this along by refusing to let me manage contracts I had won through competitive procurements. I was such a good proposal writer (the firm winning eight of fourteen proposals I worked on), management kept me at the job.

As an aside, some of my peers wanted me to leave. I was doing too well. One day I found an envelope on my desk with circled want ads inside. I understood the message.

Peer pressure, notwithstanding, I told the management, "If you don't let me manage the next proposal I win, I will leave." They didn't, so having painted myself in a corner, I left with nothing lined up. The rashness of youth!

My wife was incredulous and afraid, but I was confident—over confident. This brings us to MAXIMUS.

CHAPTER 5

MAXIMUS – QUICK HISTORY

I finally understood that my best chance to help reform government was to start my own company. Having resigned from Arthur Young, I now needed a job to support my family. My job would be building and managing the new company.

By explaining how MAXIMUS was built, I can highlight the differences between how government and the private sector operate. These differences vividly demonstrate why the private sector is an essential partner to government. This chapter, then, provides a brief overview of MAXIMUS and how it started and developed.

Naming the Company

My new consulting company needed a name. How are companies named anyhow? I didn't know, so I developed several criteria to help me.

- I did not want my name to be the company's name, for example, David Mastran & Associates. I am basically an introvert and didn't want my name in lights. This would happen if the company became highly successful, or for that matter, somehow attracted negative press.

- I didn't want the name reduced to a simple set of initials, such as IBM, TRW, and EDS—there were too many of them around.

- I wanted an X in the name. Many successful, publicly listed companies at the time had an X in their name, for example, Xerox, Exxon, and Xtra.

- Since my company would likely consult in quantitative areas and computers, I wanted some quantitative connotation, for example, something like "max" or "optimal" as part of the name.

- I didn't want the name to say what the company did, for example, Advanced Welfare Systems. This would limit what the company could do in the future.

- Finally, if it was ever to be international in nature, I wanted a name that could be understood almost anywhere.

The name Maximus popped into my head. It is Latin for "the greatest," a bit presumptuous to be sure, but it was a strong name. I liked it, and it fit the criteria.

I decided to capitalize all the letters in Maximus in the legal name of the company. If we were going to be MAXIMUS, it seemed that all the letters had to be caps. The press, the courts, and other organizations didn't always refer to us in all caps, even though it was our legal name.

MAXIMUS was born in a corner of my basement in Great Falls, Virginia, and was incorporated on September 18, 1975. I opened for business on October 1, and was now on my own and eager to get going, at age 32. Less than two weeks had transpired between incorporation and initiation. This rapid transformation could only have taken place in the private sector.

Starting the Company

I spent the first year consulting on small-time contracts—working for other consulting firms, writing their proposals. My first job was writing proposals with Booz Allen Hamilton. I had beaten them several times while at Arthur Young, and they wanted me on their side. They were good guys, and they supported me.

Some of the people who worked with me earlier at SRS had moved on to other federal agencies. They also awarded me a few very small contracts. I loved the work, and MAXIMUS was profitable from the first month. This was a recurring theme. I was motivated to help government, not to make a lot of money, but somehow helping government was always financially very rewarding.

It is fair to say I was extremely afraid of failure—not financial failure, but failure to control my own destiny. I had a mission, and I wanted to be my own boss. I didn't care what other people thought.

Fear of failure drove me harder than any other motivation. But I pushed forward, working long, hard hours frantically doing things I had never done before—like cold-call marketing. I became submersed in MAXIMUS, sometimes to the exclusion of everything else, including my family. My wife would "drag" me on vacations, and I would work the whole time. My brother complained that I brought MAXIMUS work when I visited him. This pattern would continue for years, until I had more help running the company. As my ex-wife later said, "MAXIMUS was your mistress."

In January 1976, I won a small contract in New Hampshire to calculate and implement statistical profiles of people defrauding Medicaid. For the next three years, I worked part time on that contract and developed an automated system that would identify recipients who had a 60 percent chance of being ineligible. New Hampshire's error rate went down.

In April 1976, I/MAXIMUS won a $45,000 contract, the first competitively won contract with the federal government. The contract concerned designing new sample frames for Medicaid Quality Control and was related to some of the work I started in New Hampshire. I hired three people and moved out of my basement into a one-room office in McLean, Virginia.

I remember thinking this was it—MAXIMUS was really going to make it! I had won a decent-sized contract, at least at the time. Barry Manilow was on the charts with the song "It's a Miracle." I played the song over and over—I was so happy! First year revenues ended up at $69,000. No debt. The MAXIMUS fiscal year coincided with the government's fiscal year—October 1 through September 30 since I started the company on October 1.

The second year, MAXIMUS experienced more wins, and I hired more people—revenues tripled to $223,000. Still, I was working as hard as I could. I was constantly fearful of running out of work and being a failure. The fear of imminent failure is not present in government—maybe for politicians running for reelection, but not for the average government bureaucrat.

Amazing and healthy growth continued in successive years, with MAXIMUS revenues reaching $351,000, $780,000, $1,554,000, and finally $1,772,000 in 1981, six years after starting. All revenues came from consulting, primarily with the federal government.

MAXIMUS consulted on much more than social welfare programs in those early years. We worked with most of the federal agencies, performing a considerable amount of systems work. These contracts allowed us to survive as we worked our way into the social welfare program market. Competition from other companies was fierce everywhere we turned. Growth was much slower than anticipated. *I had much more to learn than I realized.*

The business was labor intensive—no products—and little commercial work—just a few small state government clients and the federal government. All our revenues were based on labor billing hours, so the staff had to stay billable.

MAXIMUS Grows to the Next Level

In 1984, I realized I needed help to capitalize on the opportunities before MAXIMUS. I hired Raymond Ruddy, the Managing Consulting Partner of the Boston Office of Touche Ross (another Big Eight Firm). Touche Ross had considerable experience in state and local government consulting. The Boston Office competed with MAXIMUS on a number of state and local government consulting contracts. And MAXIMUS often won, including a large engagement for New York City to reduce the city's welfare error rate.

Ray led the New York City proposal effort for Touche Ross; I led the proposal effort for MAXIMUS. Later, he told me that he and his partners worked on developing that proposal for over a year. When we won this large contract, he believed MAXIMUS would be very successful in the future, so he asked to join me. After a while, I agreed and let him buy one-third of the company's stock. I retained control.

Ray helped develop the state and local government business for MAXIMUS. He later brought several senior consultants with him, including Lynn Davenport. Lynn turned out to be a great asset for MAXIMUS, providing a significant boost to a fledging consulting service we had called Revenue Maximization.

This service helped states claim money from the federal government—money they weren't aware they were entitled to. The work was all contingency-based; MAXIMUS received a percentage of the new money found for the state. Revenue Maximization was very profitable. Ray and Lynn added a strong sense of profit to our secular missionary culture.

By 1987, our revenues had grown to $6.9 million. This seemed like huge growth at the time.

MAXIMUS was still primarily a government-consulting firm, pursuing my goal of reforming government. Most of our work was now with state government social welfare programs, since those programs were our true purpose for being.

Growth through Government Privatization

Then in late 1987, something very big and very unexpected happened! MAXIMUS won the first privatization contract in the United States of a government social welfare entitlement program. We finally could have a major impact on government programs. Instead of being only advisors or consultants, we were actually going to manage a program with real recipients in a major city. This was the chance I had been waiting for since I left government.

As you've read, MAXIMUS privatized the Los Angeles County Welfare-to-Work program called GAIN (Greater Avenues for Independence). We achieved astounding successes—beyond anything that had been expected, as described later. At the same time, we attracted powerful foes determined to stop the privatization of social welfare entitlement programs right there.

Although the journey was extremely difficult, over the years we won even more privatization contracts in more welfare-to-work programs, in Medicaid managed care, in child support enforcement, in child care, and in child health insurance. MAXIMUS had shown that privatization worked.

By 1994 our revenues had grown to $57.4 million, up 700 percent in six years. We had established ourselves as the go-to company for privatization. By 1997, MAXIMUS revenues had rocketed upward to $173.4 million. Throughout this three-year period and beyond, we were continually assailed by the unions, the press, and liberal politicians. We grew anyway.

MAXIMUS was soon recognized as the largest company providing privatization and consulting services to government social welfare programs. We became a strong advocate for governments to privatize their programs. And our successes became a compelling reason why governments increasingly considered privatization.

MAXIMUS accumulated a detailed knowledge base and understanding of the operation of these programs throughout the country. This allowed us to apply proven methodologies, specialized skills, and specific systems solutions to new projects in a cost-effective and timely fashion. We also worked in more traditional government agencies and developed a wide range of automated systems for them as well.

MAXIMUS had distinct advantages over our emerging competitors, Policy Studies, Inc., Dean Curtis & Associates, Benova, and others. These smaller firms often had limited resources and skill sets. We also frequently competed against nonprofit organizations like The Salvation Army, Catholic Charities, and Goodwill Industries. These nonprofits had noble missions to advance, but tended to bid only on those contracts consistent with their mission statements. Goodwill Industries filled a tremendous void by hiring the disabled.

MAXIMUS also had advantages over the large consulting firms like Accenture and Affiliated Computer Services, Inc. that served multiple industries but lacked the focus necessary to understand the complex nature of government social welfare programs. Being "first to market," we had the largest market share. MAXIMUS was tough to beat when Request for Proposals were issued for privatization services.

During my tenure, MAXIMUS was responsible to government for some aspect of the social welfare of over twenty-two million Americans, four million Canadians, and several hundred thousand people in Australia. The numbers are even higher today with some very large contracts won in the United Kingdom and Israel.

We were pursued by many firms who wanted to buy MAXIMUS. Instead, we held out and went public under the symbol MMS on the New York Stock Exchange on June 13, 1997. Other companies wanted to own our growing revenues and high profitability, but none really understood what we did.

By the year 2000, MAXIMUS revenues soared to nearly $400 million, and then up to over $603 million by 2004. Even though we acquired companies, the vast majority of our growth was organic. Approximately $100 million in revenues was added after 1997 by acquiring a number of smaller companies.

When I retired in 2004, MAXIMUS had 5,500 employees and 245 offices in the United States, Canada, and Australia. MAXIMUS had contracts in all fifty states, forty-nine of the fifty largest cities, and twenty-seven of the thirty largest counties. The growth was phenomenal.

On the next page is the revenue chart for the first sixteen years of MAXIMUS, up to 1991.

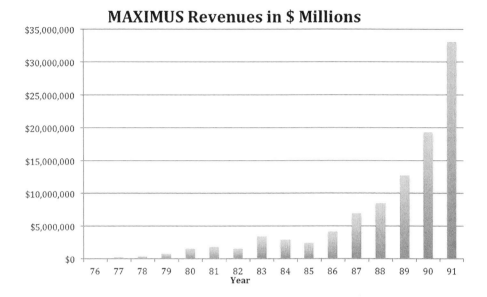

Exhibit 1 – Revenue Growth of MAXIMUS 1976–1991

The second chart includes the first sixteen years and goes out to the twenty-ninth year when I retired. Notice how insignificant the first sixteen years look.

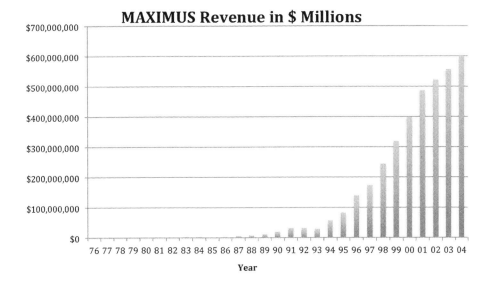

Exhibit 2 – Revenue Growth of MAXIMUS 1976–2004

The company as of this writing has a market cap of $1.9 billion, nearly 9,000 employees, and is still going strong.

CHAPTER 6

MAXIMUS – MORE CONTEXT

The overview of MAXIMUS concludes in this chapter, providing more context for the stories and lessons that follow.

Three Businesses

MAXIMUS evolved into three major businesses: consulting, systems, and government operations, or privatization. Each business had a different business model. Each business reinforced the other. Consulting work identified the need for systems and privatization; privatization work gave us more credibility in consulting and systems; systems work made us better in privatization and consulting, and so on.

Consulting was our first business. A consulting business is very easy to start since there are low barriers to entry—just hang out a shingle. However, government consulting is not nearly as profitable as commercial consulting. Government consultants are generally paid for actual hours worked and are regularly audited on the rates charged. Both government and commercial consultants are predominantly senior professionals with considerable experience.

Privatization (sometimes called government outsourcing) of social welfare programs is an entirely different business. In this business, private sector workers replace government workers serving people in need. The work is repetitive, so the operations can be optimized. The private sector workers whom MAXIMUS hired were often former social workers or psychology and sociology majors just out of school. So the pay scale in privatization is much lower than for consultants. The ethnic diversity of the workforce is also much greater than in consulting.

The systems business was different again. Here, we had highly trained professionals, but they were computer types and very technically-oriented as opposed to being management-oriented. These people were also very well paid, comparable to the consultants. MAXIMUS ended up specializing in all types of automated government systems: court systems, health care systems, fleet management systems, school systems, and government accounting and personnel systems. We had some eight hundred systems staff when I retired.

At one point, I tried to change our business model to parallel the government programs we served, such as health care, child support, welfare, financial management, and the like. For example, I created a health care group that operated all three businesses: consulting, systems, and privatization. But it didn't work well.

The consulting, systems, and privatization businesses were very different and required staff with totally different knowledge and skills. It was far more effective to transfer government program knowledge across the three businesses lines than to combine the knowledge and skills into one business. I ultimately did split privatization into different government program areas but kept systems and consulting as separate groups, serving all programs.

As we grew, my flexibility in changing our business model could never have been matched in government. As a private firm, MAXIMUS was very agile and could easily adapt to changing market opportunities. We simply could move much faster than government.

Our Detractors

Because MAXIMUS was providing services to the poor and disadvantaged and making a healthy profit, entrenched government stakeholders regarded us as the enemy. As I mentioned earlier, these stakeholders included government unions and liberal politicians, and sometimes Republicans when they were not the political party in power. In addition, we had the investigative media after us, which continually sought to manufacture scandals involving MAXIMUS and our competitors.

While the investigative media published a great number of accusatory articles against MAXIMUS that implied wrongdoing, there was never an indictment on any charge, much less a conviction, during my tenure. This is true despite the extensive investigations we experienced on almost a yearly basis by multiple government agencies as well as the media.

However, if we made any mistakes, and we did make some, the mistakes were magnified many times over, and almost unrecognizable, when reported by the media. "Bad decisions make good stories." We were living in a fishbowl, with hostile adversaries watching and reporting our every move.

The government unions—the American Federation of State, County and Municipal Employees (AFSCME) and the Service Employees International Union (SEIU)—mounted continual and ferocious attacks against MAXIMUS privatization efforts. We spent multiple millions of dollars and many person years of effort defending ourselves. I am sure the attacks are still going on today.

MAXIMUS was also in the spotlight because we sometimes denied benefits to persons who were found ineligible. They would often complain to the press or to our government overseers. We had to prove conclusively that the complainers, in fact, were not eligible for benefits. In addition, we collected child support from absent fathers who vehemently did not want to pay. We located them, took them to court, and forced them to pay. They didn't like us, to say the least. We also had recipients who were determined not to comply with government program rules, and we had to impose sanctions on them, according to government policy.

Because of the huge number of recipients we served, MAXIMUS always had to deal with complaints. We finally implemented a formal system of escalation so our government clients would know what was going on. It took a while to develop these complaint-tracking systems, though, and we often learned our lessons the hard way. However, we quickly became more responsive than traditional government to the program recipients.

Reflections

Almost every year, I found myself managing a company larger than I had ever managed before. MAXIMUS was constantly growing. Every year I had to learn how to overcome problems I had never seen before. Since I had no real experience in another large private company, other than Arthur Young for seven months, I had no role model or business practice to emulate—which in some cases turned out to be an advantage.

I learned that solving management problems was pretty much like solving math problems—management problems just weren't as well-defined or with such uncontestable answers. In both, I had to analyze the problem, break it down to understand the variables or dimensions and their relationships, and then derive or construct a solution.

I also learned to do what was right for the people being served by the government programs, regardless of the implications for MAXIMUS.

This was the only way to survive in the long term, and doing so reso-nated with the principles I was brought up with as a child.

Impossible Odds

I initially titled this book *Impossible Odds*—how come?

To begin with, MAXIMUS helped fundamentally change how many state and local governments managed their social welfare entitlement programs—the largest programs in their budgets. Many chose priva-tization over unionized government employees at great political costs, something they had never done before, and the programs helped more people, more accountably.

Second, there were many powerful foes opposing MAXIMUS and what we stood for in terms of privatizing government. We totally disrupted the status quo. The government unions and the investigative press harassed us relentlessly, and in my opinion, unfairly.

Third, in the face of that opposition, MAXIMUS revenues still grew at the astonishing average rate of 36.5 percent over the twenty-nine-year period I was CEO. To put this in context, if you had invested one dollar in a savings account earning 36.5 percent when I founded MAXIMUS, your one dollar investment would have grown to $8,750 by the time I retired. MAXIMUS was profitable every year and never went into debt! As my father often opined—"Find a need and fill it."

The irony is that our prime focus was on reforming government social welfare entitlement programs, not on being financially successful. But, in the end, it was our financial success that proved we were successful in helping improve these programs. We were on the New York Stock Exchange. That fact our detractors couldn't refute.

Finally, MAXIMUS was led by me, a person with essentially no previous business experience and no real influence.

Simply stated, if someone had told me what was going to happen when I founded MAXIMUS, I would have said the odds of that are—simply impossible.

So how was it done? Let's find out.

PART II:
BUILDING THE FOUNDATION

OK, now that you have the background on how all this got started, let's get down to how to build a company. I'll cover what social welfare programs are later. This block of chapters provides lessons learned in building MAXIMUS. They present practical solutions to real problems and provide a blueprint for those of you thinking about taking on a similar crusade.

CHAPTER 7

MAXIMUS VISION

A company starts with a vision. During my two-plus years working for the government at the Social and Rehabilitation Service, I learned how desperately the poor and disadvantaged of this country needed help—and I learned the help wasn't coming from government in the most efficient or even most compassionate way.

Welfare creates dependency; social workers aren't the best administrators; and the entitlement programs were out of control. Something needed to be done. And I wanted to do it through MAXIMUS.

Purpose of MAXIMUS

So, as you've read, I decided to start a consulting company to help federal, state, and local governments reform their social welfare entitlement programs. This was the purpose and the vision of MAXIMUS. It was a big one, but why not think big? I had personally seen how distressed and hopeless people were who had to accept welfare. I had visited many of them in their "homes." I knew how they were treated by government, and I knew the complex rules and cumbersome administrative procedures they had to follow to receive benefits. And I felt this had to change in America.

To communicate this vision succinctly and to give the name MAXIMUS more context, I decided to focus on the idea that we would be helping federal, state, and local governments do a better job in serving disadvantaged people.

At that time, the nation was celebrating its Bicentennial—the two hundredth anniversary of the founding of our country. There were strong feelings of patriotism and nationalistic pride. People were talking about the Declaration of Independence and the Constitution of the United States.

The Constitution starts with the words "We the People"—powerful words for a mandate. Taking this as a lead, I formed the MAXIMUS vision statement (or some might say the company mission) as "Helping Government Serve the People."

I added this statement to our logo after a couple of years. The logo consisted simply of the word MAXIMUS in Friz Quadrata font with "Helping Government Serve the People" centered underneath it. So it remains today.

That pretty much said what we were about. The mission statement was important, so those already in MAXIMUS and those joining the company would know what we were trying to do. We were not just a profit-making company; we were a change agent for government. That was our key message. Every company needs one.

A company's mission has to be clear and compelling. In a strange way, we became the preferred employer for frustrated government employees who wanted to serve disadvantaged people and change government. We had a noble mission everyone could relate to and work hard for.

MAXIMUS had many ex-government employees join us because we were like the government, but without all the constraints and bureaucracy to slow us down. We were making things happen in a positive way. They wanted to be part of that.

Our common passion was helping people in need. All our staff felt good about what we did. We continually received feedback from people we were helping, and they were grateful.

Operating Philosophy

Our mission statement had to be fortified with an operating philosophy. We couldn't just be idealists. We had a business to run!

Our operating philosophy was captured in the slogan *"Quality, Profitability, Growth."* A sign with these words was prominently displayed in every MAXIMUS office. The meaning was taught in every new hire introduction to the company, and in ongoing training programs. The order of the words was important.

Translated, "Quality, Profitability, Growth" means that quality comes first before profitability or growth. We needed to provide quality services to government, meeting the highest standards of excellence. We could not sacrifice quality for profitability. That was something I continually preached because the temptation in any business is to sacrifice quality for profitability.

If MAXIMUS couldn't do a quality job, we didn't deserve a profit. In addition, we surely didn't want to grow and produce more inferior work. So quality was also more important than growth.

There is no other logical order for "Quality, Profitability, Growth." If we put profit first, our quality would suffer, and we wouldn't grow. Our government clients wouldn't want us back, and our reputation would put us out of business. If we put growth first and weren't profitable, then we would run out of money or have to go into debt or dilute our firm. That wasn't the answer either. Quality had to be first; profitability second; and growth third.

I continually worked to ensure quality was achieved before we focused on profit. Profit represented a measure of the value of the services we were providing. If we could not make a profit providing quality services, then we needed to go into some other business—do something else. Let another company have the business who could make a profit and provide a high level of quality.

Note that these principles apply to any business—not just MAXIMUS, nor just companies working for the government.

What Mahatma Gandhi Said

Quality was also reflected in the customer service we provided our government clients and recipients of social welfare programs. Exceptional customer service had to become an important part of our culture in serving the government. I saw a quote from Mahatma Gandhi in my later years with MAXIMUS that was so inspiring I directed it also be placed in every MAXIMUS office.

The message is worth repeating here because it exemplifies the values I tried to instill in our staff. Mahatma Gandhi actually was a small business owner at one time. He referred to his clients as his customers. In his words:

> The Customer is the most important visitor on our premises. He is not dependent on us. We are dependent on him. He is not an interruption on our work. He is the purpose of it. He is not an outsider on our business. He is a part of it. We are not doing him a favour by serving him. He is doing us a favour by giving us an opportunity to do so.

Both the government agency staff and the welfare recipients were our customers. We needed to treat them as such. If government had this philosophy, we would not have won as many contracts. This is not to say that there aren't many great publicly managed programs for welfare recipients. But there are enough bad ones to justify the existence of MAXIMUS and other contractors devoted to helping the disadvantaged.

Profit Is a Growth Hormone

As I've mentioned, many MAXIMUS staff came from government; they had a hard time understanding why profit was an important part of our culture. Profit is a "dirty word" in government and in the nonfinancial media as well. I told our people *"Profit is a growth hormone."* Profit helped us grow so we could help even more people.

I explained that profit gave us discretionary funds so we could do what we wanted.

- We could guarantee high quality work for our clients by using retained earnings, or our past profits, to absorb any losses we incurred by underestimating costs.

- We would not have to borrow money from the banks and be under their control since we could use our profits to provide the cash flow needed for growth.

- We could invest our profits in developing new products or systems that MAXIMUS would own and later leverage for more business.

- We could give bonuses not otherwise considered allowable costs by the government to staff and, which therefore had to come from profit.

Profit gave us freedom, but we had to earn it.

Proactive or Reactive Sales Strategy

Another element of my vision was whether MAXIMUS was going to be proactive or reactive in securing new business. Even though we were very creative and good planners, I chose to be reactive. This may again seem counterintuitive—but when working with government agencies, we had to acknowledge that all levels of government are slow to make decisions and slow to act. Government contract spending is not that predictable, especially with regular state and county election cycles and changing administrations and their priorities. So I decided MAXIMUS would react to what the government did rather than predict what it might do.

As MAXIMUS grew larger, we naturally reached out to current and potential clients about the best practices we were implementing across the country and other innovations taking place. We pointed out the successes of our services, whether revenue maximization or privatization. We attended state conventions and conferences. We participated in panels to help people understand why MAXIMUS was truly a *national resource* that could be tapped to make government more efficient. So we were proactive to a degree, but mainly, we were reactive.

We clearly were not the source of all ideas on how to make government more responsive—there were plenty of others. However, MAXIMUS was definitely a leader, and we were continually spreading the word that there was a better way to do business in government.

After a while, several other companies were founded committed to reforming government. And there was a large contingent of far-sighted thinkers within government working for reform in social welfare programs. This contingent also had a wealth of ideas. MAXIMUS was definitely riding a government reform wave. I believe we initiated the wave by showing real reform was possible. At the very least, we significantly amplified the wave. Again, MAXIMUS was at the right place at the right time.

When our staff was proactive and tried to sell a specific reform or improvement idea to a government agency, it could take eighteen months or longer before a contract was signed. The process was a lengthy one. The steps to convert an idea into a government contract are as follows:

- We had to secure a private meeting with the agency management to discuss the project idea.

- We had to sell the project idea to the agency management and recruit champions within the agency to move the project forward.

- The champions had to obtain formal signoffs on the project and sometimes approval from the legislature.

- The agency had to find money for the project and make sure it was in the budget.

- The Request for Proposals (RFP) for the project had to be written and approved.

- The bidder's conference had to be scheduled and held.

- The bidders had to prepare and submit their proposals.

- The proposals had to be evaluated by the government and the selection made.

- Any award protests had to be reviewed and resolved.

- The contract had to be negotiated.

- The contract award had to be made and properly registered.

It was far more efficient to "sow corn" on a broad basis and then wait on the sidelines to see what happened. The corn represented our ideas for privatization, new systems, or consulting help the government needed, and it was "planted" in every state, major city, and county. We sent out lists of ideas and sample RFPs for agencies to consider. We answered any questions and follow-up as indicated. However, much of the time, the "corn" fell on infertile ground.

We could not predict in advance where the ideas would take root—we just kept a vigilant watch across the country until we found any growing and then capitalized on the find. Often, our ideas weren't the ones that took root.

We found it easier to be reactive—to adapt to the government's procurement cycle, tracking what RFPs were being issued and then responding to them. We needed sales people, but not nearly so many. By being reactive, we cut twelve to fifteen months out of the procurement cycle by eliminating the first four steps described above. MAXIMUS always had opportunities arising in different numbers in different states, counties, and cities across the nation.

To be effective, however, we needed to build an elaborate infrastructure to make sure we learned about all RFPs being issued anywhere. Our people systematically searched for notices of government RFPs, whether issued in Hawaii or in Florida, or in Seattle or in Atlanta, or in Fairfax County, Virginia, or in Clark County (Las Vegas), Nevada. We didn't miss many.

After ordering and receiving the RFPs, we quickly scanned them and decided whether to bid. A daily report listing all the new RFPs was sent to our senior executives, so those interested could request copies for review. Frequently, we had only weeks to make a decision, not months.

Thus, our staff often had very little time to study the RFP requirements, learn what was needed in that particular agency, and provide a quality response. We had to write outstanding, competitive proposals in amazingly short time periods in order to be successful.

This meant MAXIMUS needed an effective intelligence network, very fast reaction times, encyclopedic knowledge of government programs, and up-to-date information on the latest innovations in government. Many of our competitors had commercial clients, and were awarded contracts without any competition. Those firms could not compete effectively against MAXIMUS in government because they were not used to intense competition.

Additional Advantages of Being Reactive

Choosing to be reactive rather than proactive held other advantages for MAXIMUS. Foremost, being reactive made us win through competitive procurements. We could not wait for sole source justifications, and even if we did, they were political firestorms. *We had to win competitively, and winning competitively meant we had to be the best.* Not second best.

Being the best required that we monitor our competitors and continuously evaluate our relative position in each market. We had to know more than our competitors, have better people, understand government programs better, have stronger client references, write better proposals, and have lower costs. All these requirements were healthy for MAXIMUS. We could take nothing for granted since we were on the competitive battlefield virtually every day. Did we win every proposal? No! But we won more than our fair share.

Being reactive also meant there was no sense in developing long-range forecasts of government procurements. MAXIMUS did not have to deal with the uncertainty of predicting when and where specific procurements were to materialize. We simply relied on the macro trends occurring in government procurements. Of course, if we heard of an impending procurement, we tracked it. *Moreover, we made sure we knew when our competitors' contracts were expiring and up for rebid.*

If MAXIMUS had been a commercial business, we might have needed to forecast technology breakthroughs or consumer sentiment, but we weren't. We didn't have to manufacture and stock inventory, or estimate demand for a product. Being in the government service business had its advantages—we simply had to learn over time how to operate in the unique government procurement environment.

So, we had a vision and operating philosophy, and we had a sales strategy for MAXIMUS. This was the foundation for building a growing company and reforming government. In fact, many of our competitors started following our lead and adopting our strategies.

CHAPTER 8

OUR CORPORATE CULTURE

While MAXIMUS had a mission statement, an operating philosophy, and a sales strategy, we still needed to add more substance to our corporate culture in terms of infrastructure. This infrastructure consisted, in part, of a number of operating principles. I believed these principles needed to be emphasized continually.

"The Star Spangled Banner" is traditionally sung at every major sports event, and the "Pledge of Allegiance" is repeated in school every day—or at least it was. Many Americans go to church every Sunday and follow the same rituals. Why? Why so often? Because it's needed. We human beings need to be continually reminded of our beliefs and our principles. So I repeatedly hammered home MAXIMUS principles to our staff. All companies should take inventory of the principles on which they operate and do the same. Here are some of ours.

The Standards MAXIMUS Upheld

To develop into a truly great company, MAXIMUS needed truly great people. *The caliber of a company is defined by the caliber of its people.* Therefore, we had the serious and ever-present goal of developing our employees, stretching them into jobs they hadn't done before, and challenging them to achieve levels of excellence they had not yet experienced. I also had to instill in them a higher ethic and value system consistent with our definition of what MAXIMUS represented. It was a constant challenge.

The caliber of the company, and therefore its people, is most visible through the standards it upholds. When a government agency bought our services, it bought MAXIMUS standards. Therefore, we had to keep our standards high. The first principle of Quality, Profitability, Growth (QPG) discussed in the last chapter emphasized that standard—quality.

However, the word "Quality" meant more than the quality of the services we provided the government. It also referred to the quality of our people, the quality of their experience at MAXIMUS, and the quality of our surroundings—our offices and technology. Quality was meant to be interpreted broadly to characterize important attributes of the whole company. So we had standards in many different areas.

A company justifies its existence, in my opinion, by ensuring the sum of its parts is more than the individual parts summed separately. Otherwise, you don't need a company. This synergy is achieved, in part, by the standards the company sets. *A company has to expect more from its employees than the employees expect of themselves.* This expectation is essential to generate the additional value needed to be competitive and provide quality services.

I was forever saying, *"You get what you accept."* If our standards were low, we experienced low performance. If our standards were high, we ultimately experienced high performance. I also believe, *"Only excellence survives."* Sometimes excellence doesn't survive, but mediocrity never does. We had to do an excellent job to have any chance our recommendations would be implemented by our government clients. If we wanted to leave a lasting mark, we had to achieve excellence.

I employed another message to help MAXIMUS staff understand these standards, *"Seven drafts to excellence."* This meant we had to do and redo our work products, possibly seven times, to raise the quality where it needed to be. The products could be management reports, proposals, client briefings, system screens, or other project deliverables. After the first draft, a second draft, a third draft, and up to the seventh final draft could be required.

This was very frustrating for many in the company, and I received continual complaints. But as progress was observed with each new draft, the staff began to understand what excellence meant and what our standards meant. Even today at my new business, QuaverMusic.com, which is developing great teaching resources for kids' music programs, we have "Seven drafts to excellence"—and they are usually needed.

The more difficult a task, the more value we create when we complete it. The ability to complete the most difficult tasks is a key differentiator of the best companies. It seemed MAXIMUS could do anything we wanted, and this was because of our commitment to high standards.

As an aside, one of our government clients once cautioned a prospective client who was checking our references to be careful with MAXIMUS. Specifically she warned the prospective client, "Be careful about what you ask MAXIMUS to do." The prospective client became concerned and asked why. She was told, "Because they do it." I loved that kind of endorsement.

Honesty

Honesty was a key principle in our culture. I believe honesty is one of the most important traits a company can promote. Business is essentially commerce among people. And commerce has to be honest to continue and thrive. People within the company have to be honest with one another so trust can develop. Dishonest contractors go to jail or go out of business.

Make no mistake, honesty costs money. I had a number of opportunities to be less than honest, and save MAXIMUS a lot of money. One particular time I recall involved very little money, but the incident had a big impact. I could have ignored a likely unenforceable "no hire" agreement, and saved MAXIMUS $25,000. A "no hire" agreement prevents a prime contractor from hiring employees away from a subcontractor without compensation to the subcontractor. We had hired a staff member from a subcontractor. I told the General Counsel to pay the firm anyway. He was surprised, and became a loyal supporter of me from then on. Plus, he got the message—we honored our commitments.

Our employees also needed to know we honored our commitments. Verbal agreements were frequently made without much forethought and as often not honored. *Once the staff learned MAXIMUS honored its commitments, they were much more careful about making them.* This strengthened the company. A simple handshake signified an agreement, and at MAXIMUS, had meaning. Nevertheless, we tried to ensure our agreements were in writing and unambiguous, to avoid misunderstandings.

I implemented a policy that my initials or signature was required on all internal decision papers; otherwise, the decision was not binding on me. Some staff would say I had a selective memory, claiming I had verbally approved something, which I could not recall. There was no documentation either way, and it caused big problems.

I initiated the policy so I'd be less likely to forget my commitment, and so no one could claim I'd made a commitment when I hadn't. If my signature or initials were on a decision paper, the decision was honored. This kept me honest, as well. I found I was as fallible as the rest and sometimes had to honor commitments I couldn't believe I'd made.

I also tried hard to be fair. My brother reminded me of the time when he and I spent one evening writing a lease for a landlord who didn't have a standard lease. We made sure the lease was fair to both sides. The landlord was apparently new and had written his own lease from scratch. His lease didn't have the protections normally afforded a landlord. After we gave him the new lease, the landlord always went out of his way to help us.

There is an old saying—*"Character is who you are in the dark."* How you behave when you think no one is watching, is who you are. I can't relate the number of times when I thought no one was watching me, but they were. Nothing does your standing better than for others to see you being honest when you don't have to be.

I tried to set the example for MAXIMUS. If they see the leader is honest, they will be honest. If the leader cheats, then they can cheat, as well. My father taught me *"to take the harder right over the easier wrong."* It's actually part of the West Point Cadet Prayer, and I follow that advice to this day.

Why is honesty so important? If someone tries to sell you something and you detect even the slightest dishonesty, you generally turn away. Honesty and trust are required to build successful relationships and a successful company, and the culture of the company must reinforce those values.

Management Reporting

Honesty also involves faithfully reporting bad news—notifying MAXIMUS management and the client about a problem as soon as it is discovered. We wanted to advise the government project manager about a problem before he or she found out from another source. We wanted the project manager to trust MAXIMUS. Unfortunately, our people sometimes made mistakes, and it didn't always work out that way.

MAXIMUS employees were required to report problems as soon as possible, so they could be solved at an early stage, rather than wait until the problem became much larger. Employees were not fired for causing problems as long as they were acting in good faith. They were fired for not reporting them. More people seem to go to jail for the cover up than for the crime. Most of the big problems we experienced occurred because a senior person chose to conceal the problem until it became too big to hide. We'd find out when the client stopped paying our invoices or complained to the corporate office.

Related to the issue of reporting problems is reporting successes. I sought to minimize the reporting bias in MAXIMUS, but it was difficult, despite our policy of honesty. For example, I knew that information was filtered before it came to me, giving me a "rosier" picture than actually existed. Whether the information was financial results or progress on a project, there was always a strong urge to minimize the negative and amplify the positive. I kept telling our people that honesty and truth were intimately connected. We all had to be truthful in our reports.

To bring home the point of reporting bias, and how it can affect decision-making, I told the following story in training classes.

> Dolphins are known for pushing drowning swimmers to shore, saving their lives. As a result, dolphins earned the reputation of being man's true best friend. Some scientists decided to find out why dolphins did this. What the scientists found was that dolphins push drowning swimmers (or any other objects) in a random direction. Only those drowning swimmers who were pushed to shore lived to tell about it. The others never got a chance to file a report. So the conclusion about dolphins was incorrect because it came from a nonrepresentative sample of drowning swimmers.

As CEO, I always heard more quickly about successes than about failures. I heard right away when we won a proposal but rarely when we lost one. I had to ask. It was surprising how many times I was misled by less than the full story. This may not have been intentional because of basic human nature. But it happened so often, I became skeptical, especially when the news was too good to be true. The sample was biased or nonrepresentative.

Our managers always needed to consider the possibility of reporting bias. Each report needed to be questioned to ensure there was none. In our corporate culture, we tried to make people as honest and truthful as possible. By making them aware of reporting bias, they were less likely to submit misleading or incomplete reports.

Training

Obviously, a commitment to training was another major part of our culture. Training was essential to pass on the knowledge and values we wanted our employees to have. When MAXIMUS was smaller, we scheduled a day of training away from the corporate office. Sometimes, we invited guest speakers, but most of the time, we trained ourselves. Later, we held multi-day meetings every October away from the corporate offices, which we called the Company Off-Site. Training, socializing, and recreation were the primary objectives. We made sure the employees were well informed of the progress MAXIMUS was making in helping government. I traditionally gave a one-hour kickoff speech at the meetings to inspire the staff to perform at even higher levels.

As MAXIMUS became larger, attendance was limited to the top 450 people in the company. The administrative staff would book a hotel in Puerto Rico, California, Arizona, Florida, or some other resort area. We then developed elaborate schedules of training classes, dinners, and recreational activities so the staff could socialize and enjoy each other's company. Everyone had a good time at these off-sites, and it became a real reward to be eligible to go.

You may recall the movie *Gladiator* starring Russell Crowe as the Roman General Maximus Decimus Meridius. Before the movie was released on DVD, I obtained a clip from the studio, which showed the entire Colosseum chanting Maximus! Maximus! Maximus! I played the clip at an off-site, and our staff loved it. At another off-site, I showed a video of Sasha Cohen scoring a perfect ten in figure skating at the 2002 Winter Olympics. I used the video to show excellence. All this was done to build a company that could better help government serve the people.

The need for training grew more intense as MAXIMUS grew larger. We employed trainers and equipped training rooms in each of our large privatization projects. Because of the natural turnover in case management staff, we were continually training new recruits on our corporate culture and operating procedures.

Toward the end of my career, we created a formal, fully-staffed MAXIMUS Training Center. At the entrance to the center in McLean, Virginia, we had a large sign:

> Tell me and I will forget.
> Show me and I may remember.
> Involve me and I will understand.

We wanted our training to be retained, and not be a series of lectures. Each new employee was assigned required classes and given one year to complete them. The classes were as interactive as possible to involve the employees in the subject. We would break the trainees into groups and have them complete assignments in each topic area as teams, so they were involved rather than listening to lectures. Basic classes included the following topics:

- History of MAXIMUS

- Corporate Culture

- Administrative Compliance

- Quality, Profitability, Growth

- Customer Enthusiasm (Satisfaction wasn't enough!)

- Diversity

- Supervisory Training.

More advanced classes included the following topics:

- Leadership

- Project Management

- Client Handling

- Marketing

- Writing Proposals

- Preparing Reports

- Conflict Resolution

Each of these classes was customized to MAXIMUS requirements.

The MAXIMUS Training Center, our training facilities for large projects, and our company off-sites all helped establish a strong culture for MAXIMUS. A comprehensive and pervasive training program is a requirement for any successful company, so we were not much different from other successful companies in this regard.

Learning Organization

A growing organization needs to be a learning organization. I'm not talking about the learning that takes place in training programs, but about learning from experience, learning from our mistakes in operating our company and serving government clients. If we kept making the same mistakes, we couldn't move forward. We would waste time and money fixing the same problems.

One of the areas of earliest learning for MAXIMUS was in Human Resources (HR). Our HR manual grew every year, as we learned what to do and what not to do with employees. One employee stands out in my memory. Joyce Keller, on her own, helped double the size of our HR Policies and Procedures Manual in the early years. She unwittingly and seemingly at random tested every nook and cranny of the existing manual. This made the manual grow. She managed to uncover situations requiring policy definition we never thought of.

For example, one day Joyce was working in our production room where we assembled proposals. MAXIMUS had all the equipment needed to mass produce multiple four-hundred-plus-page proposals simultaneously, including huge copying and binding machines and even drill presses for drilling holes in paper, so the pages could be inserted in three-hole notebooks.

She was drilling paper one day, and her hair became caught in the rubber belt of the drill press. She let out a blood-curdling scream as the machine pulled a swatch of hair from her scalp. Everyone was upset. After that, our policy manual required that anyone operating drill presses use hairnets. Later drill presses included a safety cover for the rubber belt.

On a more relevant note, many of the lessons learned in Human Resources came from employee grievances against MAXIMUS and from lawsuits filed against the company, as described later. We took all of these very seriously and changed our HR Manual continually. And if I may say so, MAXIMUS became extremely proficient in managing large numbers of diverse employees.

Another key area where we were constantly learning from our mistakes was proposal writing. One of the earliest lessons we had to instill in the staff was to read the RFP carefully and respond to each and every requirement. It's amazing how difficult this seemed to be. Another area was allowing enough time to review the proposal before it was submitted. And there were many more lessons to learn about proposal writing.

We learned something in most projects we did for the government. And we learned primarily from the mistakes we made. I once told an evaluation committee in Florida that MAXIMUS was the most experienced firm for their project because we had made more mistakes on similar projects than any other firm. I'm not sure they bought the point, but it was true.

When we were making new mistakes, we were learning. I remember criticizing one manager for not making enough mistakes; he was too cautious. We just didn't want the same mistakes being made repeatedly.

Changing Staff Behavior

In order to benefit from these mistakes and the consequent lessons learned, we had to change behavior within MAXIMUS. This was no small challenge. In my experience, changing human behavior and solving problems shared five stages:

      Stage 1 – We don't know we have a problem.
      Stage 2 – We detect symptoms of a problem, but don't
              know what it is.

Stage 3 – We identify the problem, but don't yet have a solution.

Stage 4 – We develop a solution to the problem.

Stage 5 – We implement the solution to the problem.

Most organizations and people become mired in Stage 4—they know they have a problem and they know the solution, but they don't implement it. Or, in behavioral terms, we know the behavior is wrong, we know how to change it, but we keep making the same mistakes. This is what learning is all about—not just knowing the answer, but implementing the answer—acting on it—changing behavior. When we learned from experience, we had to implement what we learned.

I would tell new staff coming into MAXIMUS that it was imperative to apply what they learned in training. Otherwise, they would be making the same mistakes employees before them had made. Why should MAXIMUS continue to pay the price for different employees to make the same mistake? *The school of hard knocks is the best place to learn, but we couldn't afford to pay every employee to go through that school.*

When you manage a growing company with ever-arriving waves of new employees, you end up paying for the same mistakes many times over. So a company must make great efforts to minimize these unnecessary costs.

Institutionalizing Change

In many cases, we could force behavioral change by institutionalizing what we learned. This could be done, in part, by implementing the following types of management tools:

- **Checklists** for staff to follow when performing specific tasks, such as developing a proposal plan

- **Logs** to record when certain events occurred so they could be monitored, such as backing up a system

- **Posters** to remind staff of our corporate culture, such as Employee Rights

- **Training Handouts** to remind staff what they learned in training, such as Steps for Conflict Resolution

- **Updated Policies and Procedures Handbooks** to incorporate the latest lessons into our daily operating procedures

- **New System Functionality** to implement improved procedures, such as streamlined data entry, to guide our staff

- **Updated Administrative Manuals** for use by staff in carrying out administrative tasks, such as conducting exit interviews

- **Automated Library of Past Reports and Proposals** so staff could reference our best practices and reuse available materials, or the latest "boiler plate," reflecting our new knowledge.

Changing behavior requires tremendous work and discipline. Despite our best efforts, we weren't always as successful as we should have been. At times it was maddening. Quite frequently, learning from experience takes multiple tries—the pain of the mistake has to be much greater than the pain of the change required. *We hadn't learned the lesson until we implemented the solution.*

There are many other important aspects to corporate culture. The next chapter provides more context for understanding MAXIMUS and how it became so successful.

CHAPTER 9

OTHER MULTIFARIOUS FACETS OF CULTURE

This chapter provides more in-depth explanations of the corporate culture of MAXIMUS, covering other facets.

Employee Rights

Basic to any organizational culture is how employees are treated. I didn't elaborate on employees in my earlier explanation of Quality, Profitability, Growth, but Quality also meant providing a quality experience for employees. After many years, we decided to codify what Quality meant in terms of employee rights and post them in every MAXIMUS office. Some of these rights were based on lessons learned, as described in the previous chapter.

At MAXIMUS, employees at all levels were entitled to the following, at a minimum:

- **Meaningful Job** – The job had to be meaningful and contribute to the goals of the company.

- **Congenial and Supportive Work Environment** – The work environment in each office had to be friendly. We would tolerate no sexual harassment, discrimination, or hostility.

- **Professional Treatment** – Each employee had to be treated with dignity and respect.

- **Competitive Compensation** – Salaries and fringe benefits had to be competitive and opportunities given to employees to participate in performance-based bonus plans.

- **Regular Performance Evaluations and Career Counseling** – Each employee would be regularly evaluated and provided career counseling, if requested.

- **Fair Consideration for Promotions and Raises** – Full and fair consideration had to be given to each employee for promotions and raises, regardless of race, religion, gender, or age. MAXIMUS would also look first to promote from within the company.

- **Fair and Timely Grievance Process** – Grievances had to be processed in a timely and honest manner, without fear of reprisal.

- **Effective Affirmative Action Program** – An Affirmative Action Program would be implemented to achieve diversity in MAXIMUS.

Writing these rights down and posting them in our offices actually helped improve employee welfare. We should have done it a lot earlier. Employees and their supervisors now had a basis to discuss their jobs and how they were being treated.

Compare these rights to those of government employees. MAXIMUS guarantees a meaningful job and treatment of each employee as a professional. In MAXIMUS, there are no limitations on the timing and extent of promotions, pay raises, and bonuses—not so in the government. We could also bend the rules to take care of employees in need, as explained below—not so freely in the government. People were our asset, and we took care of them.

MAXIMUS employees had an excellent fringe benefits package with subsidized health, dental, and life insurance. They had generous vacation and holiday leave, as well as paid sick, jury, and bereavement leave. MAXIMUS matched contributions to their 401(k) plans. The government unions kept painting us as having no fringe benefits at all, and they were dead wrong.

Taking Care of Employees in Need

My parents lived through the depression, and I could see how it permanently affected their behavior. My father, for example, was very risk averse, and my mother was very frugal. I found myself being shaped by hard times as well.

During the first couple of struggling years in MAXIMUS, I had a very hard time recruiting employees. When someone did join me, I was truly grateful that he or she bet their future on me. And I carried that feeling with me throughout my tenure. I was always grateful to people who joined MAXIMUS, and I felt responsible for them.

When someone became truly ill, or when his or her family was in real distress, I ignored our written policies. I granted administrative leave with pay for months at a time to many, even though some may have been terminally ill. I paid out money we did not technically owe to spouses who had lost their partners at MAXIMUS. We were a responsible corporation. It was the right thing to do, and the staff knew we were looking out for them—beyond what was required. We called ourselves an extended family, and we were.

Administrative Culture

Many manifestations of the culture of a company are of an administrative nature. For example, for the longest time, senior MAXIMUS staff did not have secretaries. Secretaries were gatekeepers and weren't really needed with PCs in ascendency. We had an executive assistant pool senior staff could draw on as needed.

Later, I had a dedicated Special Assistant, Paul Mack, who was assigned special projects. He did not screen access to me or type my thoughts or correspondence. He helped assemble the Management Book for the monthly management meetings discussed below, and faithfully supported me in other ways on special projects.

I kept an open door policy, rarely scheduling appointments to meet with members of my management team. They could just walk in and talk to me whenever they wanted, or wait in line, if there was one, outside the door. I also walked in on them unannounced when something arose. It was very hard to schedule my time as we grew. As more and more problems came my way, I began to feel like an emergency room doctor. *Emergency room doctors don't schedule appointments.*

In our corporate office in Reston, Virginia, I had all the doors constructed with large glass panels so everything was visible. A transparent company has few secrets. Anyone could see what the others were doing. All our conference rooms were glass enclosed. Our staff needed to see what was going on.

Communications/Meetings

Another dimension of culture is how people communicate. In the early eighties I may have coined the phrase, *"Management is a contact sport."* To manage people, you have to stay in close contact with them. We encouraged communications up and down the corporate hierarchy. *I believe the volume of communications taking place within an organization is the single most important indicator of its health.* MAXIMUS published a newsletter, MAXNEWS, which was distributed to all employees. We were among the first companies to institute company-wide e-mail. We had conference rooms in all our facilities.

I also maintained continual contact with our senior staff in group meetings. As we became much larger, I held monthly management meetings with all division presidents and other key personnel in the company. Everyone was required to attend these meetings except for the president in Australia. That meant monthly travel for many of these division presidents. I wanted to see them face-to-face.

The meetings started at five p.m. and ended at eight p.m. We served a light dinner in between. The agenda began with a financial report by the CFO on how the company was doing as a whole and how the divisions were doing individually. Then, senior staff presented topics on recent contract wins, major project developments—both positive and negative, how we were helping government serve the people, and other subjects. This was done to bring everyone up to date on what was going on in MAXIMUS.

These meetings were a way of keeping everyone informed, letting them know they were accountable for their results in front of their peers, showing off our successes, learning from our mistakes, and creating an identity for MAXIMUS as a whole.

In addition, the meetings provided the opportunity for socializing. People could interact with their peers before and after the meeting. We enjoyed being with one another since we were all friends.

Dress Code

MAXIMUS had a strict dress code. I believed high standards required a strict dress code, even though Apple, Google, and others thought otherwise. But MAXIMUS had government officials who would come visit us at any time. And our caseworkers dealt face-to-face with program recipients on a daily basis.

We required a shirt and tie and long pants for men. For women, we did not allow any cutoffs or jeans. They had to look nice. On more than one occasion, a state or county project manager visiting our offices would compliment us on how professional our staff looked. In addition, we were setting good examples for the welfare recipients we served.

The staff felt like professionals when they dressed like professionals. The recipients were greeted in a business-like setting and were treated like valued customers. We were a professional company, and the dress code helped make us so.

As an aside, the very first person to join me at MAXIMUS, Dr. Stephen Stollmack, told me something surprising many years after he had left to form his own company. He remarked that I always wore a suit, even when we were in a one-room office. He said I always believed in MAXIMUS.

Subliminal Messages

One important lesson I learned about corporate culture came from another CEO. On an unusual government project we had with the US Army, I ended up visiting the offices of SKF Industries. SKF Industries is a ball bearing manufacturer headquartered in Pennsylvania. On arriving, I couldn't help notice the campus-like setting. The grounds were stunning, like greens on a golf course.

When I met my contact there, I remarked that SKF had a beautiful campus. His response surprised me. He said, yes, but the CEO was an obsessive-compulsive—he kept the grass mowed to a height of three-quarters of an inch all the time. The campus must have been fifty acres.

Riding back to Washington DC on the train, I thought about what my contact had said. This CEO was sending a message to all employees. If anything, a ball bearing manufacturer has to maintain the strictest tolerances in manufacturing. The CEO was simply expressing his standards in the height of the grass.

Perhaps he was giving his employees a subliminal message that SKF Industries was a precision company. I never got the chance to ask him. But I liked what he did and tried to keep it in mind, as we kept our offices neat and clean and our staff well dressed. No cardboard boxes or handwritten signs were allowed in MAXIMUS offices. Everything had to be professional in appearance.

Too bad all government doesn't have the same standards.

Employee Recognition

For convenience in tracking employees, we assigned them all employee numbers when they were hired. We naturally assigned them in numerical order—I was 001. As the company grew, it became more and more a sign of achievement to have a lower employee number. One's status in the company was, in part, determined by the order in which he or she joined. Some who left and rejoined later wanted their old employee numbers back.

People want recognition, and the employee number was an easy way to give it. Because the staff valued their tenure so much, we also started awarding one-, two-, five-, and ten-year anniversary pins that could be worn on their clothing. Before I retired, several employees even earned a twenty-five-year pin. Gifts were given for longer tenures. Staff were always pleased to be recognized. Napoleon once observed, "Men will do almost anything for colored ribbons." Recognition was an important part of our culture.

In fact, at our company off-sites, each division would nominate three people to win the division award. And like the Academy Awards, we would have a panel select the winners and announce them at a special dinner. Great fun!

In summary, I had tremendous flexibility in determining the culture of MAXIMUS, much more so than I would have in government. Moreover, the leadership of MAXIMUS was not being replaced every two, three, or four years as often happens in government agencies at all levels. Continuity of leadership was an important factor in building our culture, and our purpose remained Helping Government Serve the People.

CHAPTER 10

THE TOUGHEST MANAGEMENT JOB OF ALL

Managing people is the toughest job of all. And managing people is fundamental to all businesses, especially service businesses. We are all such emotional creatures, ready to abandon logic at the smallest slight. We are ready to blame others for our faults. We can be very hard to deal with.

Yet at heart, the vast majority of us are good people. I believe everyone wants to do a good job and be recognized as a good worker. Clearly, I am an optimist, but I like being an optimist. *Pessimists don't belong in business—they won't be successful.*

Let's look at some of the lessons MAXIMUS learned in managing people. The first step in managing people was hiring them.

Hiring Staff

As I mentioned earlier, the caliber of the company is determined by the caliber of its people. So hiring good people was one of our most important duties. I failed surprisingly often in the earlier years and hired the wrong person. This was always costly, so I was continually looking for ways to separate winners from losers. If there was a magic formula, I never found it. No one else has found the formula either, as far as I know.

However, I have thoughts on how to hire successfully, based on hiring hundreds of people myself. In my experience, we couldn't go seriously wrong by looking for the following attributes.

- **High Intelligence** – First, is the person intelligent? Can this person learn quickly? Does he or she understand what the interviewer is saying—can he or she extend what the interviewer is saying? Is he or she pushing the interviewer in the conversation instead of vice versa?

- **High Energy** – Second, does the person have a high energy level? Does the person talk fast or slow? Is he or she animated? Could this person win an endurance race? Will this person be a prolific producer?

- **Passion/Commitment** – Third, does this person show signs of passion or commitment? Why does the person want the job? If the reason is to make more money, then this is the wrong person. Good answers include wanting to help people in need, or wanting to make a difference, or wanting to work for a growing company and grow professionally, or just being excited about joining MAXIMUS.

If the person had these three attributes, we could then assess how well his or her skills and knowledge fit the particular job in question. If the person was not a fit, then we tried to find another job in MAXIMUS where this person's skills and knowledge were a fit *because we had found a good prospective employee.*

The types of interviews that seemed best to determine skills or knowledge were those that simulated the work to be performed. Alternately, letting successful employees in the same department select the candidate also worked. They tended to choose people like themselves.

I once had a very high-level partner from another firm interview with me for a job. He was making close to $900,000 per year, considering his total compensation package. In the first five minutes of the interview, he focused on telling me what he wanted from MAXIMUS in terms of a salary, stock options, and bonuses. I listened intently.

After he was done, I asked him what he was going to do for MAXIMUS. He asked what I meant. I said what kind of revenues can you generate, at what profit levels, and in what areas?

He stammered at first, and then commented he couldn't guarantee anything because he really didn't know our business. That ended the interview—I escorted him to the elevator. We wanted people who wanted to contribute to our mission: Helping Government Serve the People. We wanted people who wanted to contribute to a higher cause, not people interested only in how much money they could make.

Hiring Large Numbers of Case Managers

In projects where we privatized social welfare programs, MAXIMUS would have to hire hundreds of caseworkers for three- and five-year terms. Most of the projects were extended with add-on contracts, but we couldn't guarantee employment beyond the original contract term.

For the California Healthy Families Project, described in detail later, we had to hire 450 case managers in one weekend. Imagine if the government had to do that!

We couldn't hire the case managers earlier than needed because we would be paying them to be idle before the project went live. Also, at this salary level, people didn't stay on the market long, so we couldn't do advanced hiring with start dates months away. They would just accept open jobs in competing companies. We had to hire the case managers all at once, just when we needed them—"just in time" supply.

To do this, we advertised in the *Sacramento Bee* that MAXIMUS would be interviewing case managers. Ads were placed four and two weeks before the weekend when the interviews would be conducted. We leased all the meeting rooms in a hotel to conduct the interviews.

We also contacted all the local welfare offices and alerted them MAXIMUS would be hiring qualified welfare recipients. Our staff set up a call center with a local number, which was included in the ads. We asked that interested candidates call in to be prescreened to receive an interview time.

To interview six hundred candidates, we established twelve panels of three MAXIMUS employees each. We provided score sheets to the panels so each candidate would be rated on different attributes and overall. We allowed fifteen minutes per interview, including time to input the scores into our computer system, MAXHIRE. The system was designed to track all the candidates, record their interview scores, and adjust for panel bias after all the scores had been entered.

To streamline the hiring process, we administered a written "trip-wire" test to candidates while they were waiting for their interviews. Any wrong answer tripped the wire, and the interview process was terminated. Examples of questions in the trip-wire test include:

- Most people on welfare are scamming the government. Yes or No

- It's OK to use drugs in the workplace as long as your performance isn't affected. Yes or No

- It's a bad idea to report someone stealing from the company. Yes or No

- Many times you have to ignore your supervisor and do what you think is right. Yes or No

- You can't trust for-profit companies—they always cheat you. Yes or No

- It's good to change jobs regularly to get more experience. Yes or No

Surprisingly, about 5 percent failed the trip-wire test, and we avoided much trouble. Any sign of dishonesty terminated the interview. We didn't have the time to explore wrong answers.

MAXIMUS ended up successfully hiring the 450 case managers. We had planned it well in advance, and this time, the plan worked. Compare this process with the Civil Service Reform Act of 1978. There is no comparison.

Types of Employees

Employees naturally come in all shapes and sizes. One particular break-out was useful to me in hiring—some employees are caretakers and some are creators. The caretakers can run an established operation and do a good job. The creators have more problems with routine tasks and need to be continually challenged.

There is no sense in putting caretakers in charge of winning new business or starting up a new project. They were great in carrying out well-defined tasks that developed into a routine, but they were not innovative. Creators, on the other hand, had to be doing something new all the time—writing proposals, starting new projects, developing new procedures, and the like. I even implemented the Myers-Briggs personality test to see if we could tell in advance which employees were creators and which were caretakers, but it wasn't really that helpful. By the way, I am an INTJ—Introvert, Intuitive, Thinking, Judging—or so they say.

Another important breakout was whether employees were committed to the company and its mission. Obviously, we only wanted committed employees, but sometimes when hiring hundreds of people for nine-to-five jobs, we hired many who were not. When this happened, we experienced higher turnover rates, which was always costly because of the training investment. It was even more costly if we made this mistake with higher-level employees.

When I assigned people to jobs, I tried to consider what type of person they were. For case managers, we needed caretaker-type employees since the work was so routine. We also wanted committed employees, and the best way to do that was to make sure they were happy in their jobs.

Our Workforce Mirrored the Caseload

Later, as we privatized more programs, I required that our workforce mirror the caseload. For example, if our caseload (or the recipients we served) in a project was 30 percent African-American, 15 percent Hispanic, and 5 percent Asian, then our staff on that project would be approximately 30 percent African-American, 15 percent Hispanic, and 5 percent Asian. This fostered better communication between our staff and the recipients. We often had a contract requirement to support specific languages in our operations. This required us to hire the different nationalities represented in our caseload. MAXIMUS was truly multicultural.

Staffing projects was even more complicated. I set a requirement on our welfare-to-work projects that MAXIMUS would hire at least 15 percent of our case managers from the welfare rolls. In welfare-to-work programs, we helped recipients find jobs. So we had to understand the training these recipients would need to become successful employees. What better way to find out than hiring them ourselves?

In sum, our human resources policies and procedures had to accommodate the cultural differences among the various nationalities and the special needs of welfare recipients in our workforce.

Working with Welfare Recipients as Employees

In our welfare-to-work programs, our case managers would have to assure prospective employers that our recipients would do a good job. We also had to explain to prospective employers the tax credits and other benefits they would receive by hiring welfare recipients. Basically, we functioned as a placement agency, placing welfare recipients into jobs.

To do this effectively, our case managers needed to understand what other employers who hired our recipients would be dealing with—recipients who may not have held jobs before and did not know how to behave in the workplace. We wanted to anticipate the problems other employers would experience, so we could address them. That's why we hired welfare recipients ourselves. To say the least, it was an eye-opening experience for MAXIMUS!

We first had to deal with former welfare recipient employees showing up on time for work. Some had no concept of hours; some had not worked for a long while; some were late-night people and couldn't get up in the morning; some were just not responsible. We had to teach them.

Then we had to address inappropriate behavior—no cursing your supervisor; no antagonizing your coworkers; no proselytizing in the office. In our Los Angeles Figueroa office, one worker, Sherrel, put voodoo signs on the office doors, including mine, to protect us—she meant well. And, most importantly, no drugs in the workplace.

Then lunch breaks—no sleeping on the desks. No hot foods at lunch with strong aromas like Chinese and Mexican food. These made the office smell like a restaurant. Every step was difficult but workable. The vast majority of recipients we hired were cooperative and wanted to keep their jobs. Some just didn't know how to behave until we taught them.

All this experience gave us material for our welfare-to-work training programs. We worked with the recipients and taught them their responsibilities as employees. We were ultimately very successful in placing them into jobs. I remember one person who became a pilot for a regional airline and another who later graduated from Stanford University—unbelievable. Sometimes we couldn't anticipate what we'd achieve.

Keeping Supervisors Supervising

We also had to keep employees focused on doing their jobs rather than someone else's. I had one supervisor who continually did the workers' jobs for them. Repeatedly, this person helped the staff with data entry to get the work done, rather than managing the process and making sure we had enough data-entry clerks. We did not want a "superworker"—we wanted a supervisor.

I solved the problem when I told the supervisor it was fine with me if she wanted to enter data. MAXIMUS would pay her as a clerk when she was entering data and as a supervisor when she was supervising. I asked her to keep the hours straight so we could pay her fairly. Well, we had no more problems after that. I let the employee decide what to do, given the choices.

Motivation

Motivating employees is obviously also crucial to success. Motivation is how you move the uncommitted to the committed ranks. I believe *Leadership is motivating people to do the right thing*. You motivate people by interesting them in what you are doing and then involving them. If they are with you, they will be motivated.

My father taught me the function of management was to "comfort the irritable and irritate the comfortable." That's another way of looking at motivation.

My experience was that money is not the key motivator. Sure, everyone needs money and wants it—but most want something more valuable—a sense of doing something worthwhile, a sense of contribution. I would tell staff sincerely, *"You are important, and what you are doing is important."* If they felt indispensible, they worked even harder. *Recognition and appreciation, earned through important contributions to the company, are the most powerful motivators.*

One of our most successful managers and best motivators was Donna Schirf, later to become my wife. She was employee "007" or the seventh person hired in MAXIMUS. She led our corporate administrative staff as the Chief Administrative Officer. Donna had the energy of ten people and was always busy doing something to improve MAXIMUS.

Donna told me a story about the time she went to see a psychic/mind reader in Venice Beach, California. This happened during one of the projects she was working on in Los Angeles. The mind reader told Donna that she couldn't read her mind because it was too busy and offered to return her money. I can relate to not being able to read her mind. But Donna was our best manager of people.

We had a major problem in Tennessee with a child support financial reconciliation project involving over one hundred employees. The project manager on site was losing over $110,000 per month because of an unresponsive staff. Many of the staff were hired for just twelve months and had no long-term commitment to MAXIMUS. The project manager was unable to train them on the complex financial procedures they had to follow and unable to generate any enthusiasm on their part for the project.

Unexpectedly, I guess in frustration and to his credit, the project manager, Bob Sarno, asked for help. He asked Ray Ruddy, who then asked me if Donna could come down and manage the project. Donna knew nothing about child support financial reconciliation. So I asked Ray why her? He said only that she was the person needed; I accepted his judgment. I asked Donna if she wanted to go, and she said, "Sure, I'll give it a try." So I sent her.

What happened next is not in any management book I know of—nor in any management principles included in a business seminar, nor in anything I've ever seen or read. I can only tell you the project turned around in less than two months and began generating a profit. Here's what happened.

In the first few days Donna showed up on the job, she went around and asked everyone on the staff his or her names and birthdays. She asked about their families and their children—nothing about the project. She genuinely wanted to know them first—that is her nature. Then, on the third day, she held a birthday party on company time for everyone who had a birthday that month.

That was just the start. She became very close to the staff and they to her. Well—talk about a 180-degree turnaround! The people loved her; they wanted to help her; and they worked hard with her to make the project a success. And it was. Soon we were making a healthy profit, and everyone felt self-fulfilled.

I don't have to say any more—management by birthday party? Not in the government!

Manage Strength – Manage Weakness

Donna clearly did not know much about child support enforcement, but she did know how to work with people. So we took advantage of Donna's skill and surrounded her with managers who knew child support enforcement.

We are taught as managers to take advantage of the strengths of our people. However, as the story showed, we also need to address their weaknesses. Our organization had to be "tuned" so that our strengths were compounded and our weaknesses neutralized. Donna had to be surrounded by people who knew the intricacies of child support enforcement.

Exhibit 3 on the next page shows an example that illustrates the principle. In this hypothetical example, MAXIMUS senior managers were rated on five attributes, as indicated horizontally across the bottom of each organizational box:

> 1 – Leadership/Vision
> 2 – Financial Management Skills
> 3 – Proposal Writing/Marketing Skills
> 4 – People Skills
> 5 – Government Program Knowledge

These were key skill/knowledge attributes in our organization. We rated every senior manager on each attribute as either poor (black), satisfactory (gray), or good (white). Notice in the chart below how there are no black boxes for the same attribute in succeeding layers.

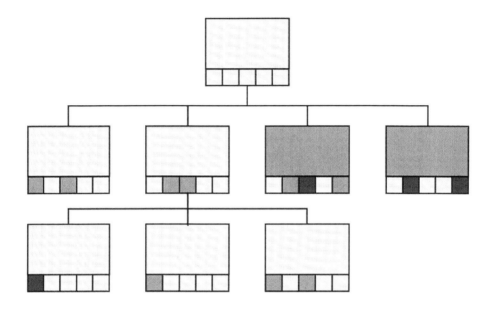

Exhibit 3 – Example of How We Tuned MAXIMUS

If a manager had great leadership qualities, for example, but was not particularly good at financial management, we had to have managers good at financial management above and below him or her.

Keeping this balance was difficult. At a minimum, we had a good inventory of our strengths and weaknesses up and down the organization.

Nonperforming Employees

So in contrast to the government, how did MAXIMUS deal with employees who were not performing? Managers, including me, often become frustrated when employees fail to do their jobs and complete assigned tasks. Our first impulse is to assume they are negligent and take corrective action. What I found was that when our people didn't do their jobs, it wasn't usually because they forgot to do it, chose to do something else, or just weren't motivated.

Many times people didn't do their jobs because they didn't know how to do them. The vast majority wanted to do a good job. So we first had to teach the employees how to do their jobs. Nonperformance most likely occurred for lack of training. If they couldn't do their jobs after training, then we would try to move them to something they could do. If that failed, they would be let go.

MAXIMUS had a Group President who was not doing well, but was very important to the firm. He had major strengths, but not in areas that I hired him to do—my mistake. I struggled with what to do. He was beyond training. Instead of firing him, I switched him to an important staff position where his strengths would gain traction and his weaknesses wouldn't matter. He agreed to try and was eminently successful in the new job, and everyone was happy with his performance. His skill set and personality were right for the new job.

Changing Someone's Basic Nature

One of the hardest lessons I learned in managing people was to stop trying to change them to fit the job. People who were not performing would come and ask me to help them change some aspect of their basic personality, such as their attention to detail or promptness in meeting deadlines. I worked with each of them and tried as hard as I could to change them, but to no avail. I was a total failure on all, and it cost years of valuable time and effort.

In one case, the person was continually disorganized. I tried to help him get organized and plan for deadlines, but he just could not do it. It seems like a simple thing to learn, but he could not. He left the company. I tried to make another, Paul, a manager. He was intelligent and understood what I was saying but just could not manage. He avoided confrontation. *A manager who cannot confront a subordinate cannot manage.*

There was another fellow, Charlie, who desperately wanted to be promoted to manager. He kept asking me what he needed to do to earn the title. Finally, I told him, "Write a proposal and win a contract, and I will make you a manager." Well, he did. In a fun ceremony, I went into his office with a pointer and dubbed him a "manager."

So Charlie had the title. Not even three weeks later he came into my office and complained. He said no one was doing what he told them to do—they weren't paying any attention to him. I sighed and said, "Charlie, a title does not make you a manager. You have to be a manager. Now go out there and tell them if they don't do what they're told, you'll take them off your contract." And he did.

MAXIMUS did best when we found people who were naturals in the job they were assigned. If the job requirements went against their basic nature, we had to remove them for their own sake and ours. Hiring people and then placing them in the correct job was always a challenge.

So who said hiring and managing people is easy? There are seemingly an infinite number of considerations to weigh in making good personnel decisions.

In the next chapter, I elaborate on some even harder decisions I faced in managing people—determining pay raises and awarding bonuses, addressing racial discrimination charges, resolving conflicts within MAXIMUS, and letting people go.

CHAPTER 11

THERE'S EVEN MORE?

Yes—there's even more. This chapter covers some of the tougher decisions to be made in managing people. Also, the chapter highlights differences between the government and private sector.

Compensation

As I mentioned in the last chapter, most staff at MAXIMUS were not motivated primarily by money, or to be more specific, by salary. However, bonuses were a little different, as will be seen.

MAXIMUS had a policy of *not* keeping salaries secret. This practice was highly unusual since most companies did. Moreover, many companies severely reprimanded individuals who revealed their salaries.

All raises at MAXIMUS were given on October 1, the beginning of our fiscal year. In privatization projects, raises were given on the anniversary of the project start date. Adjustments to salaries could be made at other times if warranted.

Since consulting billing rates were based on salaries, it was difficult to keep salaries confidential, so we didn't try. *I believe our transparent salary structure led to a fairer compensation system in MAXIMUS.* The transparency caused many problems, to be sure—but then—our policy worked. Since most staff knew each other's salaries, they also knew their raises at the end of the year. We had to be fair or lose our staff.

Sometimes, employees complained they didn't feel their salaries were fair and wanted a raise. However, many employees would never complain, even if they had good cause. We especially had to watch out for them to make sure they were treated fairly.

I remember when Nick, a senior executive at the time, came to see me. He said his $110,000 salary was too low, and he deserved a bigger raise. I told him I thought his salary was fair, based on what comparable people were being paid at MAXIMUS and in the industry. He said he didn't think so, and he would quit if his salary was not raised. I asked him to give me a week to do some research, and he agreed.

The next day, I asked our Human Resources Department to put a want ad in the *Washington Post* with Nick's job description and salary to see if there were any takers. We received over 150 resumes within a few days.

After reviewing them myself, I called Nick in and showed him the want ad and the resumes. I told him we would not be raising his salary. But if he was going to quit, would he mind looking through the resumes and picking out the best-qualified candidates for us to interview for his job? I think you can guess what happened. Again, I let the employee make the choice.

Bonuses

Bonuses were different in terms of motivation. They were awarded annually and could change dramatically from year to year, based on how well the company and the person did. I tried half-heartedly to keep bonus amounts confidential. The bonuses were not part of the billing system and were, in fact, one-time decisions. But the amounts got out anyway.

Bonuses were used for many purposes:

- Rewarding a specific major accomplishment

- Rewarding good, steady work

- Making up for a poor raise decision

- Making up for a poor bonus decision the previous year

- Compensating for a salary that couldn't be raised because it was already at the top of its range

To avoid contention, some managers wanted to award everyone the same bonus amount. So I instituted the policy that not all bonuses could be equal—after all, we were not communists! Managers had to vary the bonuses recommended for their staff. We wanted rewards proportional to contribution, and that meant recognizing the varying contributions of the staff.

I had the final decision on all bonuses for the top five hundred employees. I rarely overturned a recommendation; however, by approving the recommendations, I was the one to blame if someone became upset.

What is noteworthy about bonuses is that acceptance by an employee is relative, not absolute. For example, we typically received complaints at bonus time something like, "John's bonus was $4,000, and my bonus was only $3,000." The next year—a good one for the company—we would hear the same thing, even when the bonuses were higher: "John's bonus was $11,000, and I only got $9,000."

Naturally, we pointed out that the person complaining had received $6,000 more than the previous year. Didn't matter. The person wasn't happy. Bonus differences matter, but the unrest and problems that ensued were, in my opinion, still worth it.

I'd like to comment on how difficult it was for me to be responsible for raises and bonuses. Every year, I had to make decisions about staff I really cared about, good friends employed in the company, and even some family members working at MAXIMUS. The compensation decisions I made would affect their sense of self worth, their standard of living, and their feelings toward me. What was fair? How do you make such crucial decisions involving people you feel strongly about? What is the proper "social distance" you should maintain in your relationships with them? This is a common problem many managers face.

It took me a while to find the simple answer. There are really two relationships with the same person in this circumstance—one outside the company and one inside. I would work to help the person understand that the relationship inside the company was strictly business, and their raise or bonus did not reflect how much I liked or even loved them. In addition, their raises and bonuses had to viewed by others in the company as absolutely fair, or they would not be accepted. That is what guided me, and they came to understand it. Nonetheless, every year, bonus time was still very stressful.

Conflict Resolution

We also sought to maintain a spirit of teamwork and congeniality among our staff. We didn't want a "bare knuckles" culture. We wanted our own people and our government clients to view MAXIMUS as a friendly organization without inner conflicts. We needed to like each other and work hard together.

However, conflicts are inevitable with high-energy, intelligent, ambitious people—and even with those who are not. My observation was *"Packing high performers together in an organization is like packing uranium together in a reactor. If you pack it too tightly, it goes nuclear. If you keep it at the right level, you have a powerful energy source for your organization."*

After MAXIMUS had grown quite a bit, we were having trouble with some of our senior executives who didn't like one another. They were continually engaged in conflicts detrimental to the company. That was not the culture we wanted for MAXIMUS. We certainly didn't want conflicts with our government counterparts.

The conflicts among MAXIMUS staff in one particular office became so serious, we hired a business psychologist to help us develop a conflict resolution training program. In training, we set two executives in a role-playing game to resolve their conflict. They would have to follow a set of rules to complete the training.

Here are the simple rules we developed to solve our particular problem at MAXIMUS. The advice to each person in conflict was as follows:

- First, recognize you are in a conflict situation, and you should want to resolve the conflict amicably for your own good and for the good of the company.

- Second, assume the other person has good intentions. You may not agree with him or her, but assume they were taken in good faith.

- Next, don't talk to anyone else about the problem before talking to the person you are in conflict with.

- Use "active listening" to ensure you understand what the other person is saying. Repeat back what you think you heard.

- If you arrive at an impasse, express that conclusion, and then involve your immediate supervisor. Either person can make the decision to involve the immediate supervisor, but he or she must inform the other person before doing so.

- Seek win-win solutions in which each of you gives a little or in which one person gives in this time but is "owed one" next time.

- Accept there will always be conflicts, ambiguities, and tensions within the company. Try to minimize them, but know they will always exist, and they do not mean other people are against you.

We wanted our culture to accommodate powerful people, but they had to follow socially acceptable behavior and act as professionals.

I recall one time when two senior executives could not get along, even after following the conflict resolution rules. I called them both into my office. I told them they were both important to the company, but that they were causing serious problems in staff morale and productivity. If they couldn't get along, I was sorry, but I would have to fire one of them.

I told them they had thirty minutes to resolve their differences in my adjacent conference room. At the end of the thirty minutes, they were to come back into my office and explain to me whether they had agreed to work together amiably thereafter. I added that if they did not have such an agreement, I would flip a coin in front of them to decide who would stay and who would be fired.

After a half hour, they came back into my office, patting each other on the back and smiling. I didn't have any trouble from them again. This is the same lesson as before—let the employees decide for themselves what consequences they want.

Racial Discrimination or Poor Judgment

Racial discrimination is an ever-present threat in a large organization and an especially sensitive issue in a company doing business with the government. The problem is that discrimination is often a *perceived* phenomenon.

MAXIMUS became more than 50 percent minority after we started winning privatization contracts. As I explained earlier, we tried to have the ethnicity of our government operations workforce mirror the ethnicity of the people we served. This was done to ensure we understood and communicated effectively with that minority.

One interesting note is that we did not form ethnic Supervisory Units —that is, units in which everyone was either Hispanic, Vietnamese, Chinese, etc. When we tried this approach, we had considerable problems between the Supervisory Units. Cliques formed, and we had trouble. After that, we mixed ethnicities in the Supervisory Units.

We also tried to match ethnicity in our other businesses and at higher management levels, but we were not as successful because of the dearth of qualified candidates. We maintained a continual lookout for qualified minority managers. I implemented a policy that we had to interview at least one qualified minority for every job opening at MAXIMUS.

Unfortunately, with 5,500 employees, we were subject to a number of racial discrimination charges. What I found in the vast majority of cases was not racial discrimination, but poor judgment by management. An example is telling an employee not to play religious music out loud—to use headphones. This was interpreted by the person as racial discrimination since he was African-American—and the only one playing the music. Rather, there should have been a written policy that no religious music could be played out loud in the office, and that policy applied to everyone.

Management makes mistakes in every organization—no matter how well the managers are trained. When a mistake is made concerning a minority employee, it is often called racial discrimination. Again, managing people is not easy.

Letting People Go

One of the hardest things to do in MAXIMUS on an emotional level was letting people go, even those people who were clearly not performing. That is the last thing anyone wanted to do for the following reasons:

- These people were our friends;

- They may have really needed the job;

- We didn't want to hurt them or make them enemies;

- We didn't want to alienate their friends in MAXIMUS;

- We didn't want to be viewed as hard-hearted.

In government, there were even more reasons not to fire someone. As shown earlier, the government process was extremely lengthy and tedious and not always successful. And it consumed a great amount of time and effort, as explained.

If we tolerated subpar performance, then subpar performance became our standard. We could not accept that standard if we were to overcome the limitations of government and bring value. *We had to let nonperformers go, and we did it quickly, although it was always painful.*

Keeping a company healthy and highly productive is essential to growth. As my Uncle Johnny (Harvard graduate and Vice President for

Organizational Development at RCA) used to tell me, *"You have to cut back the bush, so the root ball supports it; otherwise, the whole plant dies."*

Jack Welch of GE had a policy of culling the weakest performing 10 percent of the organization each year. I believe this actually is an excellent policy, but we found it almost impossible to do. What we did do, however, was strongly encourage people to leave voluntarily who could not keep up their consulting utilization rate or who were just not performing. We felt they would be better off in another job where they were not failing. It was good for them and good for MAXIMUS that they leave.

I fired very few people, myself. I was often accused of keeping people much longer than I should have. I was known as "a sheep in wolf's clothing." When I did fire someone, the reasons were either insubordination, disloyalty to the company, or having a character not consistent with our corporate culture. It was hard for me to fire people. As I mentioned earlier, I was grateful they were there. To be perceived as fair, though, meant being more than fair.

When we let someone go, we did it with dignity. We did not escort the person out the door with security staff that very hour, unless it was required in our contract. Nothing can be more humiliating.

MAXIMUS required exit interviews to determine what the person thought of the company as he or she was departing and to uncover what grievance he or she might have had that never came up. Sometimes these interviews were illuminating and helped us uncover problems not yet perceived by management.

If the person tried to be a good employee but just couldn't make it, we gave separation pay. How you treat people is observed by all. We dealt with terminations humanely.

We worked hard at managing people, and it was, indeed, hard work.

CHAPTER 12

PLANNING AND EXECUTION

Managing the business meant, in large part, planning and executing one-time projects since projects were the heart of our contract work. All our business was based on completing government-funded projects. Project management is pretty much the same for governments and for commercial clients, though government work did have its unique attributes. Here is what I learned about managing projects, in particular, and the business of MAXIMUS in general.

Planning in General

All projects at MAXIMUS started with a plan, usually developed during the proposal writing process, and later revised if we won the contract. A plan in our world was essentially a to-do list with due dates, people responsible, and costs.

By their nature, plans are temporary. They become obsolete when a project is over and sometimes even before the project starts. To be useful, however, plans in general, and project plans in particular, need to be dynamic, adjusting to changes in circumstances, achievements, and failures. Plans need to be updated continually, which, for some reason, nobody wants to do. We would say, "Plan your work, then work your plan."

I often spent up to 10 percent of my time each week trying to decide what I should be working on—what was most important and what I could influence the most. I was planning, and updating priorities on a continual basis. Circumstances changed so rapidly that any plan relevant today wouldn't necessarily apply tomorrow. So I stayed flexible in what I did. Sometimes this frustrated the staff.

Some of my most loyal supporters on the administrative staff used to say in response to these changing priorities, "David doesn't make mistakes; he just changes his mind." I don't know about the mistakes part, but I did change my mind a lot.

We always had plans. That was because planning was essentially collecting, aggregating, and processing information and making sense of it. We needed information that could shape our decisions. As some sage said, *"Plans are useful in their own right, even if only to set an initial direction."*

Two Types of Tasks

We encountered two different types of tasks in planning at MAXIMUS: one-time and recurring. The types are treated very differently and result in very different kinds of plans. Consulting projects generally have one-time tasks, although some tasks within the project are recurring, such as holding regular meetings with the client and submitting progress reports. Privatization tasks after startup are almost all recurring.

One of the toughest problems we had in developing one-time project plans was determining exactly how much effort a task would take. This was important since it would affect our estimates of the cost of the project. Our ability to determine task effort was closely related to establishing the time granularity of the tasks. How finely should we develop the task plan—in hours, days, weeks, or months? The answer would dictate how many tasks were in our plan.

If we had a very high-level plan, a task might be measured in months. In a lower-level plan, the same task could be disaggregated into many smaller tasks taking only days to complete. Those tasks could then be broken down further into subtasks, taking hours to complete, and so on. All the Gantt Charts looked the same; only the period changed— like stock market charts—you can't really tell the time period without a legend. I called it fractal management. When did you stop adding more detail?

The granularity of project planning depended on the size of the project and the accuracy required. If we estimated staffing requirements in person months, for example, we probably overestimated the resources required for the task. This could cause us to lose the contract with too high a bid. If we estimated the task in person hours, we tended to underestimate the resources required to complete the task. We could never anticipate all the one-hour tasks required to do the job. In this case, we could underestimate the cost of the contract, and if we won, lose money on the contract.

Person days or person weeks seemed to be the best compromise between overestimating and underestimating the level of effort required to complete a project task. So tasks, in most cases, were sized to last from several days to several weeks. When we won these contracts, we were more confident in our ability to make a profit.

Recurring Tasks

In government operations, or privatization, we planned for recurring tasks. For example, the same tasks were repeated for every new applicant entering the caseload. Through ongoing observations, we could accurately measure how long these tasks (or procedures) should take. And best of all, we could refine the tasks over time until we achieved maximum efficiency.

We were very careful, for example, to minimize the number of keystrokes required to enter forms, as these keystrokes would be repeated millions of times. One second saved represented a lot of money over a year's period. Therefore, we estimated the time required for our data entry tasks in seconds.

As indicated, recurring tasks allowed for precise process improvements. We continually tried to improve our operations to be the low-cost producer. As a result, MAXIMUS performance kept improving over time, even in the same project. System enhancements played a major role in improving our operations, as described earlier. I'm not sure how much emphasis government placed on achieving maximum efficiency, but I didn't see much in terms of an ongoing effort. There isn't much incentive in government to improve operational efficiency continually.

Managing People, Not Tasks

One of the common mistakes managers made at MAXIMUS was trying to manage tasks instead of managing people. Typically, this works as follows. A task plan is generated for a particular project. As discussed above, estimates are made on how long the tasks should take in person hours, days, weeks, or months. Staff are then assigned who are responsible for the completion of the tasks, and a resource-leveling algorithm may be used to ensure all staff and other resources are efficiently utilized. The project manager periodically checks to see the status of all the tasks and whether they are being completed correctly. Sound good?

The paradox is that plans are usually never followed. The tasks in the plan are not really what you are going to do or how long it will take you to do it—so how do you manage a plan you aren't really going to follow?

At West Point, we were taught no battle plan survives contact with the enemy. The plan serves a purpose, but is rarely followed since you have to react to what the enemy is doing. In the case of project management, all manner of unforeseen circumstances caused changes to the tasks needed to complete a project.

As an aside, I had one project in my career where we actually followed the proposed plan. Our Government Project Officer, Bill Delehey, from the Social Security Administration told me it was the first time in his career he had seen it happen. Everyone was surprised.

Even if the tasks and their sequence remained unchanged, the fact is I never met anyone who could estimate reliably and accurately how long a one-time task should take, even if it was in days or weeks. If we couldn't accurately estimate how long a task should take, we couldn't be sure a person would be busy working on the task for a specified amount of time.

People need to be kept busy to keep costs down. Someone has to over-see what each person is doing, how well he or she is doing it, and how long the task is taking. If a person is sick, someone else has to fill in. If a person can't do the job, someone else has to. If a person is confused, someone has to clarify the task. *So we had to manage people, not tasks.*

I encouraged our managers to set up a series of tasks for each staff member so he or she knew what had to be done first, second, third, etc. Since we rarely could accurately estimate how long something would take, we adjusted the workload on the staff to keep progress uniform. If the tasks changed, then we changed them for the staff.

We tried to make sure each person was productively engaged on the next relevant task. We were managing people, while keeping an eye on the project tasks. Of course, we had to consider dependencies among the tasks.

Theoretically, we arrive at the same place either by managing tasks or by managing people. But, in practice, we didn't. Managing people worked better.

Delegating Responsibility

Early in the history of MAXIMUS in 1982, I had a consultant come in and evaluate the company. He said we had a "pumpkin chart" organization—all lines came to me at the top. He advised me to delegate more to have the company grow since I wouldn't be able to do everything myself. His advice made sense.

I learned that delegating is authorizing someone to make mistakes. Delegating is also authorizing someone to do a task differently than you would. Delegating is not abdicating accountability—*you are still accountable for the person's performance.*

As a result of the consultant's advice, I started delegating. Instead of being in charge of writing all the proposals, I delegated the job to others, spreading out the workload. I focused on working on the projects themselves.

In those days, the government made most contracting decisions at the end of the fiscal year, announcing who won the competitions for the contracts. As a result, we usually had to wait until much of our existing work was completed before finding out how much new work we'd won.

Of the thirty-two proposals we submitted that year, we won just one. Our people were apparently not good at writing proposals. Typically, we would have won eight to ten of the proposals. For the first time, MAXIMUS faced what is known in consulting as "the cliff." There was no doubt our revenues were going sharply down, and I had to lay off about one-third of the staff.

I remember calling them into my office one at a time. I told each person individually that he or she was being laid off. I had tears in my eyes throughout; so did many of them. I never wanted that to happen again. I was angry with myself for making such an obvious mistake. This was the first year MAXIMUS revenues declined, and I vowed it would not happen again. We still made a profit that year, however.

I realized, then, I could make a bad decision even if it was supported by sound rationale. Though I had good reason to delegate, delegation wasn't the right thing to do at that time. Managers reporting to me in later years would sometimes recommend a decision I considered ill-advised. I would tell them, *"Having a good reason to make that decision doesn't necessarily make that decision good."* Then I would try to explain why. Managers always had good reasons for making mistakes—that's what excuses are made of.

What was the immediate lesson? *Never delegate all critical responsibilities to your staff, even if you want them to grow.* If MAXIMUS didn't win the work, the staff wouldn't be around to grow. Lead the most important and critical tasks yourself, if you're the best person for the job.

After that, I took personal charge of most of the largest proposals at MAXIMUS—even to the day I retired. My Board of Directors did not like that I was so hands-on, but they had not experienced the failures I had endured. If MAXIMUS was to grow, we needed our best proposal writers in the forefront against our competitors.

Consensus-Making Versus Decision-Making

I had a major advantage being both CEO of MAXIMUS and, before going public, the major shareholder. I could make decisions quickly and not be second-guessed. This is in stark contrast to government.

When MAXIMUS worked with the consulting arms of big accounting firms, we had to deal with partnerships. Partnerships were difficult for us because decision-making was slower, though not as slow as the government.

I am assuredly biased, but partnerships seemed to breed "consensus-makers" rather than "decision-makers." The partners had to worry about what the other partners thought. They were somewhat risk adverse and needed "cover" on any major decisions. That's not to say many partners weren't excellent decision-makers, because each partner ran his own business. Many were very good. However, when the contracts were large enough, the decision-making turned into consensus-making. But their consensus-making was still more efficient than in government.

Within MAXIMUS, I naturally cared about how the staff regarded my decisions. Ultimately, though, I didn't have to justify myself to anyone. That was definitely an advantage, especially for some tough calls potentially risking the survival of the company. Of course, if I were making many bad decisions, my credibility as a leader would be lost.

I encouraged input from my staff, and really worked hard to see their points of view. *I learned long ago to try to understand first why someone might be right, rather than focus on why someone might be wrong.* The former was always more productive.

Before MAXIMUS, I was a referee for the *Journal of the American Statistical Association*. I had just received a Doctor of Science degree from The George Washington University and was eager to be of use to this prestigious journal. My job was to recommend whether or not a submitted paper should be published in the journal. I worked hard to determine what, if anything, was wrong with the paper, because if there was a problem, I could not recommend it for publication.

It took only a couple of times before I discovered that I was wrong in some of my assessments. I was embarrassed because I obviously didn't really understand what the author was saying. So after a few mistakes, when I refereed papers, I assumed the author was right, and I had to figure out why. My record as a referee improved immensely. I also carried that lesson into the rest of my life.

Therefore, I definitely listened to my staff and tried to understand why they might be right before making a decision to the contrary. Ultimately, though, I would say to those involved, *"It's really important to me that you understand the reasoning behind my decision. And it would be even better if you agreed with my decision…but, in the end, I am the one responsible."*

I recall one meeting with the fourteen top executives in the company at the time. We discussed whether or not to sue the state of Tennessee on a revenue maximization project. After an hour and a half of discussion, I asked those who wanted to sue the state to raise their hands. Everyone did. I never felt so useful, since I saved us from a big mistake. We didn't sue the state of Tennessee.

Yes, we were justified; yes, we probably would receive some money back. However, you can't always sue the government, even if you're right. The word would spread, and other states would be wary of working with MAXIMUS. We almost always had to act in the interest of our client, even if it was not in our interest. I think the staff eventually agreed with me.

On the other hand, if the client sues you, then you have a right to a defense. Or if the government is unfairly taking advantage of you, you can respond as we did in Connecticut, which is discussed in the Chapter 26 – Dealing with Disaster. But almost without exception, we did what was best for our client.

When to Make a Commitment

Another important area of decision-making is deciding when to antici-pate an event and react in advance and when to wait for the event to occur and then commit. For example, in hiring caseworkers, we always waited for the contract to be signed. As I have mentioned, being a reac-tive company has many advantages that may seem counterintuitive to most people. Generally, we did not spend money unless there were revenues to cover the expenditures. That's, in part, why we were always profitable.

For consulting staff, we waited for the revenue stream to materialize. Three to six months of coverage was needed before we hired additional full-time consulting staff.

Some things, however, must be committed to in advance because they take time. *"You can't have a baby in one month by having nine women get pregnant."* You have to start at least nine months early. Many decisions in business are the same way—there's gestation time. You need to commit early to be ready.

Marketing and sales resources have to be hired in anticipation of oppor-tunities. Sales precede revenues, so expenditures must be made up front. When MAXIMUS revenues declined in 1982, I mentioned we had to lay off one-third of the staff. At the same time, I added more senior staff to help with proposal writing. *It may seem counterintuitive to add costs when revenues are declining, but if MAXIMUS were to grow, that's what I had to do.* Otherwise, the company would drop into a downward spiral, from which it would be difficult to recover.

Don't Make a Decision Until Necessary

This policy is a corollary to the previous policy. Even if we committed to an action, I still tried not to make the decision or "pull the trigger" until forced. In dealing with uncertainty, I was always tempted to make the decision and get it over with. I wanted to move on to the next one. But I ultimately learned to delay the decision until it "needed to be made." That way, I had the latest information to incorporate into the decision.

So what does "needed to be made" mean? It means what it says. The decision may be needed well in advance of a particular event—so make it when you have to. The decision may require time for people to accept and adopt it—so determine when that is. If we can't reverse the decision, then making it early puts us at a disadvantage. Late-breaking information can come in that makes the decision a bad one, and it will be too late to change it.

Managing Productivity

Large privatization projects also require considerable management skills. One of our first productivity improvement efforts in Government Operations (our privatization group) came at the Health Care Options (HCO) project in California. Our HCO office was very large—several hundred people. We had the dual responsibility of processing Medicaid Managed Care enrollment forms and answering phones for people calling the toll-free number. The staff were assigned to answer phones, and when the phones were not busy, to enter a backlog of enrollment forms into the computer. This way, everyone always had something to do.

After a few months of managing the operation, I decided to post the productivity of each worker and each unit collectively on the wall near the front door. A unit typically consisted of a supervisor, six or seven workers, and a unit clerk. We had twenty units—Unit A through Unit T. Posting productivity was done first thing in the morning each workday. Computer printouts from the day before showed for each unit, and for each staff member in that unit, the number of phone calls handled and the number of enrollment forms processed.

I asked our management not to say anything about the computer list-ings to the employees. Within a few days after the postings started, we noticed the first thing staff did when coming in from the parking lot in the morning was to check their numbers. Right away productivity started to increase.

One fellow on the second floor was about twice as productive as every-one else. We went up to see what he was doing. Was he cheating? Or was he really that fast? He was really that fast. When he found out he stood out so much from his peers, he slowed down, but he still was one of the most productive workers in the facility.

Productivity basically doubled. People were taking pride in their num-bers and competing within units and between units. It was fun. No spe-cific recognition or bonuses were necessary. Everyone knew his or her scores.

We implemented a vigorous quality control program to ensure quality did not slip. If a form was processed incorrectly, it was not counted and had to be fixed by the unit that made the error. If telephone call moni-toring revealed the callers weren't being treated courteously or given the correct information, all the person's calls that day were invalidated. So there was every incentive to do a good job and be efficient about it.

I became so interested in what was going on, I initiated an experiment to test the optimal mix of phone calls to answer and forms to process. I put some of the units on pure forms processing and some on pure phone call answering, and had some units as swing units that did both. After a month, I plotted the productivity of all the units on graph paper.

What I found surprised me. Workers who processed forms and answered the phone were the least productive. They probably could not handle the transition between the two tasks efficiently. Those units that only pro-cessed forms were surprisingly more productive. They could focus heads down and get the job done, even though it might be boring. The units that focused purely on answering the phones did better than the units who did both phones and forms. However, they had some downtime during periods of lower call volumes and were less productive than the units who only processed forms.

What I did, then, was to assign some units exclusively to forms processing and some exclusively to answering phones. The number of units assigned exclusively to phones was based on the lowest call volume experienced during the slowest hour of the day. The remaining "swing units" worked like an accordion—they processed enrollment forms full time until the call volume increased—then, they switched full time to carry the additional call volume. So the number of units assigned full-time to phones varied daily, and sometimes hourly, based on the call volume.

By initiating this change, we experienced maximum productivity from our staff. I doubt whether the government employee unions would have allowed government to do that. Job satisfaction increased at the project with these productivity improvements. This was a pattern we saw everywhere. *When our operations were efficient, everyone had greater job satisfaction.*

So MAXIMUS learned to manage its business—planning and execution. The learning process was ever evolving, but we seemed to keep pace with it.

117

CHAPTER 13

SALES STRATEGIES

The sine qua non for any government contracting company is winning new business competitively. This chapter describes our sales strategies for building MAXIMUS by winning competitive procurements, our primary source of new business.

Silent Wars Going On

I understood clearly that our competitors were always actively working against us. They wanted to take over our business. Andy Grove of Intel famously warned, "Only the paranoid survive." Believe it. We may not have seen our competitors or heard about their activities, but we knew there were silent wars going on to dominate our industry.

Competitive procurements were our battleground. The competitive bidding process revealed both our strengths and weaknesses and our competitors' strengths and weaknesses. They studied us, and we studied them. MAXIMUS grew stronger and stronger because we had very tough competition.

Just because we created the market, though, didn't mean we were entitled to it. We had to learn to survive. Whenever we lost a bid, we asked for the winning proposal under the Freedom of Information Act. Often the proposal was redacted considerably because of trade secrets, but we still learned by reading what was there.

MAXIMUS competed with companies much larger and much more experienced than we were, at least in general business terms. They had sales and lobbying infrastructures in place. They had a large base of established clients who trusted them and gave excellent references, and they had top systems groups that could produce great software to compete against us.

We had to emphasize our strengths and their weaknesses to win. This is what any company has to do. Here are some of our strategies, for illustration purposes, to show how we beat the competition in the consulting and systems business—more on privatization later.

Working with Evaluation Committees

In every major competitive procurement MAXIMUS won, we had to appear before an evaluation committee who had read and scored our proposal. The evaluation committee required us to make an oral presentation about our proposal and then answer questions from committee members. Our oral presentation and responses to their questions would also be scored.

Often these oral presentations were very structured. We were given a fixed amount of time for our presentation and then for the questions that followed. Each company competing for the contract would sometimes receive a standard set of questions as well as questions specific to their proposals. Often, however, we were not told the questions in advance. The recommendations of the evaluation committees affected millions of dollars, and they wanted to be very careful and avoid the slightest appearance of being unfair. Otherwise, there would be protests.

After a few of these presentations, it became clear to me that the evaluation committees were also evaluating how well they would get along with our project staff, should we win the contract. Although not directly scored, these perceptions would creep into the scoring process. So I always instructed our people to be friendly and very relaxed in oral presentations. Be likeable.

One particular story comes to mind when a bit of humor enhanced our position. This was a project in Phoenix, Arizona, to privatize its welfare program. Holly Payne was leading our proposal effort. She was a former eligibility worker who had risen to the rank of division president within MAXIMUS. Not only was she very knowledgeable about entitlement programs, she also had a bigger-than-life personality.

In this particular oral presentation held in a government conference room, we were given a specific amount of time to answer each question. I was present to serve as a backstop in case one of our team members floundered. One evaluation committee member was assigned to flip a chart with pages indicating ten minutes, five minutes, one minute, thirty seconds, fifteen seconds, and five seconds remaining to answer the question. As time elapsed, he would flip the pages to make sure we didn't take more than our allotted time. All bidders had to be treated equally.

When Holly was answering questions, she always struggled to finish within the time allowed. She kept looking at the chart and speeding up her answer as time ran out. On the very last question of the day, she was particularly exasperated and again had to cut her answer short. She stopped mid-sentence at the end of the allotted time. With frustration painted all over her face, she looked squarely at all the committee members, paused, and then said, "Do you think I could get one of those charts for my husband?" Everybody laughed.

They liked Holly and they liked the humor, and we won. So we always made sure we didn't suppress a funny remark whenever it was appropriate.

Emphasizing Strengths/Minimizing Weaknesses

But we needed more than humor to win. MAXIMUS was always much, much smaller than our larger competitors—multibillion-dollar, international companies like Accenture, IBM, EDS, and Lockheed Martin. I won't say we were more competent than they were, but we were definitely smarter in our areas of expertise. Government social welfare entitlement programs were our core competency.

We understood these programs much better than they did because many of our people had hands-on experience in these programs working for the government. We were a government program company with business and technical skills. Our competitors were business and technical companies with some government program knowledge. In the government market, MAXIMUS knew more, and we made it known that we did.

I'd propose the idea in our proposals that *the average level of competency a client receives from a company is inversely proportional to the size of that company.* That is, smaller companies need a higher average level of competency to compete with the larger companies. The larger companies had the law of averages working against them and produced an average level of competency.

We also claimed MAXIMUS was the right-sized company for the job— small enough so the client was an important client to us, but big enough to do the job well and guarantee the results. We made many points about why MAXIMUS was the company for the job.

Let's go through a few representative competitive proposals to show how we won contracts. Essentially, we had to turn MAXIMUS's weaknesses into strengths and our competitor's strengths into weaknesses. Here are a few examples of how we did it.

Social Security Administration

Early in the history of MAXIMUS, I was summoned to the Social Security Administration Headquarters in Baltimore, Maryland, by its Chief Contracting Officer. He wanted me to explain why MAXIMUS was winning so many competitive procurements.

When we met, he asked me directly if MAXIMUS had inside help or advanced notice of the procurements. I said "no." He then asked if we had friends on the evaluation committees or in the management of the department to encourage our selection, and again I said, "no." "How then," he asked, "did you win the last three competitive procurements in a row?" I asked him to choose one, and I would explain our strategy. He selected a project to "Develop a Training Program for Welfare Eligibility Workers."

I told him that when the Request for Proposals (RFP) came out, we immediately called the known expert in eligibility-worker training to hire him as a consultant on our proposal team. To our dismay, a competitor had already hired him. (Maybe they had advanced notice?) What chance did we have with the foremost expert in eligibility-worker training on another company's team? It seemed like zero.

Well, we decided to turn our weakness into a strength, and the other company's strength into a weakness. We pointed out in our proposal that a new approach was needed for eligibility-worker training. The old approach, which had been around for years, was obviously not what was needed now, or the government wouldn't have issued the Request for Proposals.

We proposed to develop a new, eligibility-worker training program based on the latest advances in eligibility determination. These advances included recent developments in automating eligibility determination and the use of statistical profiles for identifying error-prone cases. We would certainly look at what training materials were currently available, but our work product would not be a rehash of what had already been done. I stopped to see if he was following me. I waited for him to speak.

He thought for a while about what I had said, then started to say something and then he smiled. I guess he didn't want the government to pay for something that was already available. He believed me. He understood why we had won. He stood up and said, "Thank you." We shook hands, and I left. Our contract was safe.

Massachusetts Department of Child Support Enforcement

For the Commonwealth of Massachusetts, MAXIMUS competed for a large contract in child support enforcement. The contract required a firm to review cases throughout the state and recalculate the child support due to either the state or the custodial parents, based on an array of complex decision rules. The contract involved a large number of back-logged cases.

The state was implementing a new child support enforcement computer system and needed accurate data. The state did not have the resources to conduct the reviews itself, but still needed the cases cleaned up. This is why it contracted out the work. The contract effort was a cross between a consulting contract and a privatization contract. We had to hire case-management workers for a one-time project, but we didn't replace any government workers.

MAXIMUS made the finals and was invited to an oral presentation. We had to answer questions in front of the evaluation committee. We heard our main competitor was spreading the word that MAXIMUS often used a "bait and switch" tactic. That is, we proposed very highly qualified persons for the project, and after we won the contract, switched to less qualified people.

MAXIMUS did not engage in "bait and switch," but many companies did. We realized if we claimed our company policy was not to change key personnel without client approval (unless the employee resigned), it would fall on deaf ears. So I went to a bonding company before the oral presentation and obtained a surety bond for $1 million. The bond guaranteed if MAXIMUS switched out any key personnel without the consent of the state (and if that person were still at MAXIMUS), we would forfeit the $1 million.

When the question came up in the oral presentation, I simply reached into my breast pocket and handed the envelope to the head of the evaluation committee. He opened the envelope and stared at the bond for a while, then handed it back to me, and continued on with other questions. We won.

MAXIMUS went on to open an office in Billerica, Massachusetts, and hired hundreds of people to review these cases. We built our own computer system for tracking the cases and for calculating the allocation and distribution of the child support. We had teams go out and retrieve court orders from the courts throughout Massachusetts. We had training programs and a human resources person at the office for hiring and counseling. In effect, we had established a great reference for conducting financial reconciliation projects for child support caseloads anywhere in the nation.

San Francisco Bay Area Rapid Transit

Another example comes to mind for turning weakness into strength and strength into weakness on a contract in the Bay Area in San Francisco. We were competing for a $20 million enterprise resource planning system (an accounting and human resources system) against a very large and respected company, IBM. Again, we had reached the finals. The client wanted to choose between the two companies after the oral presentation.

IBM raised a significant number of objections to the proposed contract language. The client was very accommodating and agreed to change the language in almost every case. However, before finalizing the contract language, the client wanted to know if MAXIMUS had any further objections, and if we would agree to the changes IBM requested.

I flew to San Francisco and met with the evaluation committee to go over every objection that IBM had made. We went through about thirty pages of contract language marked up in Microsoft Word and projected onto a large screen. For each IBM objection, I said truthfully that the proposed language was not a concern of ours, and either the old or new language was acceptable. In hindsight, this may have made us look more reasonable than IBM and easier to deal with.

At the end of the session, though, I suggested there was language we would like to add that IBM had not raised. Of course, the committee wanted to know what it was, and seemed a bit exasperated, since they would have to go back to IBM for its approval.

I had studied the proposed contract and realized if MAXIMUS was successful, several of the contractors working on their existing system would be terminated early because of the new system being installed. We did not want to be sued by these other contractors. Therefore, I asked that MAXIMUS be "held harmless" for performing the scope of work as outlined in the contract. In other words, if one of these other contractors sued us, the client would defend us and pay out any settlement!

The evaluation committee said they had to check with their General Counsel on that one. So they left me and my staff in the conference room while they consulted with the General Counsel some twenty floors above us. When they returned after forty-five minutes, they indicated the General Counsel had agreed to our language. He had commented that our change was the only substantive change set forth by either company.

The head of the evaluation committee then asked me why we wanted the change. I said truthfully that the other company was probably protecting itself against failure—all the changes they requested mitigated damages against a failed contract. On the other hand, MAXIMUS was protecting itself against success because we expected to succeed.

They nodded and seemed very friendly. They had to go back into consultation and weigh all they had learned and would get back to us. Well, guess who won?

As an aside, I took particular interest in this contract because the IBM proposal team was being led by a person we were particularly interested in recruiting. It is very difficult for a person in a large, well-known, respected company with great career potential to come to a relatively unknown company like MAXIMUS. We were, after all, a government contractor, serving not the most glamorous of clients.

The best way to convince this person to join MAXIMUS was to beat him. There was never any information exchanged between us about the procurement. If he reads this book, since he is now at MAXIMUS, he may find out for the first time that I led the MAXIMUS effort against IBM.

Commonwealth of Pennsylvania, Department of Finance

As you have read, MAXIMUS has a business called revenue maximization. We were able to help a state recover money from the federal government the state was unaware it could claim. We received a percentage of the claim as a contingency fee—no money recovered, no money paid to MAXIMUS.

As a matter of interest, the federal government pays a large portion of the bill for all federally-mandated poverty programs. The federal share of costs varies based on the program but is generally more than 50 percent.

127

The formula for the federal matching percentage for the Medicaid and the State Child Health Insurance Programs, for example, is highly complicated. It is based on the square of the median income of the state's population relative to the square of the median income of the US population as a whole, and other esoteric criteria. This percentage is calculated annually.

The federal matching percentage is applied to the total costs of the program as claimed by the state. The state has to make sure the program costs incurred met federal requirements, and that all the costs that met federal requirements were claimed. The more money the state could properly claim, the more the feds would pay for the program.

I recall one engagement in Maine in which MAXIMUS helped the state recover $10 million. The fix was something as simple as changing the line on a form where the cost was reported. Since our contingency fee was 10 percent, we earned $1 million that quickly. The state was happy to pay us.

In most cases though, we had to do considerable work for the state to claim federal money. For example, to be eligible for federal matching in the child welfare program, the case folder had to contain the court order that placed the child in foster care. MAXIMUS hired workers to retrieve these documents from the courts throughout the state and insert them in the case folders so the federal money could be claimed.

MAXIMUS staff were experts at government claiming regulations—much like accountants and attorneys know the tax code and reduce tax liabilities. We knew government programs inside and out—more so than many of the people working in state government. And we knew in detail the regulations through which states could claim the money to which they were entitled. Most states could not retain people with that knowledge. MAXIMUS was a gathering place for this new breed of consultant.

We were the major player for a long time. After a while, many smaller companies started competing with us—"rev max" was a very profitable business. In fact, in one year, our net profit margin reached 40 percent. Anyway, this all came to a head in Pennsylvania.

Our competitors started bidding a smaller percentage of the claim as a contingency fee. Naturally, the states were choosing these competitors over MAXIMUS. Instead of charging 10 percent, they charged 7 percent, and alarmingly, the percentage was dropping every six months or so. This was hard for states to turn down. Why pay more for the same service?

What to do? My people were at a loss and starting to panic. We didn't want to keep lowering our fee. Clearly, we had to make our competitors' strength a weakness, and our apparent weakness a strength—same story. To do this, I pointed out in our proposal to Pennsylvania the following. *The state should* not *focus on how much money the consultant will make, but rather on the net amount the state will recover from the federal government.*

If the state allowed only a 7 percent fee for the consultant, then the consultant could only undertake projects that cost less than 7 percent of the potential amount of money to be found. Otherwise, the consultant would lose money. A higher contingency percentage, on the other hand, would allow more thorough efforts by the consultant to find additional money. So, in general, it behooved states to pay the higher fee.

Moreover, MAXIMUS was a large company, and could invest much more money up front to find the unclaimed funds. The smaller companies could not operate without regular payments to meet their cash-flow needs. Since a company was paid only after the state was paid, a company often had to wait a year before being paid. MAXIMUS's ability to cover the cash-flow needs for these types of projects gave us significantly more resources to find more unclaimed funds than our smaller competitors.

The basic question, or bottom line, was something like this: "Would the state rather have 93 percent of $500,000 or 90 percent of $2,000,000? The state had to focus on what it was receiving and not on what it was paying. When the evaluation committee figured this out, the answer was obvious, and we won the Pennsylvania contract at a higher fee than our competitors.

State of Utah, Medicaid Program

Here is one final example to drive home the point of turning our weakness into a strength and our competitors' strength into a weakness. This procurement involved our systems business. The project required the development of a large health care system in Utah to help caseworkers enroll recipients into the Medicaid Managed Care program. Recall, Medicaid is the health care program for the poor, and it is very complicated and costly.

Again, we were pitted against a major firm—specializing in large systems. Compared to the other firm, MAXIMUS was a small player and could not match the other firm's credentials or credibility. So what did we do? Our weakness was that we were smaller and not a systems firm. Their strength was they were much larger and a systems firm.

We first pointed out that by being a smaller firm, MAXIMUS would give the agency a higher priority than a larger firm would. The agency business represented a larger portion of our revenues. This was just a warm-up point.

In addition, because we were a smaller firm, I could personally watch over the contract and meet with the agency contract team every several months, or more frequently, as required. As CEO, I could make decisions on the spot, and the agency would not have to wait for a decision to work its way up through another bureaucracy. This was a stronger point for us.

We acknowledged the larger firm might be able to build a system with less risk than MAXIMUS, since it had more experience in building systems. But, we pointed out, MAXIMUS had much more experience working with Medicaid Managed Care systems and had built smaller systems that were very similar in functionality to the one requested.

In fact, we demonstrated several variations of systems we had developed for our own use in other states. One of our systems could be modified for Utah. We suggested MAXIMUS might be better at helping Utah decide what it really wanted the system to do and how the functionality could be adapted to the workers' actual needs. After all, we were the Medicaid program experts and managed similar programs elsewhere.

We observed, finally, that the state had a choice between a smaller company with less systems experience, but far greater Medicaid program experience, and a larger company that had built many more large systems, but with little Medicaid program experience. While the larger firm may seem less risky in building a large system, the system MAXIMUS would build, in all likelihood, would be significantly more useful to the Medicaid caseworkers. We couldn't say how useful the other company's system would be.

The state bought our argument, and we won. We went on to build the system for Utah using Oracle system-development tools. Many states would not purchase our own homegrown MAXSTAR system since it was not available in the open market. We overspent the Utah contract to build an open system we could sell to Medicaid Managed Care programs in other states.

While we ultimately lost $4 million, the new system set the stage for winning the California Healthy Families managed care contract and many others over the next couple of years.

Each competitive procurement has an interesting story because it was a battleground. I could write another book on how we won and lost many other contracts, but the point has been made. *We turned our weaknesses into strengths, and our competitors' strengths into weaknesses.*

Dishonesty in Contracting

I am pleased to report MAXIMUS was never asked to pay a bribe in the United States, Australia, or Canada. This covers every state, most cities, most counties, and the federal government. I know such bribes are regularly reported in many city newspapers, but I never encountered one. However, we sometimes were asked for a campaign contribution to meet with the governor of the state.

We were asked to pay a bribe of $10,000 to a government official in Egypt. This was the condition to win a $5 million follow-on contract to a contract we had recently successfully completed. We turned down the bribe request and lost the work. That was OK by me. See, honesty costs money.

Even though the government procurement process varies widely from state to state, and to some extent within the federal government, the procurement process is basically very honest. *If the procurement process weren't predominantly honest, MAXIMUS could never have been successful.*

Of course, government evaluation committees have favorites, and there are leaks and flaws in the system. But I am unaware of any money changing hands in the business in which MAXIMUS was engaged. The one exception occurred in West Virginia, where we were duped, as will be explained. In a later chapter, I also discuss the impact of politics on procurements. Politics plays a confounding role in winning business—but an understandable one.

More contracting invites more opportunities for corruption. As the government relies more extensively on the private sector, it will need stronger mechanisms to ensure contracting is honest. Government bureaucrats should not be able to steer contracts to their friends or bene-factors. Government must ensure the integrity of the procurement process, or the whole system will be compromised.

Let's move on to the next block of chapters and learn exactly what MAXIMUS did to help government serve the people.

PART III:
CORE COMPETENCIES

This block of chapters explains how we helped government in our three main businesses, which represented our core competencies. The skills required in each of these businesses are very different, but we managed to continue to provide quality, profitable services to government in each.

CHAPTER 14

CONSULTING – THE HEART OF THE BUSINESS

In this initial chapter, I explain what consulting is all about, since for the first twelve years, that was the primary business of MAXIMUS. Consultants are change agents, and our mission was changing government. Here is what we did and learned.

Organizational Change

I believe a typical government organization uses 99 percent of its capabilities to perform its current mission, leaving at most 1 percent to invest in change. High-level government officials often feel too busy fighting fires to do anything else. That's why it's so hard for government to change. So when there are ways to become more efficient, the government has a difficult time taking advantage of them. Consider how hard it would be for an agency to privatize its field operations, changing almost everything. Extremely difficult.

Even small changes take time and energy, and the organization has to expend those resources to effect change. Change challenges the status quo, which automatically invites resistance, further making change difficult. Therefore, before MAXIMUS consultants recommended changes to improve government efficiency or quality of services, we considered the following:

- Is the change really necessary? Is it required by new federal or state programs or regulations, or a governor's initiative?

- Will the change really improve the agency's performance? How will that improvement in performance be measured in terms of efficiency and effectiveness? What is expected?

- Does the leadership have the capability and political will to effect the change? Are unions involved?

- Does the agency have the resources to change? If not, can the agency procure the resources to change through contracting with the private sector or through interagency agreements?

- How has the agency changed historically before? What lessons were learned from that change? What mistakes can be avoided?

- What is the cost of the change?

These are the typical questions we asked. The point is that each change is difficult, and each change causes major disruptions in the agency's business. This disruption could last for months or even years. So change had to be clearly worthwhile to initiate, and often when it was, the government still did not change.

Government Needs Vs. Wants

There was a question I always asked my classes when teaching consulting at MAXIMUS. The question was whether we should give our government clients what they wanted or what they needed? Answers were divided about equally.

Those who argued for what the client wanted said MAXIMUS should make the government happy, even if the government was wrong. Those who argued for what the client needed said that it was our responsibility to do what is right for the government—after all, we were "Helping Government Serve the People." It seemed like a dilemma with no good outcome.

Some government agencies know exactly what they want. Others are at a loss, and have no idea. Each type of client needs to be handled differently. For those that know exactly what they want, it's best not to argue. For those who don't know exactly what they want, there are more options, such as educating the client about what they might need.

I believe the consultant should always give the client what the client wants. As explained above, each organization is unique, and consultants don't always have all the information necessary to determine what the client actually needs. We don't know whether a solution similar to the one we advocate has already been tried and failed. We don't know whether our solution is also being advocated by political adversaries of the agency leadership. There are too many land mines hidden from view.

On the other hand, we have a duty to educate our clients on what we believe they need to better carry out their mission. We would explain our rationale carefully, and then let them make the decision. If they did turn out to want the solution we proposed, then we had a win—they wanted what they needed, at least in our opinion.

I should also mention that no contract MAXIMUS signed ever guaranteed our government client would be friendly, knowledgeable, or even reasonable. It was the luck of the draw. Sometimes the clients were very difficult, but then again, maybe that's why we were hired to help them.

In this vein, I sometimes found it difficult to switch personalities between being the CEO of MAXIMUS and being a consultant. As a consultant,

I was reporting to someone as if he or she were my boss. In one role, I could be decisive and make things happen. In the other role, I had to make suggestions and accept decisions I may never have made. The transition back and forth was not easy. If I started MAXIMUS to be my own boss, I soon learned that I would never be my own boss, at least while I was a consultant.

The Government's Interests Come First

One of the toughest lessons to teach our consultants was the government's interests always came before MAXIMUS's interests. The client cannot trust your company if you place your interests above theirs. This means you may have to forego more business and shortchange your project, or even—perish the thought—help a competitor! When you do this, though, your client will know what you are doing. If there is potential business with that agency in the future, I can almost guarantee it will be yours. Relationships that last are built on trust. And a client who trusts you will always find ways to award you more business.

Here is a story that illustrates how having a good relationship almost backfired. I was contacted in 1990 by Lou Iannuzelli, a professional colleague I'd worked with twenty years earlier while I was in the Air Force. He asked me to come to Rock Island Arsenal in Iowa to help him with a problem. As a favor to him, I did—no contract involved. Upon arriving, Lou asked me if MAXIMUS knew anything about the A-10 Magnetron. I had never heard of the A-10 Magnetron, and I didn't think anyone else at MAXIMUS had either.

Lou wanted to award a contract to a qualified company to help him. If we were qualified, he had the authority to make a sole-source award, an award without competition. This was possible, since the contract amount was below a specified dollar threshold and the problem was urgent.

I told him no one at MAXIMUS knew anything about the A-10 Magnetron. I suggested he would be better off giving the contract to a company that did. He said he had brought in a number of companies, and they all said they were qualified to solve his problem with the A-10 Magnetron. However, he strongly believed none of them was qualified. I was the only person who admitted we were not qualified, and so he wanted to award the contract to MAXIMUS. "Would you please take the contract, Dave?" I didn't want it, but I said, "OK, Lou, as a favor to you."

Well, we managed to find the specialized expertise to perform the contract. Lou called me again to work on another contract. MAXIMUS knew nothing about that one, either—the M110 Loader Rammer—whatever that was. I said OK, as a favor, and we did that project too. Lou called again—and we had to test how quickly ball bearings rusted in nuclear artillery shells. OK, we did that too. By the way, that's how I ended up at SKF Industries in Pennsylvania.

Lou called again and I finally had to tell him we were not really in that line of business—Army ordnance. I explained MAXIMUS was in the business of reforming government social welfare programs. I begged off on the contract and suggested another firm that might be interested in learning and working in Army ordnance. I had done my research.

In most cases, however, by working in our clients' interests, we were also working in our long-term interests. In the case above, we were just doing someone a favor.

Meaning of Objectivity

Consultants are expected to be objective—that's often why we are hired. I learned the true meaning of objectivity in working with the Assistant Secretary of Defense for Health Affairs. And now you can also benefit from that experience.

In the early consulting years, MAXIMUS won a contract to "Assess the Army Veterinary Corps." The question was, "Why are there still 10,000 veterinarians in the Army when all the horses are gone?" That's the same number of veterinarians needed in 1910 when the Army had 100,000 horses. Why were the veterinarians still around?

Apparently, there had been eighteen or more previous studies over the last forty years with the same question—all going nowhere. Yet the question remained. Congress wanted an answer, even though everyone knew the answer was politics. The Army Veterinarians were a politically powerful group. This was another extreme example of noneconomic decisions being made by government.

I divided our study group into two teams, each with different assignments, and sent them out to get the answers and develop recommendations. Each team traveled for about six weeks, came back, and drafted chapters of the report. When I read the draft chapters, one team had recommended the Army eliminate the Veterinary Corps, and the other team recommended the Army keep it. I'm thinking to myself—"What is this? Now what?"

A former Navy health care officer at MAXIMUS, Dr. Bob White, led the team that recommended keeping the veterinarians. The team that recommended eliminating the veterinarians was headed by a "young Turk," Howard Miller, who was a cost-effectiveness expert. He had never been in the military. Both teams spent considerable time with the advocates of each position. Both teams, then, became advocates for their positions. What was I to do—the report was due? And we didn't have an answer.

After a great deal of thought, I decided to start the report as follows. "In this report, we present the arguments for keeping the Army Veterinary Corps as viewed by those who advocate keeping it, and the arguments for eliminating the Army Veterinary Corps, as viewed by those who want to eliminate it."

Throughout the report, I articulated the arguments of both sides, better than the advocates ever had. Then having presented both arguments, I sorted through them, to the best of my ability, and came up with a set of recommendations that seemed to make the most sense.

Essentially, the Army veterinarians were being used as meat inspectors and for treating pets on Army posts. We suggested Public Health Specialists be phased in to replace the veterinarians who were inspecting meat. Public Health Specialists didn't cost as much as veterinarians and were trained to inspect meat. Moreover, veterinarians went to school to treat animals, not inspect meat. Treating animals was a far better use of their skills, even if it meant leaving the military.

We testified before Congress. Our report was well-received by each side, since we had made their points for them. They may have disagreed with our recommendations, but they liked the report. *They felt it was objective and provided a basis for further negotiation.*

I found in conducting this study that objectivity does not mean walking a fine line between two sides. Being objective does not mean making sure not to take sides—just the opposite. You need to take both sides of the argument and live and understand each perspective well enough to articulate it as well, or better than the advocates. You can consider yourself objective only when you understand both (all) sides thoroughly.

I learned over time a simple lesson I recounted to my staff: *"The truth has many facets, and we rarely see them all."* You have to take the time to understand as many facets of the truth as you can.

Post Script. In the end, Congress left the Army Veterinary Corps alone, and eliminated the Air Force Veterinary Corp. I didn't even know the Air Force had one. Such is politics—forget economically rational decision-making—do what is politically correct.

Program Evaluations

MAXIMUS had the honor of winning a contract in the early 1980s to conduct the National Evaluation of the Child Support Enforcement Program, another congressionally mandated study. Recall, this program collects child support from absent parents, and distributes the money to the custodial parents and to the state when the custodial parent is receiving welfare payments. What did I learn of value from this experience?

The directors of Child Support Enforcement Programs in all fifty states were naturally intensely interested in what we would say in our final report. The program had been operational for only six or seven years, and already there were many critics.

I wanted to include the program director's comments, both assenting and dissenting, as an attachment to the report. This way MAXIMUS would be considered fair, and hopefully objective, as in the last example. I asked to brief the directors on the draft report at their annual meeting. We distributed copies ahead of the meeting, so they could all read the report.

Our findings were far more positive than negative. However, I knew the group was fundamentally opposed to being evaluated. There were some very vocal and very intelligent members of the group who would try to discredit our report, no matter what it said. I knew what we were up against.

Therefore, in advance of the meeting, I listed all the possible objections to our report the state child support program directors could raise. I addressed each of these objections in preparing my presentation. And, at the meeting, I presented the study results along with our responses to the possible objections.

When I addressed these objections before they could, I took away their ammunition. Here are some of those objections I countered.

- The study was premature—the program wasn't ready

- MAXIMUS was not qualified to do the study

- The evaluation team didn't understand the program

- The evaluation team was biased against the program

- The evaluation time period was too short

- The conclusions were already formulated before the study began

- The caseload samples were biased and not representative

- Key data were missing

- The data were not accurate

- The analysis was flawed

- The conclusions did not follow from the data

- The recommendations were blue sky—could not be implemented

- Outside pressure influenced the recommendations (not theirs, of course)

- Nothing new was revealed in the study.

So if our report was going to be criticized, we learned to criticize it first. While we didn't convert all the program directors to our way of thinking, we did convert key members of the group, and received a good grade from Congress.

So if you are presenting results to a hostile audience, use their ammunition before they do.

Implementing Proven Solutions

Another hard lesson we learned in government consulting was that each government agency is unique. There are no "cookie-cutter" solutions in government. That's true, even if the agency is administering the same government program, but in a different state, or even in a different county in the same state.

Each government agency has a history of trying different solutions to different problems—some worked, some did not. Each agency has different capabilities to carry out a solution. Each has different leadership capabilities with different risk-reward tendencies. Because a particular MAXIMUS program worked in one state, didn't mean it would work somewhere else. In fact, it usually didn't, unless we tailored the solution to the specific agency requirements.

I remember one consulting engagement in Rhode Island when MAXIMUS was brought in to solve a welfare error rate problem. It was in the early days of MAXIMUS, so I personally worked on the project. We had learned by then a solution that worked somewhere else would not necessarily work here. Therefore, after careful analysis and much consideration, we came up with a solution to the agency's problem, which turned out to be a variation of a solution we had implemented elsewhere. If I recall correctly, the solution was to implement error-prone profiles specifically tailored to each welfare office, based on the types of errors the case managers in the welfare office were making.

When I explained our solution to the agency director, Joe Murphy, his response was "That's obvious—we already knew that!" My first reaction was to be defensive. But I quickly realized if our solution was obvious, then it must be correct! If it was that obvious, why were we called in to find it? Why had they not implemented that solution before? Because the solution wasn't obvious, until we showed it to Joe.

There are many ways of solving problems. Through the process of *analysis*, a problem and its component problems are broken down into smaller subcomponents and solved. Most consultants can analyze a problem to death, creating more and more detailed breakouts of different components of the problem and presenting solutions to each. They then present this huge "tree of knowledge" to the client, who would be bewildered about what to do with it.

The essence of good consulting, in my opinion, is simplification. The best consultants simplified the problem and its solution for the client. That meant we had to take the detailed breakout we developed and reduce it to less-detailed breakouts—*de-analyzing*, so to speak. This required finding the simplest solution that solved all the component problems. When we reduced the component solutions to the simplest form possible, we had the overall solution.

By analyzing the problem in great detail, we understood every facet of the problem. Then, reaggregating that detail, we could express the problem and its solution in much simpler terms. When this was done, we often found the solution was obvious. This is what happened in Rhode Island.

Recall the old dig about the definition of a consultant. "When asked what time it is, a consultant will borrow your watch and tell you." That's not so bad if you learn what your watch is for and how to use it.

Ten Commandments of Consulting

We also wanted to establish a set of principles for our consultants at MAXIMUS. Ray Ruddy, a top consultant in his own right, developed the Ten Commandments of Consulting we had printed on a framed poster for every consulting office. The Ten Commandments in Ray's words are

I.   Treat the client as you would want to be treated were you the client.

II.   Provide good service.

III.   Learn about the client (business and personal).

IV.   Stop in to understand the client's concerns.

V.   Stop in to explain progress.

VI.   React immediately to client concerns and problems.

VII.   Remember that you are the "consultant," not the boss.

VIII.   Never speak disparagingly of the client.

IX.   Never speak disparagingly of the firm.

X.   Be yourself.

So we did the best we could to be good consultants to government, and we built a strong government consulting practice, thanks to the great people we had. Despite our efforts, though, government was still slow to change.

CHAPTER 15

BUILDING SYSTEMS THAT WORK

Building systems that work is a core competency of MAXIMUS—our smallest business and perhaps the most difficult. As mentioned earlier, we had approximately eight hundred systems consultants and programmers in our Systems Group, so it wasn't that small. Our initial forays into the systems business involved providing systems consulting services. In the early years, we also programmed a few small systems for federal agencies.

Systems Consulting

MAXIMUS started by helping various federal government agencies design their large operational systems. These systems consisted of communications networks, mainframes, minicomputers, and hundreds, if not thousands, of user terminals. Millions of lines of software code were programmed to operate these systems that did everything from determining eligibility to paying benefits.

MAXIMUS did very little programming work on these large systems ourselves, helping mainly in the conceptual design phases. The work was very interesting and helped us learn to develop our own systems.

Later, MAXIMUS helped state governments plan for their large social welfare systems. We wrote Advanced Planning Documents (APDs) for states to help them secure federal matching funds. The APDs included a General Systems Design, a draft Request for Proposals to hire a contractor to build the system, and a Quality Assurance Plan to monitor the contractor's progress.

APDs were approved by the federal agencies responsible for the programs. The agencies could authorize up to 90 percent funding for the systems. Ten years ago, to develop a statewide system for a social welfare program cost anywhere from $30 million to $200 million, depending on the size of the state. So federal funding was critical if the system was ever to be developed.

As MAXIMUS grew larger, we started developing large systems for our own operations. The state did not need to procure a system for Medicaid Managed Care, for example, since we provided it as our own proprietary system. This saved the states considerable money and the responsibility of developing the system on their own. That's another one of the key reasons state governments wanted to privatize their programs.

MAXIMUS also started developing systems for states, using open-source technology—or technology available on the open market. This took us past the planning phase and into the actual development of systems. This was always tricky business, as described below.

Plan on Building the System Twice

Building a system for a government agency can easily turn into a disaster. The government client often doesn't know what an automated system is capable of doing or not doing, so the client really doesn't know what to ask for. Our government clients were often not up to date on the latest technology, despite our efforts to educate them.

150

After we completed programming their specifications and they were able to see the system in use, the clients would change their minds. MAXIMUS would have to go through the whole process again.

We ultimately learned to budget so we could build the system twice. The first time we built the system would be according to what the government agency said they wanted. The second time would occur after the agency learned what they really wanted. At any rate, MAXIMUS was usually blamed for the first system since we helped facilitate the development of the specifications.

After a while, I learned what to do. MAXIMUS won a contract in Maryland to develop a statewide child care system. I was determined not to make the same mistake again. A child care system, by the way, is designed to fund subsidized child care for working mothers who have left the welfare rolls. Eligibility of both the family and the child care provider (like KinderCare or a private individual providing day care) is established, and payments are made to the child care provider for the hours of care provided the child(ren). Child care is different from child support.

Our project manager asked the child care agency to form committees to develop the specifications for various modules of the system. There must have been fifty or sixty government people participating on ten different committees. A MAXIMUS consultant was assigned to work with each committee to guide them. The committee developed specifications for the tasks the system would perform and the management reports the agency would receive. We then assembled a book of these specifications called the Functional Requirements Document.

Not to be fooled again, I did something different for this client. I asked each of the ten committees to sign each page of the Functional Requirements Document that contained their specifications. This would allow us to begin programming the specifications, or functional requirements, described on the approved pages. We said MAXIMUS would not program specifications on any pages not signed.

The strangest thing happened! The committees said they were not authorized to approve the Functional Requirements Document. What! You developed it? We said sorry, but we weren't going to program the system until we had their initials. An impasse.

The result was the agency leadership dramatically changed the composition of the committees. Higher-level people were brought in to work with us to develop the Functional Requirements Document. The original people were those who were not that busy in the organization and could be spared to work with MAXIMUS. I suspect many were the nonperformers.

I don't have to tell you the new Functional Requirements Document looked substantially different from the first. We obtained a clear and unambiguous sign off by the agency on the entire Functional Requirements Document. We knew if we had to build the system a second time, it would be on their nickel and not ours. I wish systems problems were always that easy to solve.

Relying on the Government Agency to Complete Tasks

Our government clients usually had the best of intentions. However, if we had a task on the "critical path" that depended on the government completing the task, we were asking for trouble. The critical path represents those tasks that define the shortest amount of time it would take to complete the project. If any of those tasks was delayed, the entire project was delayed.

We had a policy to make sure MAXIMUS was responsible for all tasks on the critical path. In some cases, we just did the work for the client. In others, we helped them complete the tasks. When we relied on our client to do a task, we were mixing two different accountability and productivity models, which usually does not work for either side. But MAXIMUS usually paid the price.

Systems development was always difficult, since the system either worked or didn't. The client could tell right away if there was a problem. We needed very experienced people to be in the systems business. This was why government tended to contract out systems work. It was just too hard.

One of our many secret weapons was Pam Tomlinson, who knew these systems better than anyone inside or outside of government. That's what we needed to stay ahead of everyone else—top systems people. They were an invaluable resource to MAXIMUS.

MAXIMUS later acquired several systems companies that worked for state and local governments. These companies provided additional expertise. Their systems included fleet management, courts, schools, ERP systems, and others.

MAXIMUS Proprietary Systems

MAXIMUS started developing its own proprietary computer systems in 1984. I believe companies should develop their own proprietary computer systems to gain a competitive edge and to create intellectual property of value.

The origin of all our proprietary systems was a system we built under contract for the Social Security Administration (SSA) to monitor fifty state Disability Determination Services. These state agencies decide who is eligible to receive disability payments from the federal government, which currently numbers about ten million beneficiaries.

With this new system, called the Cost Effectiveness Measurement System (CEMS), SSA could rank order and compare the performances of the fifty state agencies along a variety of performance measures. The system was a precursor to Executive Information Systems to come along later.

We built CEMS so we could adapt it easily for use in other applications. CEMS evolved into our own Executive Information System, which then evolved into our own Relational Database Management System. From these systems, we created our own accounting and project management applications and the applications we used to manage our privatization business.

These proprietary systems gave MAXIMUS a significant advantage in bidding on government privatization projects. We had no license cost, and we could adapt these systems exactly to what was needed in the government program. Other companies had to license Oracle or other company software, which was very expensive. Our systems were also already "templated" for government operations and could be adapted more readily to each program.

This strong systems capability was the driving force behind MAXIMUS growth. We would not have been nearly as successful, if we could not build, adapt, and extend systems we needed in our privatization contracts at a cost much lower than our competitors.

Systems Institutionalize Best Practices

Our proprietary systems also made us smarter because they embedded the lessons we had learned managing government programs. Our case management staff were quickly brought up to speed when they learned how to use our systems. The systems represented a repository of knowledge about these programs.

MAXIMUS systems were programmed to take our employees through specific steps to accomplish tasks. Whether performing eligibility determinations for people in need, calculating child support amounts, searching for enrolled recipients into managed care plans, or whatever, our system was the guide. We built our best practices into the functionality of the systems. When we trained our staff to use the system, they effectively had been trained to employ our best practices.

If you want to change an organization fundamentally, change the functionality of the system it uses. I'd make the following analogy when we bid on a contract to replace a government's outdated system with a new system. *"Replacing an agency's system is equivalent to giving the agency a heart transplant."* MAXIMUS essentially engaged in a heart-transplant operation when we replaced a client's day-to-day operating system.

In our proposal, we emphasized the need to keep the agency doing business as usual while we implanted the new system. We had to remove the old system carefully, and replace it with the new system and not disrupt the business of the organization. We had to make sure the agency remained healthy throughout the process.

Many times a government agency that contracted out system development was left with a new system that didn't work, causing major program disruptions. MAXIMUS tried to avoid this as much as possible by educating our clients on what to expect. But when a problem occurred, the media, the politicians, and everyone else got involved in the mix. It was mayhem. Considering this not-so-unusual outcome, the six stages of systems development have been described as follows:

> Stage 1 – Wild Enthusiasm
> Stage 2 – Disillusionment
> Stage 3 – Panic
> Stage 4 – Search for the Guilty
> Stage 5 – Punishment of the Innocent
> Stage 6 – Praise and Glory for the Nonparticipants

How true!

Systems Have to Be Used Properly

On one contract we had with a federal agency, MAXIMUS developed software that performed complex mathematical calculations. We had to deliver the computer program to an office located in the Midwest. I was asked to bring punched cards, so the program could be loaded into their computers. At that time, punched cards had all but disappeared from use.

I told the client we didn't have access to a keypunch machine, but I would bring the printout with me and have the cards punched at the client's location. Then, we could load the program into their computer, and I would explain how the program worked.

I flew in the night before and met the client at his office early in the morning. After a brief chat, we went down to the keypunch room, which was spread out over an acre of office space, packed with keypunch machines and keypunch operators. Everyone looked very busy.

I estimated the computer program would require about three hundred punched cards. We dropped the "job" off at nine a.m. When we came back at ten a.m., the supervisor told us the job was not yet ready. We were surprised since it had received the highest priority.

I asked the supervisor what the problem was. He said the job took much longer than normal because to punch an alpha character (a to z), the keypunch operators had to hold the Control key down and press three numeric keys—this instead of pressing just one alpha key. I asked him why.

He said they had too many keypunch operators, so they had to slow the machines down to keep them all busy! Therefore, the jobs took three times as long to finish. Wow! We finally received the punched cards about eleven a.m. I barely made my two p.m. flight back to Washington, DC.

You learn something new every day. This was the first time I had heard of computers making people less productive. *This is a perfect example of a noneconomic decision made by government.* This would never have occurred in the private sector, where keypunch operators are hired as needed.

Since it was very difficult to lay off keypunch operators in government, the solution was to slow down the machines. This function clearly should have been outsourced.

Here's another story where the system caused a problem—this time because of me. As a hands-on CEO, I liked to dive into the code of our computer programs. One night I thought I had found a way to make our computer program more efficient, and changed the way a basic calculation was made. The programmers tolerated me because I often had good ideas and, of course, I was the boss.

I changed the subroutine that sent recipient names and addresses to our mail house. The mail house sent packages of materials to the recipients using the information in the file. The package of materials included information on each health care plan so recipients could choose the plan that best fit their needs. The packages were phone-book size! Unfortunately, my logic was faulty, and I forgot the logic to change the next address to store in the file.

A couple of days later, some unlucky household in Santa Clara County, California, had two moving vans pull up to their driveway and attempt to deliver 8,000 seven-pound packages. The mistake I made caused the same address to be repeated 8,000 times. The mail house didn't have the sense to stop the shipments. MAXIMUS paid for that one. I always wondered what the look on that person's face was when the deliveryman came to the door.

Computers can make more mistakes per second than you can imagine.

Developing User-Friendly Systems

To keep our staff and our clients happy, we had to develop user-friendly systems. To do this we adhered to certain principles of design. One of the most important is simplicity—a recurring theme. For readers responsible for systems, here is how MAXIMUS built user-friendly systems. We would try to

- **Place a "Help" Button on Each Screen** – The Help would explain each option on the screen. There are many models for providing help—nowadays, a video tutorial for each screen is perhaps the best approach.

- **Assure Consistency in Terminology** – We needed consistency of terminology throughout our screens. This is a key element of simplicity. Once the user learned one term, it applied throughout the system to the maximum extent possible.

- **Assure Consistency of Functionality** – Once the user learns how to perform a certain function—say enter a date—it is done that way every time.

- **Use Repetition of Look and Feel** – Each screen had a recognizable layout. Functions were located in the same areas of the screen—exit, menu, help, etc. Repetition makes things simple.

- **Minimize the Number of Steps** – A task should be performed with the minimum number of steps, data-entry strokes, and/or clicks of the mouse. Example of steps we would take include the following:

- ○ *Prefill Data Fields.* We had dates automatically entered along with other fields that could be prefilled with the most likely answers—like yes/no questions. The user would just change the answers that were different.

- ○ *Use Pull-down Menus.* We used pull-down menus when there were many choices, with the most likely choices at the top.

- ○ *Put Forms on Screen Next to Data-entry Fields.* We used pdfs of handwritten forms displayed side-by-side with the corresponding data-entry fields, so the data-entry clerk could enter the form easily.

- **Employ Color-coding** – Color-coding is an easy way to make the system more understandable to the user. Color-code the different modules or types of functions.

- **Put the "Fun" in Functionality** – If you can make the system fun to use, all the better. Think about it when you design the system.

I once calculated that saving one second on one data-entry screen in one of our largest projects could save the company close to $35,000 per year in data-entry costs. Consequently, the effort devoted to achieving simplicity was worth it.

MAXIMUS maintains a strong systems capability even today since such a capability is the key to success. About three years after I retired, MAXIMUS sold off the nonwelfare system companies it acquired in order to focus on social welfare entitlement programs. The systems business was just too hard.

CHAPTER 16

REPLACING GOVERNMENT

Privatization (also called *outsourcing* in government) became the prime core competency of MAXIMUS and the largest of our three businesses.

Privatization in Government

What exactly is privatization? Simply stated, privatization is replacing government workers with private-sector workers. But it's a little more complicated than that. In this book, privatization is replacing permanent public-sector workers with permanent private-sector workers.

Many tasks in government are one-time tasks and are contracted out. Tasks like cleaning up the records in a child support enforcement caseload—going through all the cases and making sure they are accurate—are one-time tasks. The government does not have the resources to do this job and concurrently manage its child support caseload. So I would say they "outsource" the task rather than privatize it.

Another example involves automated systems. The government generally does not have the resources or technical ability to build large, automated systems for itself. Government outsources this to large systems-development companies. And government often brings in consultants to help it make better decisions, but the consultants are not a permanent part of its operations either.

The privatization this book addresses is taking over government operations by the private sector. Many state governments initially privatized Medicaid claims processing by hiring EDS—then Electronic Data Systems, Inc.— avoiding the need to add additional government employees. Other states elected to process their own Medicaid claims and hired new employees.

The military privatizes base operations throughout the United States and overseas. A private contractor is responsible for managing the military base. The Forest Service privatizes concessions in the National Forests. Government personnel do not run concessions. And in many government buildings, maintenance is contracted out to a private contractor. Privatization is fairly widespread in government. So what's the difference in privatizing social welfare entitlement programs? There is a big difference, as you will see.

Privatizing Social Welfare Entitlement Programs

An entitlement program is just that. If a person meets the eligibility requirement, that person is entitled to receive cash, food stamps, medical help, housing, day care for his or her children, child support collection services, or whatever the program provides.

In government, there is a major distinction between discretionary duties and ministerial duties. For the longest time, determining eligibility for entitlement programs was deemed a discretionary duty. This meant that only government employees could determine eligibility.

What does discretionary mean? Basically, it means a judgment call. We all understand judges have discretionary power. We rely on their personal judgment when the law is ambiguous to determine how a civil or criminal case will be heard and, in some cases, decided. Governors, as well, have discretionary power to make some decisions independent of the legislature. So does the President of the United States when he issues Executive Orders. Some decisions are so complex they cannot be dictated by policy and procedure, and so the government relies on judgment, or the discretion of the decision-maker.

MAXIMUS was a party to the lawsuit in Los Angeles that first caused eligibility determination to be deemed a ministerial duty, at least at the state level. A ministerial duty is one with a fixed set of policies and procedures that anyone can carry out since no discretion is involved. *We showed that eligibility determination had to be ministerial to be equitable.* Soon after our GAIN contract was terminated by union influence, new federal legislation came along to affirm the benefits of privatization.

Major Welfare Reform Legislation

The Personal Responsibility and Work Opportunity Reconciliation Act (PRWORA) of 1996, passed under the Clinton Administration, created widespread privatization opportunities in social welfare entitlement programs. States were allowed, for the first time, to privatize eligibility determination in the federal TANF program—the core welfare program of the country. From my perspective, this new flexibility in contracting with the private sector stemmed from the successful privatization of the Los Angeles County GAIN program by MAXIMUS. We showed that a private contractor could be responsible and do an excellent job at lower cost.

The Act also required every state to have a welfare-to-work program, similar in purpose to GAIN. States could hire private contractors to operate that program as well, and they could pay the contractors based on achieving specific goals if they wished. Employees in government

163

unions don't work on a pay-for-performance basis. So many states privatized these programs, and government became more effective.

Ever wonder why the national welfare rolls fell so dramatically after welfare reform was enacted? Many pundits claimed it was the time limits on welfare eligibility—a family could be eligible for welfare for only a limited number of months. Time limits were important, but the main reason, in my opinion, was that the power of the private sector was unleashed to place welfare recipients into jobs. And we did in record numbers. About 1.4 million welfare recipients left the rolls in the first year after President Clinton signed this welfare reform law.

The State Child Health Insurance Program (SCHIP) was enacted into law a year later in 1997. Again, there was no limitation on the private sector managing this program. In fact, the private sector could determine eligibility for this program, even though it was still not allowed to determine eligibility for Medicaid. Again, this program was heavily privatized by the states, aided by the fact that there were no existing union employees. Government became more efficient through privatization. Chapter 19 – Enrolling the Poor in Health Plans explains why in detail.

MAXIMUS Experience in Managing Social Welfare Programs

Even though MAXIMUS had never managed a social welfare program before 1988, we had done just about everything else. Our staff worked regularly with government officials who were managing social welfare programs and with government systems staff who supported these programs.

We even worked with caseworkers in these programs to help them do their jobs better. MAXIMUS helped develop policies and procedures as well as train government caseworkers on how to carry them out. We had been "spectacular", as one client testified, in helping government improve the eligibility determination process to minimize agency errors and client fraud and abuse. Eligibility determination was a core competency of MAXIMUS.

One early project, in particular, gave MAXIMUS an excellent reputation—helping the New York City Human Resources Administration reduce the error rate in its basic welfare programs. This was in 1984, as I mentioned earlier in the book. Basically, we were successful in significantly reducing the welfare error rate in New York City, below that of all the other counties in New York State.

To provide a visceral understanding of what social welfare entitlement programs are like, I'd like to describe a typical welfare office in New York City at the time MAXIMUS was consulting there. This will help explain why we did what we did.

I'll focus on a welfare center I personally visited and worked in for about a week on a consulting assignment. My team was working with city government caseworkers and their supervisors who were determining eligibility for Food Stamps, Medicaid, and Welfare. As I recall, the center was in Williamsburg in Brooklyn. This description could apply equally to a welfare office in Los Angeles, Chicago, or in any other large city in which MAXIMUS consulted. I don't know what you would find today, but I wouldn't be surprised if little has changed.

The welfare center in Brooklyn was in a poor, dirty, and dangerous neighborhood, with walls covered with graffiti. There was an armed guard at the entrance of the center and one inside. The windows were barred. We walked into the waiting room, which consisted of row after row of chairs facing a bulletproof, cashier-type window. There were some torn, stained posters on the wall, required by program regulations. The furniture was cheap and very old. In one area, we could see a shattered window.

The people in the waiting room were sullen and quiet. The eligibility staff working with these people seemed to be taking their time and were not at all animated. They too, in fact, were poor and not much better off than the families in the room living on welfare payments.

At the time, I remarked to our government project officer it seemed strange that eligibility workers were being paid only $30,000 a year to administer programs that dispensed at least $1.2 million a year through each worker's caseload. Since the average eligibility worker was making mistakes at a 6 percent or higher rate, their error costs alone exceeded their salaries by at least a factor of two! Something was out of balance.

The idea of welfare is to provide temporary assistance to help people achieve self-sufficiency and leave welfare, not remain in the program. This welfare office was not the setting for raising the self-esteem of those people in that waiting room. It was not the place to give them hope that they could ever find a job and raise their standard of living. This was a place of dependency and despondency. I could not believe government was associated with something so clearly wrong. Surprisingly, the welfare offices I visited on Long Island were even worse. Something had to change.

I know many states, counties, and municipalities made the welfare application and redetermination process deliberately cumbersome and unpleasant. This was done to control the size of the welfare rolls. They didn't want everyone applying for benefits. I remember talking to one administrator, who by the way was a very good manager, about a new check issuance procedure being implemented. He told me he had to add steps to make picking up a check hard to do. He made it hard by requiring the check be picked up at an out-of-the-way welfare center. At first, I thought he was joking, but he was not.

So when I saw these conditions, I was determined to find an opportunity through privatization to make the recipient's experience entirely different from what they were currently experiencing. We were not going to take over a dysfunctional program unless we could substantially improve it. Moreover, MAXIMUS employees were not going to work under disreputable office conditions. Either we were going to manage the program properly in a decent setting (even accepting a loss of profit), or we were not going to compete for such a contract. This experience was the early motivation to administer one of these programs ourselves.

Welfare Recipients

Let's discuss the recipients of these welfare programs. There are many stereotypes that come to mind, but in my experience, these stereotypes were off the mark and misleading for the vast majority of these people.

In our capitalistic society, there are inevitably disadvantaged people who cannot earn their own way and fall into poverty. People end up on welfare for a number of different reasons, both long term and short term. These include growing up in a multigenerational welfare family, having little or no education, lacking any marketable job skills, being in poor physical or mental health, not having any employment opportunities, engaging in substance abuse, going through a recent divorce, and just plain hard luck, among others.

People in these circumstances need help. We would say MAXIMUS was "caring for the casualties of capitalism," when we were doing our jobs, and to some extent, that was true. Our government has to provide a safety net for those not able to cope in our capitalistic society, and we were part of that safety net. The difficult task for government is drawing the line between capitalism and socialism. The best course of action was to help people overcome the reasons they were on welfare so they could support themselves.

Without claiming to be too precise, in my experience about one-third of welfare recipients could recover from their poverty-inducing condition and go off the rolls. Another one-third would take longer but, with concerted government intervention, would make it off as well. The last one-third would be problematic. Either they had been born in the culture of dependence, or surprisingly were satisfied with their low-standard of living, or just didn't have what it took to support themselves. Obviously, government could make the most difference with the middle third.

So let's take a look at someone in the middle third. Recall most families on welfare are women-headed and have at least one child. There are other programs that help two-parent families, but they are rather small in number by comparison.

Through The Eyes of the Recipient

Dealing with the conditions in the welfare office was one thing—the other was seeing the welfare program through the recipients' eyes and understanding the burdens they faced. We had to understand what we were requiring of them to be able to design a helpful program.

Imagine you are a single mother in Brooklyn, New York, on welfare with two children, aged two and six. You live in a high-rise project apartment in dire need of repair. You have to rise early in the morning to feed your children and get them off to day care and school. No one is there to help you. Obviously, you first needed to find a day-care provider you could trust. You had to apply for a child care subsidy, going into the welfare office to have it arranged. Every time you go to the welfare office you have to wait—and wait.

You also have to find transportation to take your two-year-old to day care so you can come to training classes. You have to make sure your six-year-old gets on the bus to go to school. Once this is done, you can go to the training site mandated by the terms of your welfare grant, often by bus or subway.

You sit and participate in motivation and training classes for up to four hours a day. You are asked to go look for a job afterward, and sometimes the case manager will arrange the job interview and accompany you.

Your case manager may talk to the employer and explain the benefits of hiring a welfare recipient and vouch for you.

After your mandatory classes, you have to pick up your child at the day-care center. You don't have a car, but you do have travel vouchers issued by the government agency. You have to pick up your six-year-old after school at the bus stop or arrange for someone else to take care of your child. You know if you find a job, your daily schedule will be even more difficult.

The father of your children has stopped paying child support, so you are required to go to the child support office to help establish a court order to enforce support. This takes even more time, and you may be required to testify in court. If you don't cooperate without "good cause," your welfare grant will be terminated.

You are also required to reestablish eligibility for food stamps, Medicaid, and Welfare every six to twelve months, depending on whether you have a part-time job or other indirect income. As a result, you may have to visit the welfare office again to provide current information. If you do earn any money on a part-time job, you have to declare those earnings and have your grant reduced by a predetermined amount.

Then, you have to go to the store to buy food with your food stamps to feed your children. Obviously, you need to wash their clothes as well and take care of your apartment, pay the rent, and the like. And when your children get sick…and on it goes.

The burdens of single mothers on welfare are enormous. We tried as best we could to take into consideration what the recipients had to deal with and accommodate them. This was our edge in understanding social welfare entitlement programs. We understood the programs and the people dependent on them. Our welfare offices looked nothing like the one described above.

This is the privatization I am talking about. It is not processing claims in a professional building far removed from the recipients of the program. It is working individually with people who are disadvantaged and highly stressed and having a difficult time getting by. Establishing eligibility for these programs is the deepest level of privatization, a level that had never been breached before MAXIMUS. Eligibility determination is a function that significantly impacts the quality of life of millions of people.

Though I cannot find precise figures, there are likely a hundred thousand or more government eligibility workers in the United States. Until MAXIMUS came along, in government entitlement programs, they were all government workers.

MAXIMUS was the first private company of any size to win contracts to staff a welfare office and determine eligibility. Our case managers/eligibility workers interacted individually face-to-face with recipients and their families in their native language to help them navigate the complexities of the application and redetermination process. Our people collected income, assets, and other data and entered the data into state- or county-provided systems, which computed the eligibility.

We performed many other tasks as a privatization contractor in addition to determining eligibility, as described below.

Motivating Welfare Recipients

A key task at MAXIMUS in all programs was to motivate recipients to find jobs and become self-sufficient. No work we had was more satisfying than doing this.

The federal government offered substantial tax credits to employers who hired welfare recipients. The tax credits currently are worth up to $9,000 over a two-year period if the employee has been on welfare for eighteen months. MAXIMUS was very successful in placing recipients, in part, because we informed prospective employers of the tax credits. So they were more motivated to give the recipients a chance. In fact, in one contract in Fairfax County, Virginia, we essentially placed almost every job-ready recipient into a job—we worked ourselves out of a contract. But that was OK.

To explain what we did, I've chosen to tell the story of my brother, Joe Mastran. He was a trainer and motivational speaker for MAXIMUS on a contract to help welfare recipients find jobs. Some of his experiences make great illustrative examples.

In his training classes on motivation, Joe would challenge the recipients to make something of themselves. He would entertain them and work with them individually to become proud of who they were. He could get them to try anything. One time Joe's supervisor caught him with all his recipients standing on top of their desks. Since this was dangerous to say the least, we had to tell him to stop. But the recipients loved him because he talked their language, and they responded to his message.

Joe told me about the time he took a piece of chalk and wrote a big "1.69" on the blackboard. He didn't explain it to the class. After a while, however, the recipients became curious and wanted to know what it meant. He asked if they could guess, and they couldn't. So he told them. He said, "That was my grade point average in high school." He then asked, "How many of you had a higher grade point average?" Well, over half the hands went up. Then Joe said if he could make something of himself, then surely they could make something of themselves. Incidentally, Joe graduated with a B.A. from the University of Hawaii and was a captain in the Air Force.

Joe also told the following story to motivate the recipients:

> Scientists placed a barracuda in a long fish tank along with a small fish that barracudas like to eat. They also inserted a pane of glass in the middle of the tank, so the barracuda could not get to the small fish. The barracuda banged against the glass repeatedly, failing each time to reach the small fish. As time went on, the barracuda attacked the fish less and less frequently. Finally, after several days, the barracuda stopped attacking. This is when the scientists removed the pane of glass from the middle of the tank. The barracuda never swam over to eat the small fish, though there was nothing in the way.

Joe said that is where the welfare recipients were in their lives. They had been unsuccessful in being what they wanted to be for so long, that they just quit trying. He told them the pane of glass was just a mental block, and it wasn't there any more. All they had to do was go look for a job, and they would find it—and they did.

There were a lot of people like Joe in MAXIMUS—maybe not as clever, but certainly as motivated. His was one of the best jobs in the company because it was so satisfying.

My Mother and Welfare

I am clearly proud of my brother. So I want to tell you a bit more about him. This is a story my mother told me, and I repeated it at one of our off-site meetings with all the top executives present and then many times again in front of new employees.

One day, many years ago, my mother was shopping in Walmart in Alexandria, Virginia. She happened to be wearing a MAXIMUS pin on her blouse. The sales assistant who was helping her noticed the pin and said MAXIMUS had helped her get her job at Walmart. My mother said that was wonderful.

Then the sales assistant asked my mother if, by any chance, she knew a person at MAXIMUS by the name of Joe Mastran? After a short pause, studying the woman, my mother said, "Yes—he's my son." The sales assistant was speechless with gratitude. She said Joe was the person who changed her life. She hugged my mother and thanked her so much. She went on and stayed with my mother until she left the store. My mother thanked her, too. What a great feeling of pride that brought to my mother and me. That's what MAXIMUS was all about.

Finding Jobs

To motivate recipients to interview for jobs, we had to build their self-esteem and confidence that they could actually get a job. Recipients had to believe in themselves, or little could be accomplished. This was not an easy task since many had very low self-esteem. Every day they saw on TV how other people lived, and they knew they weren't living that life. They didn't believe they could live that life.

So we made sure when we placed a recipient into a job, everyone else participating in our program knew about it. Our case managers focused hard on helping the recipients look at their strengths and not at their weaknesses. Our job was to make them feel good about themselves and give them hope.

I taught welfare recipients myself very briefly. I remember being in a conundrum about whether to teach astrology to the recipients. In a few classes, I asked the recipients for their astrological sign and then gave them the personality traits associated with that sign. The traits were all very positive, and knowing their positive traits helped build their feelings of self worth and a sense of identity. And, of course, they loved it.

However, MAXIMUS couldn't have the media saying we were teaching astrology to welfare recipients, so I had to stop. Too bad—it worked very well.

We also worked hard to teach recipients interviewing techniques and videotaped their mock interviews. When they were done, the class critiqued the interviewees to help them improve their performance.

We taught recipients how to dress for an interview and behave in an acceptable manner—no chewing gum and the like. We worked hard to help them help themselves. And of all the jobs we had at MAXIMUS, this was the most dramatic. When they finally got a job, the excitement was overwhelming. In our first year, MAXIMUS found jobs for over 20,000 recipients.

Life Skills Training

Before recipients could work, they had to be able to take care of themselves and their children. MAXIMUS won a contract early on in Texas to help recipients learn basic life skills. We opened offices in Dallas, Houston, and San Antonio to provide life skills training to welfare recipients. Our contract payments were based on the number of recipients who completed our program—a pay-for-performance type contract government employee unions could never accept.

We developed our own courses to teach life skills to recipients. These people were often confounded by life's challenges and unable or unequipped to cope. As mentioned earlier, many came to accept their low standard of living—it was OK with them. We had to work with the recipients to raise their sights and create a desire to achieve a higher standard of living. We had to teach them the basic skills of living.

Among the courses we developed, in addition to how to interview for a job and proper behavior in the workplace, were the following:

- **Money Management** – This course taught basic budgeting and how to open and use a checking account.

- **Parenting** – Basic ways to be a good parent, including disciplining children, were covered in this course.

- **Personal Hygiene** – This course taught recipients how to take care of themselves and their children, including bathing and brushing the kids' teeth.

- **Health Care** – This course showed recipients how to get basic medical care and the coverage of Medicaid and Medicare.

- **Self Assertiveness** – This course taught recipients to stand up for themselves and be assertive.

- **Legal Rights** – This course explained their legal rights in the workplace as well as entitlement to government programs.

Many on our staff thought these courses should be taught in high school since everyone needed them. But they weren't.

In summary, MAXIMUS tried very hard to identify with the welfare recipients. We tried to "walk in their shoes" to design a program that worked for them. In the vast majority of cases, we were successful. And that was good.

Handling Recipient Complaints

Recipients have complaints like anyone else. And it was important to us to handle these complaints properly.

In privatization projects, MAXIMUS was interacting with tens of thousands of people every day, face-to-face and over the phone. Complaints were inevitable, even though we were trying our best. So our project management systems in privatization contracts had to handle complaints as one of the functions of the system.

I remember my first encounter with complaints against MAXIMUS was with the then Mayor of Nashville, Phil Bredesen. The complaints came from our Davidson County Child Support Enforcement Program. He called me in and said that his office was receiving ten complaints per week, and what were we going to do about it? I was caught off guard, and blurted out, "Is that all?"

He was surprised at my answer. He asked me what I meant. I said we had over 60,000 of the most contentious types of cases in social welfare programs, and ten complaints a week was an extremely small number. It must be a sign we were doing a good job. In the past, when the DA operated the program, complaints did not go to the mayor's office. Now they did.

I told the Mayor that MAXIMUS took each complaint very seriously and bent over backward to resolve the complaint satisfactorily. I suggested, though, that it would be helpful if we were notified immediately of any complaints to his office. We wanted to resolve them, if possible, and then send the disposition back to his office. We set up a communications system that kept his office informed. I don't recall any problems with the mayor after that.

Over time, we had to develop even more sophisticated systems for recording, resolving, and reporting recipient complaints. We also had to establish a liaison in the governor's office to report complaints back to MAXIMUS. We tracked these complaints in our own system. We reported the facts and disposition of the complaint in a timely manner to our client manager, or to the governor's office, or to whomever the agency designated.

Of course, if we found the complaint was valid, we took corrective action to ensure we did not see that complaint again. If the complaint involved one of our employees, the employee went into customer "enthusiasm" training.

Naturally, opponents to privatization tracked these complaints and grossly exaggerated them in an attempt to discredit MAXIMUS. As I explain later, our "customer" satisfaction ratings were off the charts, compared to traditional government. However, reading the media, at times you wouldn't have thought so.

It was important the recipients see MAXIMUS as their ally in the complex system they had to navigate.

In the next block of chapters, I explain how this all got started.

PART IV:
SOCIAL WELFARE PROGRAMS

This block of chapters will give you a clear picture of selected social welfare entitlement programs in the United States. The chapters describe how privatization first started in welfare-to-work programs and the obstacles that had to be overcome. This discussion is followed by a description of how other social welfare programs were subsequently privatized.

CHAPTER 17

THE FIRST WELFARE PRIVATIZATION

In this chapter, I explain how the first welfare privatization contract came to be. The federal program, known as TANF (Temporary Assistance to Needy Families), is the basic welfare program that provides money to families in need, as well as money for emergency assistance. This program is defined under Title IV-A of the Social Security Act. The amount of the monthly grant payment to a family is based on the number of children in the family and the state where the family lives. If the welfare recipient receives any earned or unearned income, then the grant amount is adjusted, depending on the type and amount of income received.

Some states experimented with programs in the 1970s requiring adult welfare recipients to go to job training and find a job while on welfare. The California Work Experience Program (CWEP) was one of the first programs to do this. Later in 1987, California enacted a successor program—discussed earlier—called the GAIN (Greater Avenues for Independence) program. Nine years later PRWORA, the federal Welfare Reform Act of 1996, made participation in welfare-to-work programs mandatory in every state.

The Decision to Privatize

MAXIMUS won a contract in early 1987 to train prospective GAIN case managers. At about the same time, the Los Angeles County Board of Supervisors decided to see whether privatizing the entire GAIN program in Los Angeles would be cost effective. They would have had to hire more county employees to administer this new program, which they didn't want to do.

I'm not sure how the supervisors made that historic decision to privatize GAIN, but Jack Svahn, president of one of our divisions at the time, played a role. Jack was a former commissioner of the Social Security Administration and the Domestic Policy Advisor to Ronald Reagan in the White House. As mentioned earlier, I had worked under Jack Svahn at SRS. He met with the Los Angeles County Board of Supervisors sometime earlier, explaining the potential benefits of privatization.

The three Los Angeles County Supervisors who approved the privatization of GAIN were Pete Schabarum, Mike Antonovich, and Dean Dana. They deserve credit, in my opinion, for giving the movement its first chance. Don Knabe, Dana's Chief of Staff, also contributed heavily.

Anyway, we reasoned if MAXIMUS could train GAIN case managers, we could manage them as well, so we bid on the contract. MAXIMUS had tremendous experience in welfare programs, as you have learned.

After a lengthy proposal process, the evaluation committee selected us. County financial analysts testified at a subsequent board hearing that MAXIMUS would be more cost effective to manage the GAIN program than using county employees, saving $4 million per year in full operations. The Department of Public Social Services recommended that the Board of Supervisors award MAXIMUS the contract.

The Service Employees International Union (SEIU) immediately understood privatization was a threat to its membership, and the union pulled out all the stops to fight it. We had never encountered a union before, and were stunned by the intensity of their campaign against us. They were experts at intimidating government.

During the hearings, the union brought in hundreds of demonstrators, all in red T-shirts, to fill the Hall of Administration. They chanted anti-MAXIMUS slogans as the Board of Supervisors considered the recommendations of the financial analysts and Department of Public Social Services. Despite the union demonstrations, the supervisors approved the contract.

Now, 175 new GAIN case manager positions were going to the private sector instead of becoming new, dues-paying union members. No existing Los Angeles County employees were affected. The SEIU was and still is an aggressive union with powerful political influence in Los Angeles, and nationwide for that matter. The union immediately sued MAXIMUS and Los Angeles County, claiming eligibility determination for GAIN was a discretionary activity that could be performed only by government employees, and that our contract was illegal.

The union lawsuit required me to make a strategic decision. The Department of Public Social Services notified MAXIMUS that if the courts ultimately declared the contract illegal, the county would have to recover all the money it had paid us during the course of the court battle—millions of dollars. Did we want to continue?

I determined the risk was worth it, since this was the first privatization contract ever for eligibility determination. As Ronald Reagan said a few years earlier, "If not us, who? If not now, when?" I felt the same way. Therefore, we stayed to fight, even though MAXIMUS's financial survival was potentially on the line. (Thankfully, I was the majority shareholder and could make the decision.)

After a long court battle, the union lost. (Incidentally, it lost a similar lawsuit years later after we won another GAIN privatization contract in San Diego.) The ruling was that eligibility determination is defined by a set of rules anyone could follow. Otherwise, caseworkers could decide arbitrarily whether or not someone was entitled to benefits. MAXIMUS was merely collecting data and entering it into the computer. Complex rules of eligibility determination would be applied by the computer; and, therefore, were not under MAXIMUS control.

This is what we argued—that eligibility determination was governed by a strict set of policies and procedures. MAXIMUS was simply hired to carry out these policies and procedures. The court agreed—the Los Angeles GAIN program could be operated by a private, for-profit contractor. *This was a landmark decision!*

Program Operations

Unfortunately, while all this was going on, I was in the middle of a "friendly divorce." My wife of twenty-three years had had enough of me and filed for divorce. There were no shouting matches or displays of anger—it was just very sad. I left the house and moved into an apartment complex in McLean, Virginia. We split everything fifty-fifty. I bought her shares in MAXIMUS—she sold them to me instead of Ray Ruddy, who asked to buy them.

The divorce was so painful, I decided to move to Los Angeles and personally manage the new privatization project. I stayed in Los Angeles for two years, learning to accept what had happened to my marriage. My son David was just entering college, and my daughter Susannah was a sophomore in high school. She came out to visit me. Donna, who I would later marry, was also going through a divorce and would come later to Los Angeles to work on the project sporadically. Otherwise, I stayed very busy.

I personally managed the Los Angeles GAIN contract for MAXIMUS for the first two years. I set out to make a huge difference, showing how well a private company could manage a social welfare program. I hired the top people I could find. MAXIMUS operated five regional offices located throughout Los Angeles County. Initially, we were asked to lease the buildings since the county leasing procedures were burdensome and taking too long. At the last minute, we were called off, and the county leased the buildings.

The buildings were modern office buildings with new furniture. We created a reception area (aptly called a "waiting room" in welfare offices) and made sure no one waited more than fifteen minutes for an appointment. We provided free coffee to the recipients and cookies for their children. We arranged the reception area in small groups of chairs around coffee tables with current magazines for recipients to read. We had stanchions to guide a line for those checking in for their appointments. For all intents and purposes, it was a large, modern reception center in a professional office building. This was culture shock for the recipients.

MAXIMUS case managers were taught how to help recipients deal with their frustration and anger and to motivate them to free themselves from welfare dependency. We treated recipients as equals who needed our help. We explained their benefits and tried to enroll them in schools. At the end of their visits, we gave them a Customer Satisfaction Survey to fill out anonymously and drop in a collection box.

I monitored our recipient ratings relentlessly—and across all five centers in Los Angeles, the average rating was over 99 percent satisfaction, with over 80 percent of recipients submitting forms. At first, we could not believe the ratings, but then recipients saw how different our offices were from their regular welfare offices and how differently they were treated.

I implemented an Executive Information System that tracked statistics for every case manager in every supervisory unit in every regional office.

We gave the county monitors access to the system. The systems displayed waiting times and satisfaction ratings for a wide range of services MAXIMUS provided. Incidentally, we served recipients in fourteen languages, using forms in the corresponding languages and alphabets.

To show the power of our Executive Information System, I remember discovering a supervisory unit in our Van Nuys office that had an 85 percent satisfaction rating, the worst of any supervisory unit in our whole operation. I personally went to Van Nuys with our project manager, Fred Gustafson, to find out why. Fred was a very qualified manager who had recently retired from the Department of Public Social Services.

It turned out the unit had two Armenian case managers and, therefore, had Armenian recipients. The reason for the lower ratings was the survey form was translated into the wrong dialect of Armenian. The form had led the recipients to say "No" when they meant "Yes." When the form was corrected, the supervisory unit satisfaction rating soared back over 99 percent. Would government have done that?

Because of the unions, California democrats were also after MAXIMUS. I was subpoenaed to appear before the California Senate to explain how MAXIMUS won the Los Angeles GAIN contract, as described in the prologue and later in the book. We were continually under fire from powerful politicians—Maxine Waters, Bill Greene (before the hearing), and Diane Watson. I was told SEIU had targeted MAXIMUS as their number-one priority in California. They had!

Public Private Partnership

MAXIMUS worked in close partnership with the Department of Public Social Services. Eddy Tanaka, head of the department, and his staff supported us 100 percent. We published a brochure called the "Public Private Partnership" that showed the advantages of government and the private sector working together. The department loved what we had the freedom to do, and we made many long-lasting friendships there. Of course, they monitored us extremely closely and watched every move we made. But that only made us better.

The Los Angeles GAIN contract term was five years. Every year, the union fought to have the contract terminated. Every year, the Department of Public Social Services explained that MAXIMUS was more cost effective than having county employees do the work. However, as explained, the unions ultimately won the battle, and our contract was terminated. Nevertheless, privatization of the most sensitive components of social welfare entitlement programs had been successful. The privatization wars were in full force!

Learning How to Privatize

In the early days of privatization, government officials had to learn how to construct privatization contracts that met their needs. Over time, the government learned how to obtain what it wanted. The early privatization efforts that failed with other companies had poorly constructed contracts.

In some privatization contracts, the government provided contract language antithetical to its interests. The contract officers had to learn that the contractor was going to follow the scope of work exactly. So they had to learn to define clearly the behavior they wanted from the contractor.

As mentioned earlier, we won a second GAIN privatization contract in one region of San Diego County. Since the County Board of Supervisors understood the benefits of privatization, they didn't care that Los Angeles County had deprivatized its GAIN program.

Our San Diego contract called for providing training programs for the recipients and arranging child care while they were in training. OK. We did a great job! We developed a first-class training program, which participants rated very highly. In addition, we had excellent attendance by the participants since they liked the program and received child care assistance when needed. We had done what we were contracted to do.

When our performance evaluation was released, we were told the MAXIMUS contract was not being renewed. The reason was we didn't place enough welfare recipients into jobs. What? That was not in the contract.

We told the county project manager, if you want us to place recipients into jobs, put that in the contract. Based on our appeal, the county allowed us to continue as a contractor. The next year, we performed well in excess of expectations in placing welfare recipients into jobs. Had we not intervened, this would have been labeled by the unions as a privatization contract that failed.

So when the government defines what it really wants, the private sector can deliver.

Staff Attitudes

When MAXIMUS competed for these welfare-to-work contracts, we tried to make sure we were not perceived as just another profit-making company. We trained our case managers to be compassionate toward the recipients and ensured our people liked their jobs. We added a MAXIMUS Compassionate Care Program later to give specific additional training to our staff. We wanted our staff to go the extra mile.

MAXIMUS looked for prospective employees who were experienced social workers, social work or psychology majors, or former case managers. In fact, this was often a requirement in contracts we signed. One state, West Virginia, as I recall, required all case managers to have master's degrees.

As indicated earlier, MAXIMUS also hired welfare recipients to fill job openings. To do this, I had to lower our standards a bit for these employees. For example, I set the typing standard for a recipient applying for a clerical position at fifteen words per minute—very low. If I hadn't done this, we wouldn't have hired any recipients.

I remember one elderly woman who came in and took the test but could only type eight words per minute. I let her try again, but to no avail. I suggested she practice typing at home for a couple of weeks and then come back and try again. She came back and failed again.

Talk about heart-wrenching. Here was a very pleasant person on welfare who really wanted a job, but I couldn't in good conscience give her one, even though I was in the business of helping her. I had already set a low standard for welfare recipients, but it was a standard. I could not sacrifice that standard, or I would have no standards at all. And the work wouldn't get done.

This is a dilemma every manager faces—how to choose between compassion and the job requirements. Sadly, I thanked her for her efforts and wished her well, and with a tear in her eye, she wished me well, too. I remember it like it was yesterday.

We tried to make sure our people on the front lines achieved real job satisfaction when they helped people in need. And I believe most of us did.

Other Programs

MAXIMUS went on to manage welfare-to-work programs in Lake County, California; San Antonio, Dallas and Houston, Texas; Washington DC; statewide in Wyoming; Prince Georges and Montgomery Counties, Maryland; northern Virginia, and many other places, including Australia.

In 1997, we also won and managed the TANF program in Milwaukee, Wisconsin, called W-2. And in 1999, we won and managed the TANF program in Phoenix, Arizona. These two programs involved eligibility determination for TANF and thus involved the entire scope of the welfare program, not just the welfare-to-work component. We are still operating in Milwaukee.

For political reasons, MAXIMUS eligibility workers are still not allowed to determine eligibility for Food Stamps and Medicaid. This restriction didn't make sense because in all government welfare offices, the same eligibility worker determines eligibility for all three programs concurrently. That's the most cost-effective way to do it.

I believe the irrational restriction was the work of government employee unions and far-left politicians to ensure that privatization could not prove to be more cost effective than business as usual. The federal agencies for Food Stamps and Medicaid would not give their permission for private workers to determine eligibility, even though the United States Congress had set the precedent with the TANF program. Even today, this limitation exists.

Despite all this, we learned a great deal in these initial privatization contracts that lifted us to even greater heights in the future.

CHAPTER 18

MAKING DEADBEAT DADS PAY

The Child Support Enforcement Program was enacted in 1975 as Title IV-D of the Social Security Act. The program was designed to promote accountability among absent parents, or in the vernacular, to pursue deadbeat dads and make them pay. The law, incidentally, also applied to absent mothers.

A very large number of woman-headed families are on welfare because absent fathers won't pay child support. The law allowed states to recover money from these absent fathers (or noncustodial parents) to offset the welfare payments to the mothers (custodial parents). The program was also extended to persons not currently on welfare to ensure they didn't end up on welfare. Therefore, anyone can obtain free child support enforcement services from the government.

The program is also multistate. States cooperate with one another, sending money collected in one state to the other, if the custodial parent was in the other state. The absent parent couldn't just relocate to another state and get away without paying child support. States even have agreements with other countries.

Privatization services provided by MAXIMUS under this program included the following:

- **Locating Absent Parents** – MAXIMUS operated skip-trace units to locate absent parents, no matter where they were in the United States, or sometimes in other countries.

- **Establishing Paternity** – MAXIMUS staff took buccal swab specimens (saliva from the inside of cheeks) from putative fathers and sent the swabs to paternity testing laboratories to determine by DNA if the men were, in fact, the true fathers.

- **Establishing Support Orders** – MAXIMUS child-support attorneys filed support orders, which established the amount of support owed by the absent parent. We took absent parents to court to establish the amount of the order. Judges used federal guidelines to set the amount based on the absent parent's financial condition.

- **Enforcing Support Orders** – MAXIMUS attorneys also filed contempt orders for failure to pay child support. The court orders reset the amounts owed and often required a lump-sum payment for back child support. If an absent parent still did not pay, he was sometimes sent to jail. Other MAXIMUS enforcement staff engaged in income withholding or asset attachment. We also administered the IRS tax refund intercept program by which federal tax refunds were applied first to child support arrears and then sent to the taxpayer.

Interestingly, both liberals and conservatives voted for the Child Support Enforcement Program. The program appeals to both parties because it promotes parental responsibility.

Initially, states outsourced or privatized only selected components of the program. As described earlier, states contracted with private companies to clean up their caseloads to conform to the law. This was a one-time job that states did not have resources to perform concurrently while operating the program. So they hired a private company.

MAXIMUS was an early pioneer in privatizing child support enforcement. We won the Massachusetts child support contract in 1989, not long after winning the Los Angeles GAIN contract. We continued winning contracts in Arizona in 1991 and in Tennessee in 1993 for financial reconciliation of their caseloads. The principal work involved determining how child support debts are calculated and allocated and how the money, once received, is distributed. The financial reconciliation process is just one small component of the Child Support Enforcement Program.

Most child support cases are not current—or paid up to date. In fact, some cases are years in arrears since no payments have been made for a long time. In addition, because the custodial parent (95 percent women) can go on and off welfare, the allocation of the child support between the custodial parent and the state becomes a problem.

If the mother is on welfare, the child support payment goes to the state to help offset her welfare payments. The legislation was later amended to allow a portion of the payments to go to the mother to ensure she continued to cooperate with the state. For example, she can sometimes help in locating the absent father when he moves to avoid paying child support.

If the mother is *not* on welfare, the entire child support payment goes directly to her and nothing to the state, so long as the state account from the time she was on welfare is up to date. Our staff, therefore, had to know the welfare history of each custodial parent and the amounts collected over time from the noncustodial parent(s) to make the proper allocations.

It is not uncommon for a father to pay child support to more than one mother—sometimes up to three and four at the same time.

Correspondingly, it is not uncommon for a single mother to receive child support from more than one father if she has had children by several different men. Therefore, MAXIMUS had to keep track of the number of children being supported by each father, and the amounts paid the mother to offset her welfare grant. If she receives multiple child support payments, we had to determine whether the state could keep some of the money for child support in arrears due the state.

We also needed the history of support orders to determine how much the absent parent actually owed. There were many changes in circumstances for an absent parent that could affect his ability to pay—for example, loss of a job. When this happened, the amount of the support order changed. This also had to be taken into account to calculate the correct arrears for any time period.

Finally, we needed to know when the child reached maturity. Typically, child support stops when the child reaches eighteen years old, but there are exceptions. As a result, we had to calculate the child's age to determine the amount of support actually owed in a particular time period.

So what happened when a lump-sum payment came in because of an enforcement action? Say we collected $3,000. We had to allocate the $3,000 to different accounts by calculating the arrears (unpaid child support) going back for multiple years for each custodial parent and for the state. Then we had to determine who received how much based on the arrears owed.

Once the allocation was made, the $3,000 had to be distributed, or paid to the various parties. The amounts allocated to each custodial parent and the state had to be tracked, so we could make sure they were actually paid.

Often, there were undistributed funds in an account, and we had to go back and determine who was entitled to the money. And sometimes funds had been incorrectly paid and a correction had to be made. And this calculation changed every month!

By the way, this financial reconciliation project is the type Donna was sent to manage, as described in Chapter 10 – The Toughest Management Job of All.

In June 1992, MAXIMUS helped convince the state of Tennessee to privatize not just the financial reconciliation process, but the entire program. Fortuitously for us, the district attorney in Nashville (Davidson County) did not consider the Child Support Enforcement Program a priority because his resources were stretched already prosecuting serious crimes.

As a result, the performance of the program suffered. When asked by the state, the district attorney readily agreed to give up the contract and let a private company administer the program. As far as I know, this was the first time an entire child support program had been privatized in any state.

MAXIMUS competed for and won the contract. What we found was an indescribable mess. The DA's computer program did not work, the office was in shambles, the staff was untrained, and the collections were abysmal. The contract required that we hire the DA's workers, so we did. We didn't know what to expect from them.

We brought in our own computer system and tailored it to Tennessee's requirements. We brought in supervisors experienced in child support enforcement, and we trained the staff extensively on the new procedures we were implementing. We leased new office space and furnished it professionally, and we introduced a bonus system for achieving high collection goals.

Needless to say, the ex-government staff were elated. Their productivity jumped immediately, and by the end of the first year, collections had soared 100 percent. By the end of year three, collections were up an astounding 300 percent. We had inherited a caseload of 60,000 and were outperforming the other child support district attorneys in the state and throughout the country.

The Toughest Cases of All

Child support is one of the most emotional programs we managed because a mother and father have separated, typically under very unpleasant circumstances. When MAXIMUS staff became involved in establishing or collecting child support, there was usually palpable anger on both sides.

I would occasionally read our child support case records to keep up on our performance. These records put the daytime soaps to shame. I have never seen such rancor reduced to writing. I remember one man who would send his ex-wife Monopoly money, even after being threatened by the judge for contempt. We had to take him to court regularly to get him to pay.

Another man, an attorney as I recall making over $100,000 per year, wouldn't pay a dime. He told the judge he hated the "bitch" and would never pay. The judge said, "How about trying thirty days in jail?" So the man went to jail. After thirty days, we brought him back before the judge, and the man said the same thing—he would never pay.

So the judge said, "How about six months in jail?" The man said fine and went to jail for another six months. We brought the man back before the judge after the six months and got the same answer. The man told the judge he would stay in jail for the rest of his life rather than pay her anything. So what did the judge do? He set the man free, and we didn't try to collect child support from him again.

The case records were filled with these types of stories. People can really be unkind and unsympathetic to one another. MAXIMUS staff had to work with both parents in this program. Both parents were emotionally charged when they met at our offices or in the courtroom. We had to help them be reasonable with each other. The job was extremely stressful, but, at the same time, extremely interesting.

Child Support Is Like a Business

Child support is an easy program to privatize since it is most like a business. The program has clear measures of effectiveness—collections and the cost of collections. Performance could easily be compared with other child support programs using government employees or private sector employees. As a result of our success, MAXIMUS went on to privatize child support programs in many states.

We managed Child Support Enforcement Programs in Nashville and Knoxville, Tennessee, in 1993, and then later in Chattanooga and Memphis, Tennessee. We privatized Baltimore and Queen Anne's County, Maryland, and Jackson and Vicksburg, Mississippi, in 1995.

MAXIMUS also privatized child support programs in Augusta, Valdosta, and Columbus, Georgia; Myrtle Beach, South Carolina; and a host of other places. *We collected over $275 million of child support per year on behalf of custodial parents and their children.*

Soon, privatizing child support became an industry unto itself, and we had many competitors, including Policy Studies, Inc., also an early pioneer. It was a win for the government, a win for the government employees converted to private sector employees, a win for the mothers and children who needed the child support, and a win for MAXIMUS. OK—the deadbeat dads lost.

MAXIMUS acquired Policy Studies, Inc., along with its 1300 employees in April 2012.

CHAPTER 19

ENROLLING THE POOR IN HEALTH PLANS

Medicaid, the health care program for the poor, is the most expensive program in state budgets. One solution to containing costs is to enroll the recipients into health care plans, or managed care. The state pays the plans a fixed amount per month per recipient, determined by competitive bidding. The health care plan then takes care of the recipients and pays their claims. This program is enormously complicated, just like child support enforcement.

The federal government issued regulations for Medicaid Managed Care programs that prevented health care plans from marketing directly to Medicaid recipients. An independent, third party enrollment broker is required to serve as an intermediary. In 1995, MAXIMUS won its first Medicaid Managed Care project in Nebraska. Our job was to serve as the independent enrollment broker and educate recipients so they could choose the best managed care plan for their particular circumstances.

The contract was very difficult for us. We had to develop a sophisticated computer program on the fly that handled all the complexities involved—like repairing an airplane in flight. The Medicaid Managed Care program was so undefined at that time that no one really knew what policies had to be developed. As well, the doctors and other medical providers in Nebraska were vehemently against managed care and fought the program continually.

On one occasion, I was called to a "project review" meeting in Omaha with the medical community. For these new types of projects, I would spend three to four months on site making sure the project started up correctly. Anyway, every person around the table at the meeting railed at me about the terrible job MAXIMUS was doing. I didn't say anything other than to apologize. They didn't want to hear any explanations.

I remember in history class studying the Star Chamber, which was the English court convened in secret in England in the seventeenth century. There were no indictments, no rights of appeal, no juries, and no witnesses. That meeting was another Star Chamber as far as I was concerned, and MAXIMUS was guilty. I was embarrassed and felt terrible—their comments were all negative and unfair. MAXIMUS was doing a miraculous job under the circumstances.

After the meeting, I sat for several minutes in my rental car in the parking lot trying to assimilate what had happened and why. After a while, I heard a tap on my window and rolled it down. One of the female physicians said to me, "MAXIMUS wasn't really doing that bad of a job—everybody had to vent about managed care, and you were the available target." She was very kind to say that, and it helped.

Some of the tasks MAXIMUS was required to do in our enrollment broker contracts were as follows:

- Develop, print, and distribute brochures that explained the various managed care plans in terms that recipients could understand

- Maintain a call center so recipients could call in and have their questions answered and complaints addressed

- Integrate with the state's Medicaid eligibility system so we knew who was newly eligible and who had lost eligibility for managed care

- Send out enrollment notices for new Medicaid recipients who had to select a plan and renewal notices to those in plans who had to reenroll

- Conduct enrollment seminars in our office and around the state for those who wanted to attend classes in person and have help choosing a plan

- Coordinate with the managed care plans on who was enrolling and who had lost Medicaid eligibility and was disenrolling.

In 1997, we won enrollment broker contracts for the entire state of California, followed by Texas and then Michigan, followed in 1998 by New York City and Long Island. We ended up in many more states after that, including Massachusetts, New Jersey, Georgia, Kansas, Iowa, and Vermont. Our call centers all combined took over 500,000 calls per month.

State Child Health Insurance Programs

Recall that in 1997, the US Congress passed SCHIP—State Child Health Insurance Program—Title XXI of the Social Security Act. This program is designed for poor families who are just above the threshold for Medicaid eligibility and focuses primarily on their children. Families are required to pay a portion of the premium for the insurance.

SCHIP was the largest expansion of taxpayer-funded health insurance coverage for children in the United States since Medicaid was enacted in 1965. SCHIP was sponsored by Senator Ted Kennedy in a partnership with Senator Orrin Hatch, with support coming from First Lady Hillary Rodham Clinton during the Clinton administration.

States had the flexibility to design their SCHIP eligibility requirements and policies within broad federal guidelines. Some states also insured the parents of children receiving benefits, as well as pregnant women and other adults. Again, each state is different.

Besides administering the insurance components of this program, MAXIMUS had the additional responsibility of determining eligibility for benefits since recipients could not be eligible for Medicaid. While the federal government wouldn't allow us to determine eligibility for Medicaid, we could determine eligibility for SCHIP. *Politically-correct decision-making again.*

To determine eligibility, we had to collect income and asset information and make the determination whether or not the applicant was entitled to benefits. MAXIMUS was again engaged in doing the most sensitive job of any government worker.

In addition, we were required to collect premiums that were based on a sliding scale according to income. So we had a financial management function as well. We had to keep track of arrearages and overpayments and tremendously complicated policies, just like in child support.

In doing these things, the barriers to entry into this business became exceedingly high. MAXIMUS became an extremely knowledgeable and skilled resource for states to contract with, and the bonus we brought was the computer system we developed to operate the programs efficiently. This alone saved states tens of millions of dollars.

MAXIMUS privatized the SCHIP programs in California, New Jersey, Iowa, and numerous other states.

The next chapter discusses our California SCHIP program known as Healthy Families in much more detail so you can appreciate the complexity of child health insurance programs. The chapter also describes two other very large privatization contracts.

CHAPTER 20

MAXIMUS's LARGEST CONTRACTS

This chapter covers the largest and more prominent privatization contracts MAXIMUS won during my tenure. These contracts helped define MAXIMUS because the amounts were so large. They all involved health care in some way. I resume with the California Healthy Families contract introduced in the last chapter.

California Healthy Families

Recall, California Healthy Families is California's State Child Health Insurance Program (SCHIP). This program is partially funded by the federal government and allows low-income families to buy subsidized health insurance for their children.

In 2003, the California Insurance Board issued a Request for Proposals (RFP) to rebid this program, as well as some smaller health care programs across the entire state. MAXIMUS bid against our competitor EDS on the first contract some five years earlier but lost. Since SCHIP was a relatively new program at the time, there were no unionized government workers when the state decided to privatize SCHIP.

Some of our top executives felt it was a waste of time to go after the contract since there was a strong incumbent, EDS. That didn't bother me because bidding on larger and larger contracts was good training for everyone, and we always learned from writing these huge proposals.

We were all surprised when MAXIMUS was asked to appear for an oral exam as a finalist. The evaluation committee was prepared with many questions. The first question was a curve ball: "How could we use the data collected in our program to ensure proper medical treatment for our beneficiaries?" This question was not in the RFP.

Since MAXIMUS was a company that truly understood health care as well as program operations, the question was easy for us. We gave a great answer, surprising the evaluation committee. We handled their other questions just as easily and got along well with the committee staff. MAXIMUS eventually was selected for award, after the normal political vetting process.

John Boyer, who led the Health Care Group in MAXIMUS, was not only a Registered Nurse, but also a PhD in Public Health Administration. He had spent his entire career in health care, and the committee loved him. I was also well versed in using health data to monitor health care since I helped develop Utilization Review programs at SRS. MAXIMUS had also worked for the Joint Commission on Accreditation of Hospitals to determine how hospital discharge codes could be used to assess quality of care. So we were very knowledgeable.

Since MAXIMUS managed the California Health Care Options (HCO) program—which involved enrolling Medicaid recipients into managed care plans—we had substantial credibility to manage California Healthy Families as well. The latter also required eligibility determination and premium collection from families each month. Though the two programs seemed similar, the operations were actually very different.

To everyone's surprise, MAXIMUS won. The contract was worth $418 million over five years. Now we had to do the work. The original RFP for California Healthy Families had a penalty clause tied to twelve major tasks in the six-month startup period. Unbeknownst to me, a subsequent revision of the RFP applied the penalty to every task in the contractor's proposed startup plan. We had something like 1200 tasks in our startup plan.

Since we had so many tasks, and since the state did not expect such a detailed plan, we negotiated to change the plan to fewer tasks and then accepted the risk of penalties on the fewer number of tasks. More information on the extensive penalty and performance standards of the California Healthy Families contract is provided in Chapter 22 – Contracts, Contracts, Contracts.

MAXIMUS received essentially no cooperation from the incumbent. EDS must have really believed we would fail. Their lobbyists kept raising alarms with the legislature, warning of our impending failure and the catastrophic consequences. Instead, we created one of the most comprehensive health care administrative systems in the county and completed the startup without any penalties. MAXIMUS still runs the program today. That automated system, by the way, had its origins in the Utah system I described earlier.

This contract was extraordinarily complex. MAXIMUS had to set up hundreds of collection points throughout the state where recipients could come in and make cash payments. We worked with Wells Fargo Bank to collect the money and credit the appropriate accounts.

The Financial Management Subsystem processed checks using large check reading machines. The unreadable checks had to be adjudicated by our staff. We might as well have been a bank clearinghouse, the volume was so large. Our system had to process cash, checks, credit cards, money orders, and all manner of payments. We had to track whether or not the family was in arrears on its payments. When payments came in, we had to allocate them to the amounts overdue or to the current month (like child support) to allow coverage to continue.

Our call center, located just outside Folsom, California, employed 450 MAXIMUS staff. In the six months from date of contract award to the date we "went live," we completely gutted the building and rebuilt the interior according to our specs. The building was actually very beautiful, with skylights and large windows. We were all very proud of it. We even had a ribbon-cutting ceremony when it opened, with the client project manager using oversized scissors.

Like the California HCO operation, the California Healthy Families call center staff also processed application and renewal forms. We had ultra-modern call distribution software and multiple, huge wall displays showing the longest waiting time for callers coming into the center on different toll-free lines. MAXIMUS published statistics daily on call volumes, average length of call, and longest waiting times by language. Each language had a different toll-free number.

We staffed a mailroom to open and sort thousands of forms received every day. We attached a tracking number to each form and entered the number and form into the computer. We also scanned all hand-completed forms, converting them to pdf's. Our staff stored the image in the recipient's electronic folder, so any one of the call center staff could retrieve the form on the computer. The screen was organized so the handwritten pdf form was on the left, and the corresponding data fields from the form on the right for ease of data entry.

Then, there were the multiple eligibility decision rules programmed into the computer, which themselves were enormously complex. The income and assets of the recipients had to be determined because the program was "means tested." That meant eligibility was determined based on the "means" or financial condition of the family. This was a separate sub-system in the overall system.

We also had a mail-out subsystem as part of the larger system, where the computer automatically sent electronic files to the mail house. The files contained the names, addresses, and languages to use in the letters and informational materials sent out. An image of the letter was also provided for printing. The mail house printed these materials on demand and assembled the letters and the proper materials from pallets of materials stored in the warehouse. These mail outs represented alerts that the insurance premiums had not been received, or notifications of decisions made on the case, or general notices to all recipients. Our postal budget was stratospheric!

MAXIMUS staff worked very closely with the Managed Risk Medical Insurance Board, the independent agency in California state government charged with administering Healthy Families. They were extremely helpful and very appreciative of what we were doing. We did our best to please them, whether or not the requirement was in the contract. Later on, when they could have fined us for a mistake, they didn't, considering all the additional programming we did for them at no cost. This was truly a public–private partnership. In fact, this client was one of the best we ever had.

In this contract, we were paid based on the number of families enrolled in the program. As the number went up and down, we adjusted our staff. This adjustment could not have been done with government employees. This feature, alone, saved the state tens of millions of dollars.

Social Security Administration Disability Programs

People with disabilities are covered under Titles II and XVI of the Social Security Act. Recall, the Disability Determination Service in each state determines whether a person is disabled based on very specific criteria. One of MAXIMUS's first contracts was to develop an automated system to track state Disability Determination Service performance. This was the CEMS contract discussed in Chapter 15 – Building Systems That Work.

People with disabilities receive money to pay their living expenses. Some are also entitled to Medicare—the health insurance program for the aged, others to Medicaid, and some to both. MAXIMUS currently operates a key part of this program for the Social Security Administration—the Ticket to Work Program. Only a very small portion of the people who are disabled ever go back to work. However, with some ten million people on the rolls, it is appropriate to have a program to help them try.

In the mid-nineties, The Social Security Administration (SSA) issued fifty RFPs seeking organizations in every state to help review and manage alcohol and drug abuse cases receiving disability payments. These people claimed drug- or alcohol-related disabilities and were eligible for disability payments under the Social Security Act. SSA was interested in finding ways to rehabilitate these addicts so they could be removed from the rolls.

MAXIMUS decided to bid on every state, and ended up winning all fifty states for a total of $385 million. We explained in each proposal the advantages of a single firm taking over the program nationally. The three main advantages were 1) ease of administration for SSA (it had only one contractor to deal with), 2) consistency of administration across all states, and 3) economies of scale. By winning this large contract in 1995, MAXIMUS was on the map as a major player.

The proposal effort alone was massive, requiring MAXIMUS to lease additional floors in our building just to assemble the proposals. Ilene Baylinson, a super high-energy VP, managed the proposal process, assisted by Bob

Muzzio, a pillar of MAXIMUS. When finally finished, two trucks were required to deliver the proposals to the Social Security Administration in Baltimore, Maryland. About a year after we had won the contract, the SSA contract officer asked us to please pick up the proposals and dispose of them—they were taking up too much room in their headquarters.

Again, we thought outside of the box and bid on everything. As a result, MAXIMUS was able to establish networks of alcohol and drug abuse treatment facilities across the United States that would accept SSA beneficiaries. We coordinated the treatment with these facilities, and the program was working well.

Unfortunately for MAXIMUS, after we really became established, Congress repealed the provision of the Social Security Act that allowed drug and alcohol abuse to be considered a disability. There was considerable outrage among taxpayers that the federal government was paying people to become and remain addicts. As a result, the contract was terminated for the convenience of the government. We had received about $100 million of the total over the first couple of years. However, we had made a very favorable impression at the Social Security Administration.

What was amazing is that MAXIMUS revenues grew again the following year, despite the loss of this major contract. This growth showed everyone the power of the company.

British Columbia, Canada

Another fabulous contract! This was a $300 million contract, adjusted to US dollars, that MAXIMUS won in 2004, just before I retired. The Government of British Columbia, Ministry of Health Services decided to consolidate and contract out the administration of its Province-wide health care program. This program supported four million Canadians entitled to free health care. The scope of work included the following:

- Build a new health care management system capability, including internet access for beneficiaries, and extend the systems the Province already had

- Integrate the new systems with its old systems, and maintain all systems, thereafter

- Pay six million claims per month from doctors, hospitals, and other health care providers

- Provide customer services to beneficiaries, handling some 250,000 call attempts per month

- Provide customer services to health care providers, handling an estimated 150,000 calls per month

- Scan 36,000 documents per month, of which 7,000 would be enrollment documents, and so on.

The requirement was to absorb existing union workers under private management rather than government management. That was fine with us—we had done that before in numerous child support privatizations with great success. The difference in Canada was they would remain members of the union.

Again, we were competing with big companies. None had administered the program before. This was a new initiative by the Province, so there was no incumbent. The MAXIMUS project manager was Tom Carrato, who had been Executive Director of the Department of Defense TRICARE program. This program oversaw all managed care for all uniformed services beneficiaries and their families worldwide. The experience of our director gave MAXIMUS additional credibility.

I remember working for four days in Victoria, British Columbia, with Tom and John Boyer on a presentation lasting something like eight hours. We had over three hundred PowerPoint slides, most with detailed graphics. There were client subcommittees to work with, and a whole regimen of different activities to go through before the final presentation to the evaluation committee.

When the time came for the presentation, we were ready. We presented our case and answered questions. During the lunch hour, we played a twenty-minute video of our operations on the California HCO project. We hadn't done one for the Healthy Families project yet.

We showed a professionally narrated video of the huge warehouses containing the health care informational materials we sent out daily. The video also depicted the outside of our office building and the parking lot as staff arrived for work. We also included the inside of our ultra-modern facility with hundreds of staff answering the phones and data-entry staff pounding on keyboards across a sea of computers.

We basically demonstrated MAXIMUS could do the job. It was impressive. I don't recall how many of the evaluation committee members actually watched the video, but they knew it was playing, and it gave immense credibility to our proposal.

The major hang up to signing the contract was the Patriot Act. Under the Patriot Act, the US government can require any contractor to provide any data maintained on any person. This is true even if the contractor is working on an international contract. The Ministry of Health Services didn't want the US government requesting health data on Canadian citizens. Therefore, we signed an agreement that if the US government requested data on any Canadian citizen, the contract would immediately be terminated and transferred to a Canadian company. It hasn't happened.

Incidentally, I understand MAXIMUS has worked very well with the labor union in Canada.

These three large contracts alone gave MAXIMUS significant stature. We were a player in the arena of multi-hundred-million-dollar contracts. Had I stayed at MAXIMUS, we would have bid on more as the prime contractor. MAXIMUS did win another large contract after I retired, which involved a welfare-to-work program in England.

So how did I manage all this responsibility and growth taking place? The answer is in Part V: Managing Rapid Growth.

PART V:
MANAGING RAPID GROWTH

In this block of chapters, I explain how MAXIMUS was built and managed for rapid growth, not only organizationally, but also contractually and financially. The last chapter explains the history of overcoming revenue "stall points" so rapid growth could continue.

CHAPTER 21

KEY GROWTH STRATEGIES

I did not expect after fifteen years that MAXIMUS's growth would actually accelerate. State and county governments were learning that privatization was a solution to many of their problems and were taking full advantage. MAXIMUS was making government better. When the government initiated a new program, the easiest way to implement it was to privatize. And the result was phenomenal growth.

MAXIMUS was a different breed of company, perfect for privatization. We understood complex social welfare programs as well as the government. We could rapidly hire, efficiently train, and effectively manage large numbers of caseworkers to work closely with program recipients. We were also a technology company that could rapidly build systems to support our operations.

As I've mentioned a couple of times, MAXIMUS had a compound annual growth rate of 36.5 percent over twenty-nine years. The growth was not uniform. In some years, revenues actually declined; some years we grew at less than 20 percent; some years we grew more than 100 percent. However, even a 10 percent growth rate is challenging if it represents $10 million in service-business revenues—that's a lot of additional people to train and manage. So how did we do this? What were our growth strategies?

Metaphor of the *New York Times* Crossword Puzzle

Managing a rapidly growing company is a bit like working the *New York Times* crossword puzzle. At West Point, I had Sunday mornings to myself after chapel—about the only really down time I had. I occasionally tried to solve the *New York Times* crossword puzzle, but never got very far. I swore one day I would learn to do it.

Many, many years later, I decided to try again. I would start the puzzle early Sunday morning, and after about half an hour, inevitably conclude there was no way I was ever going to finish it. So I'd quit. I did this for many Sundays. I could not imagine any normal person could solve the puzzle. Finally, I gave up entirely.

After a few more years, I decided to try again. This time, I was determined to stay with the puzzle, even if I couldn't make any discernible progress. I was supposedly an intelligent person and should be able to do it. And so I started again each Sunday, but this time I refused to give up.

Slowly, and through perseverance on a typical Sunday, I would solve a horizontal word clue and then have some letters to use with the vertical word clues. Then a corner of the puzzle would materialize, and then more of the puzzle. Slowly it came into focus. I was always surprised I had gotten that far in the puzzle. Clearly, I must have done the easier part since the rest lay out there as a sea of blank squares. So I still had major doubts about finishing the puzzle. But at least I was making progress.

Sometimes I'd have to leave for an hour or so. When I came back, some of the answers I couldn't solve earlier became obvious. Filling these answers in moved me forward again. Slowly, I realized much of the puzzle was being solved. Eventually, to my great surprise, I would solve the entire puzzle. I couldn't believe it! It truly did not seem possible!

How does solving the *New York Times* crossword puzzle translate to managing a rapidly growing company? *I could never see all the answers in managing MAXIMUS. I had to find them slowly over time.* And one answer provided clues to the next. I gained knowledge with effort, and that knowledge led to further knowledge, with even more effort.

Faith that I could solve our problems and grow, drove persistence of effort and ultimate success. Faith in myself and persistence in dealing with uncertainty were the key qualities in growing MAXIMUS. I just had to believe and had to keep working at it.

In our case, the underlying puzzle was continually changing. As a reactive company, we had to position ourselves for growth, even if I didn't know where it was coming from. The only thing I could really do was ready MAXIMUS for the opportunities that came knocking. I knew the answers to the problems would slowly be found, even though I knew the puzzle was getting much larger.

The Look of a Growing Company

MAXIMUS was built to grow, no doubt about it. What does "built to grow" mean? To grow we needed to be top heavy. The first triangle in Exhibit 4 represents the hierarchical organization in a typical company. The shaded area represents the management or leadership portion. The next triangle shows the same triangle for MAXIMUS. Note that it's top heavy. The reason it's top heavy is so MAXIMUS could grow as shown in the third triangle.

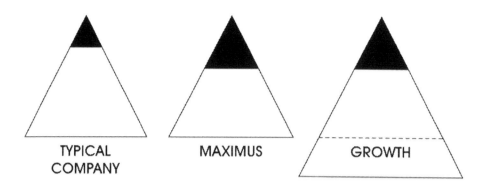

Exhibit 4 – Top-Heavy Organization

Our management infrastructure needed to leapfrog our actual organizational size. I was always trying to build the infrastructure of a company larger than we were. That was the only way we could keep pace with the growth.

I also created a target organization for a future MAXIMUS. The target organization showed the managers how we could or should look if we were 30 percent or 40 percent larger. It told us who we would need to hire and what new functions and capabilities we would need to implement. The target organization rarely materialized as envisioned, but it keyed us up for what opportunities to look for and seize upon when they appeared.

Bigger Contracts Make a Bigger Company

To pay for the larger-than-needed infrastructure, we had to grow! The source of revenues came predominantly from staff billings, not from management billings. So we had to add staff to generate the revenues to pay for the top-heavy management structure—staying one step ahead of the "repo" man.

I soon learned the best way for MAXIMUS to grow was to win bigger contracts. *If you want a bigger fire, add bigger logs.* We can use kindling all day and never go anywhere. To make the fire grow bigger, we needed to increase the size of the logs.

Therefore, we kept pursuing bigger and bigger contracts, especially in the government operations or privatization area. Fortunately, the government was awarding bigger and bigger privatization contracts as the success of and need for privatization spread. While the cost and effort required to write the proposals for these contracts may double, the contract value would quadruple or even go up tenfold. We went up against ever-tougher competition since these contracts attracted the attention of larger companies.

However, to remain competitive, we were forced to learn more about proposal writing and managing larger contracts. I think competing with a division of Lockheed Martin made us a far better company. Later, that division was bought by Affiliated Computer Services, who then became our prime competitor. EDS was also a steady competitor. However, none of these companies had the singular focus on government social welfare programs that MAXIMUS did.

As MAXIMUS grew larger, we became more and more credible on even larger contracts. We didn't need to add many more senior proposal managers. I could lead a proposal for a large contract, as well as write a proposal for a small contract. The large-contract proposals were more complicated to be sure, sometimes involving twenty-five to fifty researchers, writers, and production people, costing $250,000 to $500,000 and more to prepare. However, the strategies for winning were the same. Examples of these strategies were provided earlier in Chapter 13 – Sales Strategies.

The larger the government contract, the steeper the competition. We always liked competition because it meant MAXIMUS had to keep a razor-sharp edge. We had to know the latest developments and employ the latest technology in our proposed solutions.

Layering Existing Top Management

When a company is growing fast, you soon realize the managers currently at the top level of the organization, or any other level for that matter, may not be capable of being your managers at the next level of growth—the so-called "Peter Principle." One of the toughest jobs I had to do was overlay a management layer above existing managers, when they were no longer capable of leading the company at the higher level. The existing managers believed they created the growth and therefore were entitled to manage at the higher level. So it was a delicate situation to deal with—after all, we didn't want to lose them.

Rather than continually replace these managers or place new managers over these existing managers, I tried to grow MAXIMUS horizontally as much as possible. I did this by creating new business units. We brought in new people in new areas of growth. If the more tenured managers were capable and demonstrated they could grow with the company, we didn't place them under newer, but more experienced managers. The worst mistake was to insert a new manager over an existing one and have the new manager fail. That was disastrous for morale.

So the management layer had to grow as the company grew. This was always difficult when the existing managers themselves were not growing.

Authority Matrix

When the company grew beyond my and the other corporate officers ability to review and approve all decisions, we implemented an Authority Matrix. The Authority Matrix detailed for every management level (manager, director, vice president, and president) the limits of their authority for the following areas:

- Decisions to Bid

- Value of proposals signed

- Value of contracts signed

- New hire salaries

- Disciplinary actions

- Pay raises

- Terminations

- Value of expense approvals

- Value of overhead expenditures

- Value of vendor invoice approvals.

With our widespread organization, local managers needed to understand what they were authorized to do. The government also needed to understand what our managers were authorized to do.

The Authority Matrix was a complex delegation of authority and accountability throughout the company. We eventually automated the Authority Matrix so a manager could search for and see the extent of his or her authority immediately.

Growth through Subcontracting

Some companies elected to grow by being subcontractors to larger companies. This way they would receive exposure to different clients and add capabilities to their corporate resumes. Larger companies would look for small subcontractors with capabilities they didn't have in order to gain access to markets they weren't yet qualified to enter. This way, they could grow as well.

MAXIMUS was always tempted to become a subcontractor to a larger firm or to use a subcontractor on our own team. Ninety percent of the time, it was a mistake! The larger companies take advantage of you. The smaller ones will either try to steal your clients or won't do a good job. We had to sue a couple of prime contractors when we were the subcontractor and a couple of subcontractors when we were the prime contractor. Later, I implemented a policy that MAXIMUS would not be a subcontractor at all.

In fact, I resigned four months earlier than planned over a decision by our Board of Directors to support the Chief Operating Officer over me. He wanted to change the policy and have MAXIMUS be a subcontractor to Accenture on a large privatization contract in Texas. I knew they were rightfully grooming the COO for my job, but I didn't want to make the subcontracting mistake again. I told the Board not to do it, but they overruled me. I was not surprised after my retirement to learn MAXIMUS lost $50 million on the subcontract.

When we employed subcontractors, their standards were rarely up to ours, and we had to cover for them. I had a policy never to take advantage of a subcontractor because we had been taken advantage of so many times. I don't know that we ever took advantage of a subcontractor. We just quit relying on them for tasks in project plans. We did use mail houses as subcontractors because of the enormous set-up costs required to do the job. And our experience with mail house subcontractors was good.

I found it very difficult to grow MAXIMUS using subcontractors, and even more difficult being a subcontractor.

Acquiring Companies

MAXIMUS also grew through acquisitions. We acquired a number of small companies that specialized in state and local government systems. The areas of systems expertise included the following:

- Government financial management systems

- Court systems (criminal, civil, appeals, bankruptcy, traffic, family, clerk of the courts, etc.)

- Fleet-maintenance systems

- Government Enterprise Resource Planning (ERP) systems

- K–12 school student information systems

- Government cost-allocation systems.

We also acquired small companies in Canada and Australia that proved to be fruitful. We acquired most of the companies after we went public in 1997. All of them were peripheral to our areas of expertise. As a result, we faced a number of problems:

- Integrating them into our corporate culture, including our mission of Helping Government Serve the People

- Providing our own expertise to ensure contracts were managed properly

- Dealing with owner/managers who thought they could manage the business better than we could

- Cleaning up unknown problems that occurred prior to the acquisition.

Here is what I learned as a result of the MAXIMUS acquisition program. If MAXIMUS ever acquires companies again, I suggest it do the following:

- Acquire competitors first

- Stay in their areas of core competence

- Add new areas to MAXIMUS only if the acquired firm is very large

- Buy out the owner/ managers and replace them with your own

- Stay away from relationship-based businesses, such as consulting

- Stay away from accounting-based businesses; the liabilities linger.

In hindsight, and with eight years' visibility, I believe we would have grown faster in areas of our core competency had we not acquired most of these companies. Despite the fact that we did our due diligence, studied the books, and did everything we thought could be done to make the right decision, we made few successful acquisitions.

Only four of over twenty acquisitions really paid off:

- Control Software founded by Jim Paulits, specializing in fleet management, and was ultimately sold

- a Medicare appeals firm founded by Dave Richardson, which is really going strong now

- a firm we bought in Australia, where we replaced the owner-manager quite early in the process; and

- a small firm in Canada led by Brian Pollick, which gave us a beachhead in Canada.

In my opinion, we wasted considerable time and effort trying to make the other acquisitions grow and be profitable. MAXIMUS sold off many of these firms after I retired; others just faded into obscurity.

As I said earlier, MAXIMUS was built for growth. We were top heavy and planned for growth. We had faith and were persistent. We were opportunistic and sought bigger and bigger contracts. Our successes and those of other privatization companies created even more opportunities. We just didn't know where they would materialize. But, since we were reactive, we followed the market.

I used to tell my managers that we needed to be just a little bit out of control in managing MAXIMUS. After all, if everything were under control, we wouldn't be growing rapidly.

CHAPTER 22

CONTRACTS, CONTRACTS, CONTRACTS

As you may guess, there was much MAXIMUS learned about managing government contracts in our core competencies. This chapter addresses these lessons since they were essential for growth.

The contract is sacred. Verbal understandings aren't worth much. We had contract officers retire or be transferred, and when the new contract officers took over, the tacit understandings we had with the old contract officers went up in smoke. We learned to make sure all substantive understandings with the government were contained in the contract, and that the contract was amended as necessary to reflect them. Our people heard this all the time.

Different Types of Government Contracts

Government is not really very different from the private sector when it comes to contracting. I'll briefly summarize the different government contract types, so you understand the context for the rest of the chapter.

- **Cost Plus Fixed Fee (CPFF)** – This is a favorite contract type of the federal government and some state governments. The government often cannot estimate how much effort a project will take since it doesn't always know exactly what it wants. As a result, the government agrees to pay all allowable costs for work on the contract, plus a fixed fee independent of the costs. Allowable costs are those accepted by the government as being reasonable and include indirect costs such as marketing expenses. Our union and media critics never wanted to recognize indirect costs as a legitimate cost of doing business. In addition, the fixed fee (or pretax profit) earned on the contract could be used for anything we wanted—buying coffee cups or T-shirts emblazoned with our name, or even golf balls—no audit required.

  Normally, the contractor is paid monthly, based on approved invoices. Since the government pays only allowable costs, our costs were audited every year and payments adjusted based on the audited results. Government auditors love to retroactively disallow costs and always did. In our Wisconsin project to be described later, this was almost our undoing.

- **Fixed Price** – The most common commercial contract is a fixed price contract. Contractors review the specifications of the scope of work and bid a fixed price to complete the work. Usually the payment schedule is tied to progress in completing the work. Stiff penalties are incurred for being late or not meeting contract specifications. The government often used this contract type as well.

- **Time and Materials** – Some contracts are based on fixed hourly billing rates. This type of contract is a combination of the previous two types—fixed hourly rates but hours charged based on those actually expended. This is how most commercial services are charged—so much per hour. The nice aspect, here, is we usually don't have to be audited on the rate. Sometimes, a company is audited to make sure the time and materials billed were, in fact, expended on the contract.

- **Payment Per Recipient Per Month** – This is a typical type of contract for privatization. The company is paid based on how many recipients are served that month or on how many were in the caseload. Health plans are paid this way, as well.

- **Performance-Based** – Another type of contract pays for performance or outcomes, for example, for each welfare recipient placed in a job. The government pays for outcomes only, and proof has to be provided the outcome actually occurred. The rev max contingency contracts are a variation of this type.

MAXIMUS didn't have a preference for any type of contract. The Fixed Price and Performance-Based contracts were the most risky, but offered the highest profit potential. The CPFF contracts offered the least profit potential and were often problematic. *During my tenure, MAXIMUS never defaulted on any contract to my knowledge, nor were we ever fined for missing a "go live" date.*

Contract Negotiations

After being selected by the government for a contract, the final terms still needed to be negotiated. Terms included payment schedule, termination for convenience or for cause, indemnity, performance penalties, and the like.

I spoke briefly of our negotiation in the San Francisco Bay Area contract. Obviously, MAXIMUS was engaged in many different negotiations. This section presents what I learned about negotiations that may contradict conventional wisdom.

I won't spend time explaining the importance of being well prepared; we obviously needed to know where MAXIMUS stood and how much leverage we had. Nor will I explain how negotiations become more serious as the time remaining decreases. And I won't address holding best and final offers until late in the negotiations—we needed room to give. You can learn these lessons in other books.

What I am going to point out is that no major negotiation, in my experience, becomes serious until one of the parties walks away from the table, or at least threatens to. This starts the real negotiation. The word "Negotiation" starts with the letter N for No, not with the letter Y for Yes.

In my opinion, negotiations move more efficiently if you tell the other party what you need from them to make a decision and then ensure they understand how your decision depends on that information. If they understand you are a rational negotiator, and making rational decisions while negotiating, your task will be easier. Some experts believe you should act irrationally during negotiations. I don't.

The essence of negotiations, again in my experience, is discovering what the other party wants from you and values more highly than you do, and then discovering what you want from the other party and value more highly than they do. Those exchanges are easy and should be made. When you both have the same values, then compromises and fair sharing are required.

Importantly, negotiations are the place where we set the terms we are willing to live with. *We could not sacrifice our principles to win the contract.* We had to make sure the contract had enough funding to let us do a quality job. If it didn't, both MAXIMUS and the client would suffer.

Negotiation Training Courses

I sometimes taught courses at MAXIMUS on contract negotiations. I would break the class into teams of four. Two of the four negotiated for

MAXIMUS, and the other two for the government. I gave the MAXIMUS negotiators a project cost, and required that they could not accept a contract below that cost. The government negotiators would be given a project budget, with the requirement that the contract could not exceed the budget. Obviously, the project cost was lower than the government budget. Neither side knew the other side's number. The idea was to find out where the final price would fall between the two limits. This would show how much profit the MAXIMUS team could "negotiate." The rule was they had thirty minutes to come to terms.

If the MAXIMUS team said the company could not accept less than a 10 percent profit on the project, then that is usually where the negotiations ended. The government team would see there was no give on the point. The teams in training that educated the government on their constraints had the easier times. Those that did not had less credibility in what they were asking for and didn't fare as well.

Contract negotiations for our first privatization contract in Los Angeles lasted six weeks. At the end, each party knew everything about the other, and the resulting contract was fair to both.

Walking Away

Not all negotiations will be successful. You should walk away from some of them. I walked away from two negotiations at MAXIMUS—one was a consulting contract and the other a systems development contract. The first was with the Nuclear Regulatory Commission (NRC). In the very early days, we did everything from "welfare to warfare" to keep growing.

I had an idea for nuclear reactor failure analysis that was quite innovative and of particular interest to the NRC. The idea stemmed from my doctoral dissertation on Bayesian statistics at The George Washington University.

Instead of having MAXIMUS bid on the contract directly, the NRC decided to have a prime contractor, the University of Maryland, with an ongoing nonspecific contract vehicle, hire MAXIMUS as a subcontractor. This was often done to avoid a lengthy procurement process. So we had a prime contractor to deal with.

The University contracting staff were heavy-handed. They unilaterally dictated to us what our billing rates would be and the role we would play in the contract. And they added that MAXIMUS would have no right to any follow-on work should the contract be extended, and so on.

What arrogance! The contract terms they were imposing on us were completely unacceptable. They knew it, and I told them so. Their negotiators must have thought I was bluffing when I said we wouldn't accept their terms, but I wasn't. They didn't budge, so I walked away from the contract and never looked back. Again, there is no future in being a subcontractor.

The second time I walked away from a negotiation was in Egypt. MAXIMUS bid $25 million on a cost plus fixed fee contract. Recall, cost plus fixed fee means the government would audit our costs to complete the contract, determine what was "allowable," and then add a preagreed, fixed fee to the total. Of course, if our costs exceeded our estimate, then we were still at risk to complete the job or justify additional funds.

The contract was to develop and implement a comprehensive hospital management information system in Arabic in eighteen hospitals and two hundred clinics throughout Egypt. The Agency for International Development (AID) funded the project.

After a procurement process that lasted months, MAXIMUS was selected as the winner and called in for negotiations. I traveled with John Lau, our VP in charge, to Cairo and met with the AID contract officer. As we went through our business proposal (the money side), the contract officer told me we would not be permitted to earn a fee on the subcontractor's (NCR) hardware.

I had never heard of anything like that before. The hardware represented about 30 percent of the contract value, and we had placed a minimal fee of 2 percent on the hardware. If they were asking for that, I could see working for AID was going to be a nightmare.

I stated that it was unacceptable for MAXIMUS to give up a fee when we were taking the risk on hardware delivery and operation. Where there was risk, we had to have the opportunity to earn a profit. The contract officer firmly countered that the government's position was not negotiable. I believed him and said we had no option but to turn down the contract. He said fine. Therefore, my people and I left Cairo and returned to the United States.

Our Egyptian subcontractors were extremely upset with MAXIMUS and me. (We had to have someone who understood Arabic!) Coincidentally, the week after I left Cairo, an article appeared in *Newsweek* on me as CEO of MAXIMUS, including a photo. This gave our team in Cairo considerably more credibility and put the contracting officer on the hot seat. Apparently, the contract officer had some explaining to do to his superiors.

Six months later, we were again called back to Egypt for negotiations. The contract officer realized we had the best offer, and a 2 percent fee was not that much. We subsequently signed the contract and were successful. The systems went into the hospitals and the clinics, and health care was improved for thirty million Egyptian people. I understand our contract was one of a very few AID could count as a significant success in Egypt.

Why did I walk away? I mentioned we did not want to deal with unreasonable people. In addition, the federal government and many state governments have a clause in most contracts that they must receive the most favorable terms of any contract, the so-called "Favored Nations" clause. If MAXIMUS had given up a fee on this contract, then we would have set a precedent and may have been forced to give up fees on subcontractor pass-throughs in subsequent contracts.

Performance Penalties and Standards

Many contracts had performance penalties and required performance bonds. The willingness of a contractor to accept both performance penalties and offer a performance bond was an important consideration for many government contract officers. To grow, we had to accept them.

As stated earlier, the California Healthy Families contract was a model contract for the government. The contract carried a $400,000 penalty each time any one of twelve major tasks in the six-month startup period was late by one day. After a week, the late penalty escalated to $1.2 million per task. We had Microsoft Project and PERT charts and intensive task tracking to make sure MAXIMUS didn't incur the penalty. At one point, I had to hire some twenty Oracle programmers at $300 per hour for several weeks to make sure we completed a component of the system on time. It was extremely expensive, but worth it since we were never penalized.

The major point in accepting penalties is they have to be very well defined. The contractor has to be the sole cause of the delay—not late because of waiting for client approvals or decisions. We made sure the penalties and the conditions for imposing them were clear.

After startup, when the project transitioned to operations mode, there were other performance standards and associated penalties for not meeting the standards. I found a Contract Compliance Report Card from the California Healthy Families project in my files showing how we did in July 2004. MAXIMUS provided the client some of the data for the report card, and the client compiled the rest. The exhibit below shows an excerpt from the spreadsheet for MAXIMUS assembled by the government client.

MAXIMUS Department	Number of Contract Standards	Number of Contract Standards Met	Compliance Percentage
Call Center Operations	49	45	92%
Data Entry/Image Assembly	27	27	100%
Eligibility	28	25	89%
Mail Operations	76	76	100%
Research and Appeals	10	10	100%
Program Compliance	32	31	97%
Quality Assurance/Training	3	3	100%
Systems	41	37	90%
Premium Processing	13	13	100%
Administration	3	3	100%
Audit	0	0	N/A
Finance	13	13	100%
Project Total	295	274	96%

Exhibit 5: Healthy Families Contract Compliance Report Card for July 2004

Our payments would be reduced for failing to meet the standards, so the state had assurance our performance would be acceptable.

So the government was receiving amazing performance from MAXIMUS— far better than they could ever expect from themselves. Ever see a government agency with 295 monthly performance standards? But that's why we were there instead of government employees—to make government better.

Importance of Documentation

In another California project, the Health Care Options project discussed briefly in Chapter 12 – Planning and Execution, the state tried to penalize MAXIMUS approximately $8 million for failure to identify and process a particular group of Medicaid recipients. These recipients were a special group of cases who became eligible again for Medicaid within ninety days of having become ineligible (internally they were known as the infamous Status J cases).

After many years of working on complex projects with government clients, I instituted a new communications policy for this project. The policy required numbering each memorandum and e-mail MAXIMUS sent to the government client, and numbering each memorandum and e-mail the government client sent to us. Therefore, MAXIMUS had a complete written record of all written communications with the agency. If a decision was made, it was documented in a Memorandum of Understanding and sent to the client.

In this project, we filed some 750 Memoranda of Understanding during the first four months of start up. If I recall correctly, we asked the client in Memo #147 how MAXIMUS was to process Status J cases, the group of cases that lost and then regained Medicaid eligibility within ninety days. We asked again in Memo #620 what to do with them since we did not receive an answer to the first memo. We never did receive an answer, and to our discredit, forgot about the problem.

This group of Medicaid recipients was finally discovered because they were not enrolled in a managed care plan and were flooding hospital emergency rooms, costing the state much more money. The state computed the differential costs of not having them in a managed care plan and tried to recover the costs from MAXIMUS.

I was called in to meet personally with the Secretary of the California Department of Health Services. To say the least, the conference room was electrically charged. During the course of her questioning me in front of ten of her senior staff, I handed her Memo #147 and Memo #620. She read them carefully and understood we were totally covered. She was furious—but not at us.

The lesson was to document all our questions, answers, and decisions in our projects. It may be administratively burdensome, but when working on a high-value contract, it was worth it. Sometimes we didn't document everything and lucked out, as in California Healthy Families.

Other Key Contract Clauses

One of the most important clauses in a contract is how to get out of the contract—the termination clause. This is especially important in long-term contracts. I always paid attention to how MAXIMUS could extricate itself from a contract. We usually set up a number of conditions that allowed us to terminate "with cause." Of course, the most obvious was that if MAXIMUS wasn't paid in a timely manner, we could terminate. We made sure all our contracts had a way out!

In government contracts, another point of interest is how the government can terminate MAXIMUS, or how the government "got out" of the contract. Termination clauses come in many shapes and sizes. For example, the government always had a clause to terminate "without cause." If they did, they needed to provide a shut-down period, pay for legitimate expenses through the shut-down period, and reimburse us for expenses obligated to the point of shut down and into the future.

The government could also terminate "with cause" for nonperformance. To terminate with cause, however, the government had to explain why performance was unacceptable and allow a "cure period" to fix the performance problem. Needless to say, contractors facing this type of adverse action did not receive the same due process as government employees. We could be fired much more easily, which actually became a reason to hire us.

Another key contract clause is how the contractor is paid. There were many ways—by hours worked, by payment schedule over time, by percent of work completed, and others. We negotiated whether or not there would be up-front payments and how much the government held back until the contract was completed to its satisfaction.

How hard we pressed for these terms depended on the risk we perceived in the contract. As mentioned, we always made sure that failure to be paid on a timely basis was cause for termination by MAXIMUS. This saved us in Connecticut, as will be explained in Chapter 26 – Dealing with Disaster.

Subcontract Agreements

When MAXIMUS was a subcontractor, we had to fight for the following rights:

- MAXIMUS name and logo would be visible on the work products that we helped produce

- Our project staff would be represented in meetings where our work was discussed

- MAXIMUS would be paid even if the prime contractor was not paid for reasons not related to our performance

- There would be no hiring of our people during or after the subcontract

- Our propriety material would remain proprietary to MAXIMUS

- MAXIMUS had the right to follow-on work related to our original work on the contract.

We were always under pressure from the prime contractor. The prime contractor did not want MAXIMUS to outperform them in the client's eyes. The prime contractor always wanted to eliminate us as soon as possible. And in many cases, the prime contractor violated the terms of the subcontract agreement. After we sued a couple of them, the word got around about MAXIMUS being willing to sue. Prime contractors honored their agreements with us. Of course, by that time, I had put a virtual ban on being a subcontractor.

Additional Work Must Be in Writing

The California HCO contract taught MAXIMUS a number of lessons. California had been an innovator in the concept of an enrollment broker and had hired a small Oregon firm, Benova, to manage its program. Recall, the enrollment broker sent out materials to Medicaid recipients who had to enroll in managed care and then helped the recipients choose the best plan for their circumstances.

I explained earlier that the federal government required states to have an independent enrollment broker. When the California program was significantly expanded because of the new federal State Child Health Insurance Program, Benova just could not handle the increased volume. Its computer system did not have the capacity. Therefore, the state put the contract out for bid, and MAXIMUS won.

We had eighty-eight days to make our new system operational on a very complex program. We almost died doing it, but we met the deadline. I recall we had to be operational on January 2. We worked right through the Christmas holidays, night and day. You know you have a great staff when they work all night.

I also remember staying up all night working on a serious software bug that had to be fixed by 7:30 the next morning. If not fixed, the government project officer was going to call us in default, which would cause a great number of problems. We just could not find the bug. At 5:30 a.m., I realized I was crying involuntarily, tears streaking down my face. Many of the staff saw me. I had never experienced a failure like that. I had not cried before or after in a MAXIMUS crisis.

At 6:30 a.m., we miraculously found the bug! Perils of Pauline—saved in the nick of time! Just before 7:30 a.m., I called the government project officer, Mike Neff, at his home and announced the problem was fixed. He actually sounded disappointed.

One of the people helping me that night was Ed Hilz, a great person—a tall, handsome man with sky-blue eyes. As my Dad used to say, "He's someone I'd take into combat with me." I cried again in public several years later, along with many other MAXIMUS staff, when Ed Hilz was killed one morning driving to work. At MAXIMUS, we were an extended family. With thousands of employees, many tragic events took place that we had to deal with.

When the conversion to our system finally took place, we found the data was even worse than expected. Their automated records were incomplete, inaccurate, and almost indecipherable. After everyone understood how bad the data was, I was summoned to the government department head's office in Sacramento.

He, Stan, pleaded with me to do everything possible to clean up the data and fix the system by the end of January. He said not to worry about the money. This was an emergency—he just wanted us to do what's necessary to get the job done, even though the requirement to clean up the incumbent contractor's data was not in our contract.

Coincidentally, I had our attorney with me at the time because I didn't know what to expect at the meeting. I asked the attorney if we should do it, and he nodded yes. I told Stan, "OK, we want to clean this up as much as you do."

Well, again, we did the impossible and cleaned up the data, just as we were asked to do. However, when we tried to bill for the extra staff needed to clean up the data, the auditors came in and started disallowing everything. "Why did you hire three people in the copy room?" "Why did you hire seven extra forms processors—you only needed two"—that kind of thing.

Their disallowances added up to over $1 million, and we were never paid. I still have the memo explaining our bill. The lesson for MAXIMUS—*Make sure everything is in writing; I don't care if the building is on fire!*

Leases

MAXIMUS had a large number of leases to oversee. We had a separate real estate department that took care of the initial leasing, the build-out of the space, and the administration of the lease from our end. My brother Joe ended up in this department because of his extensive real estate background—and with a significant pay increase.

MAXIMUS required a "kick out" clause in every lease. If the government terminated our contract, we could terminate the lease. We often had to pay for this privilege in higher lease payments or in a longer than usual notification periods, but it was worth it. In one case, we saved $2.3 million by being able to terminate a lease. Recall the large SSA Disability Insurance contract that was canceled by Congress.

I also learned what an "expense stop" meant. I thought that was where MAXIMUS expenses stopped and the landlord's began. On the contrary, it's where the landlord's expenses stopped and ours began. That lesson cost MAXIMUS about $250,000. The landlord now owns the Washington Nationals baseball team. I can understand why.

So contracts governed our lives, and we had to make sure we could negotiate and manage them. MAXIMUS couldn't grow if we signed bad contracts. Contracts, Contracts, Contracts.

CHAPTER 23

CPAs AND CFOs ONLY

Financial management was also crucial to growing MAXIMUS. Like setting quality standards, we got what we accepted financially. MAXIMUS had to remain financially strong to continue to change government and grow, given the uncertainties and risks we had to take. There were many forces working against us, and we had to be able to outlast them. *We had to stay in the fight.*

Business Model

When I founded MAXIMUS, I did not have a business model to tell me what my billing rates should be or how much I should charge per hour. Many friends and colleagues told me to charge as little as possible to make sure I would be competitive. That seemed to make sense according to supply-and-demand theory. However, I decided, instead, to charge as much as possible. I was a good proposal writer and had a good track record, so I should be able to charge premium dollar for my services. And I did.

In hindsight, that was probably the single most important decision in making MAXIMUS successful—to charge as much as the market would bear. Had I not charged these high rates for my time and that of subsequent staff, MAXIMUS would not have been profitable and may not have survived. The additional money was needed to build the infrastructure of the company—even at the very low levels of revenues and expenditures in the beginning—and in later years to survive the onslaughts of the unions, our competitors, and our mistakes.

Fundamental to ensuring our profitability year after year, was to have and understand a business model. As noted earlier, I did not fully understand the relationship among overhead rates, billing rates, and number of hours billed when I started MAXIMUS. Having an advanced degree in quantitative analysis, though, I decided to solve the relationships mathematically. I developed a mathematical formula (it had to be true) that I used to govern how we set our billing rates and fees. Every business needs one. Stated in its most simple form, the formula is

Utilization Rate × Multiplier × Salaries = Total Costs + Profit

Where Total Costs = Salaries + Fringe Benefits + Overhead + Direct Costs

The Utilization Rate is the percent of the maximum hours a company can bill in a given time period, say a month. Typically, we'd shoot for 65 percent to 70 percent utilization. That left 30 percent to 35 percent for marketing, administrative tasks, vacation, sick leave, and down time. Of course, we all worked overtime, which was outside the calculation based on eight billable hours per day.

Note that marketing is an allowable expense in government. Many people both outside and inside government have no idea marketing is a necessary cost of doing business. Because it is so important, the expense is reimbursed within reason in government contracts.

The Multiplier is the markup on salaries that includes these other expenses, including marketing, to calculate an hourly rate for the consultant. For example, a multiplier of three was usually acceptable for government consulting. The more prominent consulting firms could charge as high as four or five times the hourly salary rate to commercial clients. In our case, we would take the consultant's salary, divide by 2080 hours per year (52 weeks × 40 hours per week), and multiply by three to calculate the hourly billing rate.

As an example, let's say a consultant had a salary of $60,000 per year. Dividing this by 2080 gives $28.95 per hour. Multiply by three to obtain $86.54 an hour, so we billed the person out at, say, $90 per hour.

The multiplier obviously allowed us to cover the salaries, fringe benefits, overhead, direct costs, and profit. The multiplier, however, is based on achieving a 65 percent utilization rate. If MAXIMUS had plenty of work, we could keep the utilization rate high, but if there were too little work, the utilization rate would drop since there were no projects to which we could bill hours.

Using this equation, we could solve for different variables and draw a utilization versus multiplier curve—a hyperbolic curve of the form $x \times y = \text{constant}$.

Below is such a curve with utilization on the x-axis and the overhead rate required on the y-axis. If we lowered the target utilization rate to allow more time, say, for marketing or training, we had to raise our overhead rate and, therefore, our multiplier to cover our additional marketing costs.

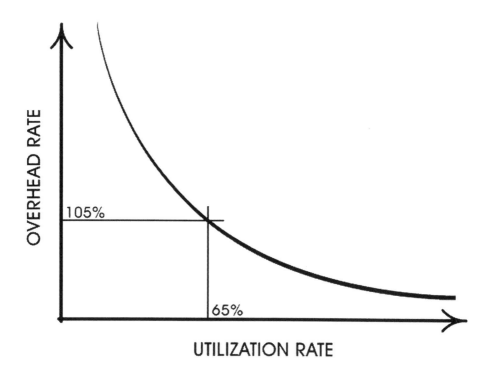

Exhibit 6 – Utilization Rate vs. Overhead Rate Curve

Without going into a treatise, suffice it to say this formula can be used to solve for fringe benefit rates, overhead rates, profit versus utilization, and any number of relationships that governed our business.

This equation gave me great comfort. I knew the forces affecting our financial performance, and I could manage them. MAXIMUS had a business model that would guide our growth.

Fixed Versus Variable Costs

One of the key advantages of a consulting firm, whether government or commercial, is that fixed costs are usually small compared to variable costs. Consultants don't need large machines or factories to provide services—just an office and an airline ticket. Incidentally, we had our own internal travel service, so our consultants would get the best price on airline tickets.

Salaries are considered variable costs since consultants can be brought on and let go as contracts are won and completed. Of course, this was no way to run our company since we wanted to develop long-term employees. Nonetheless, it still helped to understand we could reduce salaries to survive. *This knowledge helped me take more risks.*

Costs are primarily fixed in government. Government cannot hire and let go people like the private sector can. Government has to staff for the highest long-term workloads, unless it contracts with the private sector.

By contrast, the fixed costs in consulting include primarily rent and utilities. Even then, I required that every lease agreement have a kick-out clause in case we lost a contract. I could scale our administrative staff based on the consulting staff. Later, our systems staff became a fixed cost since they were needed to maintain the systems that supported MAXIMUS. The point is I always worried about fixed costs and how long those costs would remain fixed. Because of my attention to these costs, even through the revenue declines and growth stalls, we always earned a profit.

Debt-free Growth

Perhaps surprisingly, MAXIMUS never borrowed money to fund our operations. I started with $12,000 initial capital, and that carried MAXIMUS all the way to $600 million and beyond, with the public equity raised later. There might have been some debt on our books for a short period, but the debt was from acquisitions that had debt on their books. We paid it off as soon as possible.

MAXIMUS didn't acquire companies of any size until after we went public. These acquisitions were discussed earlier, and, suffice it to say, they did not play as large a role in our growth as you might think.

In order to avoid borrowing money, MAXIMUS needed to make enough profit to cover the cash-flow needs for the incremental growth. Our cash-flow needs equaled about three months' revenues since the government was a slow payer, taking about three months on average to pay. To be safe, we needed about one quarter of our annual revenues in cash to support operations without borrowing.

As an aside, the government may have been a slow payer, but the government was also a sure payer. We used to tell our contemporaries who worked with commercial clients how much we loved government. And we did love the government.

For example, we had a contract with Orange County, California, when it declared bankruptcy. Nonetheless, they kept paying MAXIMUS throughout the bankruptcy process. No government agency ever failed to make an uncontested payment to us, so we didn't have a government bad-debt line in our accounts.

Since MAXIMUS was growing at 30 percent to 40 percent per year on average, we needed to have after-tax profits equal to at least one quarter of the incremental revenue to avoid borrowing money. Well, we did it! With a 10 percent net profit rate, we could grow revenues 40 percent per year debt free as long as the profit was plowed back into the company, which it was.

Until MAXIMUS went public, Ray Ruddy and I didn't take any money out of the company for ourselves. We did draw down on retained earnings to buy back the stock of someone leaving the company. We never borrowed money from the banks either. When we went public, Ray and

I sold shares, and so did MAXIMUS. The money MAXIMUS received in going public obviously further mitigated the need to borrow money.

In all fairness, we did apply for and receive lines of credit from banks. This was done in case we ran into trouble. The banks were continually frustrated, however, by our lack of willingness to borrow. We never had to borrow from them, at least while I was at MAXIMUS.

No Administrative or Marketing Budgets

You read correctly—no budgets! This did not apply to specific contracts that we had to execute within budget. Of course, there we carefully tracked our costs versus the contract amounts. Projects had budgets; corporate management did not.

I rejected the idea of budgets in order to control corporate overhead costs. Overhead costs included administration, accounting, marketing, and sales costs. The reason there were no budgets in MAXIMUS is that most people interpret a budget as an authorization to spend up to the amount budgeted. Instead, I asked for expenditure forecasts—"How much do you think will be required to support our operations in the next quarter, as it currently looks?" I would approve a forecast, and then let the expenditures go under or over if rationally supported. It may have been a matter of semantics, but the difference was important in mindset.

Another reason I didn't set budgets was to make sure our staff weren't inhibited in making decisions. The staff were not afraid to spend money pursuing a large contract because there was no budget limiting them. Other companies did have marketing budgets. Opportunities often arose unexpectedly in our reactive culture at MAXIMUS, and we didn't always know in advance of government procurements and how much we would have to spend on marketing.

Frankly, we wanted our staff to bid on everything—forget the budget—spend as much as possible winning new business! In a reactive business, it's self-defeating to set a marketing budget you can't exceed. We had more flexibility without budgets.

Treat Profit Like Rent

Quality was not an option, nor was profit, since we were only in those businesses in which MAXIMUS could provide quality and make a profit. We treated profit like rent—you had to earn a profit just like you had to pay rent—no option for either. Since that was the standard, it was almost always achieved. We did set profit goals for each of our businesses. Naturally, we lost money on many contracts and lost money in certain businesses from time to time, *but never overall in any year during my tenure.*

Each business had a different attainable profit level. Consulting was the highest, with about 15 percent to 20 percent average. Our revenue-maximimization business was contingency-based, so we could make high profits—similar to attorneys who work on contingency. Also, because we were providing very specialized expertise in other areas, we could charge more. The consulting contracts were smaller, so the percent profit line did not bother the government contracting officers as much.

Systems work ran about 10 percent to 15 percent. There were many great systems firms out there we competed with for government systems business. Our rates had to be more than competitive with theirs. The risks of failure were higher in this business than in any other, and we probably should have charged more than we did.

Our government operations or privatization business brought in about 7 percent to 8 percent. Here, the contracts were very large, and so were the total profits compared to the smaller consulting contracts. The cost of failure in this business was immense. MAXIMUS could be wiped out in a single contract if we performed negligently. This threat kept many of the larger companies away from privatization—and kept us on our toes.

We did our best to make sure these businesses achieved their profitability goals. Ray Ruddy took the lead on this. Fortunately, the higher profit margins for consulting helped pay for the cash-flow needs of the faster growing, lower margin privatization business.

Red Flag System

When MAXIMUS grew to become really large and had some 3,000 active contracts, we could not track the contracts individually in the home office. As a result, I created the Red Flag system to identify possible problem contracts. We didn't want any problems with the government. We needed the Red Flag system to help us continue to grow.

Using our accounting system, we entered data describing each contract and then screened each contract for any of the following:

- Costs charged before contract start date

- No costs charged in the previous two months

- Costs exceeded contract amount

- Costs charged after contract end date

- No billing for two months

- No collections for two months

- Spend rate exceeded two times straight-line projection.

This system identified some 7,000 red flags the first time it was run. Needless to say, we went into "crash mode" to resolve the red flags, and we did resolve them.

Most red flags identified poor controls by project managers. However, many of the red flags in the first pass of the system were false positives— there was something in the contract terms that justified the condition causing the red flag. We didn't want these contracts showing up every time a Red Flag Report was run. Gradually, we learned to tune the system so it flagged few false positives—saying a contract was a problem when it was not.

However, the Red Flag system did find many problem contracts. In particular, I remember one contract valued at about $45,000 that a couple of staff had not worked on but charged anyway. They found the project accounting number and billed their hours against that number, and the accounting system accepted the charges. No work was being done, yet the client was still being billed.

The project manager was not doing his job. When the client stopped paying our bills, we found out about the problem. The guilty were identified and dealt with, and more controls were implemented. We still had to complete the contract and logged a significant loss doing so.

Soon the staff learned they were accountable for every contract, even if it was a small one. The Red Flag system improved our ability to manage our far-flung businesses in almost every state, large city, and county. Both MAXIMUS and the government benefited.

Watchdogs Crying Wolf?

After we went public in 1997, it seemed everyone was asking questions about our financials. In February 1999, the Center for Financial Research & Analysis (CFRA), a watchdog-type organization, issued a report on

MAXIMUS, saying we were basically "cooking the books" and misleading investors. CFRA is an organization that sells "forensic accounting research" to institutional investors, underwriters, and other financial institutions. Naturally, our stock took a nosedive, dropping over 10 percent the day the report came out.

I was very worried about the government's possible reaction to this report. Thankfully, the Securities and Exchange Commission (SEC) and our potential government clients didn't see the report because it would have seriously damaged our ability to win more business. Government agencies would be hesitant to sign any contract with a company under SEC investigation. In addition, we would have had much explaining to do to our existing government clients.

At any rate, we scrambled to find a copy of the report, so we could see what it said and respond. Fortunately, one of the stock analysts who covered MAXIMUS faxed us a copy, which I still have.

The sections of the CFRA report on MAXIMUS were titled:

- Misleading Revenue Growth for Consulting Group

- Revenue Decline for Government Operations Group

- Surging Receivables

- Deteriorating Operating Cash Flows

- Declining Government Gross Margins

- Legal Proceedings

CRFA had done an extensive, detailed statistical analysis of all our public data, and compared MAXIMUS to other "similar" companies. They left the reader to conclude we totally misrepresented our financial condition and were destined for significant financial and legal problems.

After reading the report, we were stunned and outraged. CFRA clearly did not understand our business and was cooking its own books!

Without going into great detail, they focused on Days Sales Outstanding (DSOs), gross margins, quarterly changes in operating segment revenues, cash flows, and alleged legal problems. CFRA enjoyed a good reputation among financial analysts, so we had to take them seriously. And we did.

CFRA clearly did not understand our revenue-maximization work. The Days Sales Outstanding (a measure of how long it took to be paid) looked very high for MAXIMUS, but that was because we were not paid until the state was paid in revenue-maximization contracts. Sometimes this would take over a year. And those payments represented significant profit.

Within a few days, we issued our own detailed report to our investors and the public that refuted their charges. We explained why CFRA had misunderstood our numbers.

We believed we had effectively responded to its criticisms. Still many people didn't know who to believe—CFRA or MAXIMUS? The only true test of who was right would take time—and it did. Was the CFRA prediction going to come true?

Without going into our specific defense, let's look at the top and bottom lines of MAXIMUS's financial performance during the periods in question. Let's look at 1998, the year before the year CFRA questioned; 1999, the year CFRA questioned; and 2000 and 2001, the two years after the year CFRA warned of financial collapse.

The table below presents MAXIMUS revenues and net income in Fiscal Years 1998, 1999, 2000, and 2001. See whether their alarms had any merit.

Fiscal Year	Revenues ($000)	Net Income ($000)
1998	$244,114	$15,514
1999	$319,540	$27,626
2000	$399,164	$34,118
2001	$477,260	$40,102

We grew in Fiscal Year 1999 and all the years thereafter. All our financial reports were audited by a "Big Four" accounting firm, Ernst & Young, who you can bet was extra careful. As far as I could tell, we were always truthful. I had to sign all the audit papers personally. CFRA was clearly wrong.

The organization may not have understood our business. I was told many of its subscribers were short sellers who benefited from the drop in our stock price, whether or not the report was accurate.

The lesson is that we had better know our numbers—better than anyone else, especially as a public company. We were accountable both to the financial community as well as the government. This should have given the government some comfort, knowing they were dealing with a reputable firm open to public scrutiny.

Because we were a growing public firm, our quarterly results were always carefully examined. We had to manage our finances well—and defend our numbers!

CHAPTER 24

OVERCOMING BARRIERS TO GROWTH

This chapter provides an abbreviated chronological order of the barriers to growth MAXIMUS experienced and how these barriers were overcome. Even though we were working to reform government, I still struggled to manage a growing company. We had to provide high quality services to more and more government clients.

Growing a company at a high rate is not easy, especially when selling services by the hour. With a consulting, systems, or privatized case management business, we needed to add people to grow, and this always led to complications. These days, companies like Google, Facebook, Groupon, LinkedIn, and even Amazon are growing with the Internet, where scaling operations is more straightforward. Selling labor by the hour is more difficult, so we ran into more barriers as we grew than I suspect they did.

There are plateaus or stall points at different revenue levels on the growth curve for all growth companies. This is true whether they sell to the government, to commercial companies, or directly to the public. Problems occur at these stall points that are not experienced at lower revenue levels. These problems must be solved before the company can resume its growth. A corporate transformation has to take place to be able to cross the revenue plateau and climb to the next level.

Since I had never managed a company larger than the one I was currently managing, I first had to become aware of the problem, then identify the problem, next find the solution, and finally implement the solution. Recall the stages of learning discussed in Chapter 8 – Our Corporate Culture. This took time.

Revenue plateaus occur for different reasons. The plateaus we experienced were not clearly defined levels, but ranges of revenue that required changes in the way we operated. What follows are plateaus symptomatic of a service business, where revenues are closely correlated to the number of employees in the company.

While there is no specific place where these plateaus or stall points occurred in MAXIMUS, I felt them fairly acutely at Start-up to $500,000, $2.5 to $3.0 million range, $8 to $12 million range, $30 to $35 million, $75 million to $100 million range, $250 million to $300 million range, and the $500 million range and above. Each of these levels presented different problems that had to be solved for us to continue helping government at higher and higher levels. Since the problems were solved, you might guess we never had any problems. Sure!

Start-up to $500,000 in Revenues

I faced few problems starting a consulting business by myself. I didn't need much money; by definition, there was consensus on all decisions; there were no personnel problems; I didn't need policies and procedures, and so on. It was fun and fairly easy.

After six months, when I began hiring staff and moved out of my basement, managing the business became a lot more complicated. Payroll was an obligation, fringe benefits had to be defined and became very important, office space had to be acquired, and office furniture and equipment leased, and so on. MAXIMUS actually became a small business.

This arrangement worked for a long time. As long as I could directly manage the staff and their activities, things went fairly smoothly. As we gained more and more employees, the problems magnified.

$2.5 Million to $3.0 Million in Revenues

As the company grew to the range of thirty to forty people, I could no longer manage everyone by myself. The "pumpkin chart" with all lines leading to the CEO didn't work anymore. I needed to hire additional higher-level managers and delegate accountability and authority to them. I had to rely on others. Delegating caused many problems. The new managers had to be hired, trained, and indoctrinated on my vision and standards. I had to communicate my plans and have the new managers execute the plans.

The problem became acute when we won a major contract in New York City to reduce the city's welfare error rate. This was the first significant contract away from our home office, and I couldn't be there every day. Therefore, I hired more senior people and delegated to them. Incidentally, that was the project in New York City where we reduced the error rate below 4 percent, which was a major milestone.

We beat Touche Ross for that contract. As explained in Chapter 5 – MAXIMUS – Quick History, Ray Ruddy joined me to help grow the state and local consulting business of MAXIMUS. He turned out to be the right solution. He was an experienced consultant and influenced the way I thought about the business. He also brought additional senior consultants with him.

At these higher levels of revenues, we also needed to add full-time accounting staff and other support staff to the company. We made sure we had an excellent reporting system that provided timely data on all our operations on a continual basis. Our accounting system was totally under our control and was developed specifically to meet our unique needs as a government contractor. We employed our own programmers, who maintained and developed this functionality. This capability helped us reach the next level.

$8 to $12 Million in Revenues

As we continued to win more business, it became clear we had to increase the salary structure of our company to attract even more experienced consultants. As a result, I doubled my salary, at Ray's recommendation. My salary had been below his. That gave much more room under both of us to hire higher-level consultants.

We had opened a consulting office in Boston a couple of years earlier. At this point in our growth, the office was also growing and created logistical problems of managing from afar. Ray had to travel back and forth to Washington DC every week. As we hired additional staff in the Boston area, they had to be indoctrinated into the MAXIMUS culture and our passion for helping government. At the federal level, we were winning more business, not only in the consulting area but also in developing systems. So our systems staff was also expanding.

In late 1987, we won the Los Angeles GAIN contract. *This was the game changer for MAXIMUS and the country.* Los Angeles GAIN required that we hire case managers, lower level employees who were like social workers rather than consultants. We needed to learn to manage this different type of employee. As explained later, we were also forced to deal with being embroiled in political firestorms and surviving them.

Because of the new type of employees and our other internal growth, MAXIMUS policies and procedures manuals were evolving rapidly, growing as we covered issues that needed to be resolved. The policy and procedures manuals reduced the need for decision-making by our managers since the decision was already established in policy. And the manual kept growing.

$30 Million to $35 Million in Revenues

We also began operating Child Support Enforcement Programs around the country. We managed Medicaid Managed Care programs in several small states at this level as well as welfare-to-work programs. In effect, we were creating a franchise-type businesses in these areas. This allowed us to learn in one project and transfer the knowledge to the next. We could manage multiple contracts of the same kind more easily than if they were very different. Naturally, we developed systems and training programs to assimilate and control the growing operational staff.

The value of these larger privatization contracts was their three- and five-year terms, so they provided recurring revenue. When we had recurring revenue, growth was much easier since we didn't have to replace our entire business base each year, and then some, to grow.

One of the key decisions I made to get past this plateau was to raise the salary of our project managers from the $75,000 to $80,000-level to the $120,000 to $150,000-level. These people had enormous responsibilities, and we needed more experienced, more mature project managers for these contracts.

Also, as billings soared, it became obvious we needed to have greater profits to fund our cash-flow needs and to take even bigger risks. We also needed to protect our reputation and be able to fix any problems we caused—or to go the extra mile to please a client. As a result, we raised our profit goals. Again, you get what you accept. So our profits went up.

$75 Million to $100 Million in Revenues

As the company became larger, we had to reorganize it into different business lines and social program areas. We promoted existing managers and hired even more people as new managers. It was very difficult to hire a new manager and have existing staff report to that manager. However, as previously explained, we had to be top heavy in terms of management and marketing capabilities in order to grow. I never promoted a person to manage his or her former manager. I moved them to other parts of the organization.

To grow more, we had to bid on larger contracts. We were able to develop systems under these contracts that could be extended for use by other government agencies. Basically, we let the government fund the development of our internal systems. We developed our own database management system called MAXSTAR that could compete with anything from Oracle. MAXSTAR gave us a competitive cost advantage since we did not have to pay for database systems like our competitors did.

MAXIMUS was successful in bidding on the larger contracts, which were primarily large-scale privatization contracts. We became a major player in Medicaid Managed Care, administering programs in California, Texas, Michigan, Iowa, and other states during this time.

Government social welfare programs are remarkably similar across the states, and at the same time, they are very different. We were able to transfer considerable knowledge and system components from one state to another—like a franchise business. But each state was different, so it wasn't exactly like a franchise business. We had to tailor each program to the unique needs of each state.

Throughout this growth phenomenon, it became obvious that people loved their titles. So I was liberal with titles. It helped in staff retention and helped us grow. For example, when I created divisions for the different business units, I gave the division managers the title of president. When we reached fifteen divisions, I created group presidents to manage them. By the time I retired, MAXIMUS had twenty-one or more presidents.

As the company grew even larger, we needed outside help in terms of lobbyists, law firms on retainer in each state, media relations people, and others.

MAXIMUS was receiving more than its fair share of negative attention in the media, a lot generated by the government employee unions and our competitors. Until we solved the political problems, we weren't going much further.

$250 Million to $300 Million in Revenues

By being a reactive company, we were drawn by government needs into different market areas. Therefore, we grew where the money was. And, as I have mentioned, we had to respond quickly and well to win these larger contracts.

The major change made at this revenue level was centralizing proposal writing, the heart of winning new business. We created a corporate Proposal Center with its own separate building and with its own professional staff. We needed to upgrade our proposal-writing capabilities in order to win these increasingly large contracts. I hired a professional proposal manager, Mike Humm, from one of the leading proposal-writing consulting firms. He did a great job.

The larger contractors hired firms that specialized in proposal writing to write their company's proposals; MAXIMUS wrote its own. We created an online proposal library so staff could search for topics from previously written proposals. We had four large "war rooms," where proposal teams could meet, make presentations, and post sections of the written proposals on the wall for others to comment. This was a major change in the way MAXIMUS did business—a needed change at this level.

With some two hundred or more vice presidents and directors, we also had to develop an Authority Matrix, as described earlier, that prescribed the authority of each managerial level in the company. This matrix told the different managers what they could decide on their own and what they had to elevate to their superiors for approval. It worked pretty well.

MAXIMUS also received a boost in revenues by acquiring companies with the money we received by going public. While these acquisitions broadened our service offerings considerably, and added revenues, there were a great number of challenges they presented to us. With all these acquisitions, we had to reorganize again and place these acquired companies where they fit best in the organization.

To grow more, we had to assimilate these acquired companies into our growth culture. This process was so difficult we stopped making acquisitions. Nevertheless, one by one, all these companies became profitable, at least for a while. A couple of years after I resigned from MAXIMUS, the Board of Directors decided to sell the systems companies. They were just too much trouble to manage, relative to the rest of the business.

The larger we grew, the easier it was to win more business. We had an excellent reputation with our government clients, and so we received excellent references when we bid on other jobs. When we became the largest player in a market segment, we were very difficult to beat. So growth begat growth.

$500 Million and Above in Revenues

Next was the MAXIMUS Training Center. We implemented a Training Center with a full-time staff of trainers. Courses were developed and taught. As described earlier in the chapter on Corporate Culture, there were mandatory courses and voluntary courses. The Training Center had the latest technology to train our people, which was needed to ensure uniformity of knowledge across the company. We also had separate training centers in each of our large privatization projects.

We implemented the concept, "What gets measured and rewarded, gets done." In order to manage a $500-million company with so many people scattered all over the globe, we needed clearly defined goals and expectations for each division of the company. I could not begin to meet with all the presidents. I viewed managing MAXIMUS as sitting on top of a mountain with a cloud layer halfway down, obscuring the valley. I couldn't see the valley, even though I wanted to. I wasn't panoptic, as they say.

So we developed an elaborate performance management system based on how well the company performed, how well the division performed, and how well the individual performed. Goals were assigned up and down the line on Quality, Profitability, and Growth. Bonuses were awarded based on performance. This kept everyone working in the same direction and cooperating with everyone else.

Then we placed a high priority on international business to find more customers. We bought a small welfare-to-work company in Australia. It took some time, but the company is now a major contributor to MAXIMUS, thanks to a fellow, Michael Hobday. I remember when he asked me after he was hired what I wanted him to do. I said, "Build another MAXIMUS in Australia." He just about did.

I liked what Tom Watson of IBM fame said:

> I firmly believe that any organization, in order to survive and achieve success, must have a sound set of beliefs on which it premises all its policies and actions. Next, I believe that the most important single factor in corporate success is faithful adherence to those beliefs. And finally, I believe that if an organization is to meet the challenges of a changing world, it must be prepared to change everything about itself.

If I interpret him correctly, an organization must be able to change everything except its beliefs. In a way, I could say that's what MAXIMUS did. Our mission remained "Helping Government Serve the People."

Now let's look in more detail at some of the other complications we faced in growing and how they were solved.

PART VI:
COMPLICATIONS

These chapters cover what I believe is important to teach in business schools. This is the real world.

CHAPTER 25

EXTERNAL FORCES

When a company works for the government, it has to deal with all kinds of external forces. Here is what we did and learned.

Lobbyists

Lobbyists played an important role in the growth of privatization at MAXIMUS. It's not what you think, though. We used lobbyists only as consultants, not as agents to influence legislation on our behalf. We were active in all fifty states—even as a smaller company. We needed someone to vouch for us to governors or other higher elected officials that MAXIMUS was a company that could be trusted. For a time, we had a large number of lobbyists working for MAXIMUS.

Because we were not well known, MAXIMUS was *not* awarded a significant number of contracts we had technically won. The problem was that the secretary of the department or the governor of the state had not heard of MAXIMUS and didn't want to take a chance on an unknown company, at least unknown to them. In almost all cases, we weren't located in their states.

Just to give you a sense of this, I'll cite two examples. One instance occurred in Massachusetts. MAXIMUS wrote an outstanding proposal—several hundred pages long—to manage the Massachusetts Medicaid Managed Care program. We heard that the evaluation committee was thrilled with our proposal and recommended us for award. The next thing we knew, Foundation Health Care won the contract. When we requested and received its proposal under the Freedom of Information Act, we found it was only thirty pages long and essentially nonresponsive. Why were they selected? Because the state knew Foundation Health Care and did not know MAXIMUS.

We won another contract in Maryland to conduct a management study of the Department of Human Resources. The contract, signed by the department secretary and me, went to the governor's Board of Public Works for final approval. There, legendary State Comptroller Louie Goldstein, said he never heard of MAXIMUS, and on the spot, awarded the contract to Peat Marwick Mitchell. I was an eyewitness. Everyone was shocked.

Therefore, we engaged lobbyists and educated them about MAXIMUS. We flew the lobbyists to our corporate headquarters in Reston, Virginia, so they could learn about our capabilities. We taught them how to represent us, explained our mission and corporate culture, and gave them references to other government agencies we had worked for in other states.

One time, we actually held a miniconvention, where each of our twenty-one divisions created a booth that explained what the division did. We invited our lobbyists to go around to the different booths and ask questions of our staff. It was important that they really know MAXIMUS well.

We also invited lobbyists to our off-site meetings and tried to engage them in the company's activities. The more they knew about us, the better they could represent us as ambassadors in the different states. When we were selected in a state for contract award, the lobbyist could vouch for MAXIMUS and, in most cases, we won those awards.

Lobbyists live off their personal reputations. I assured them that MAXIMUS didn't expect anything of them that would jeopardize their credibility. If the lobbyist couldn't represent us in good faith in a particular instance, that was fine with us. We just needed to know what the problem was. This way, MAXIMUS had a real partnership with the lobbyists. They made sure we were always in good standing in their particular states.

We hit a few snags, however, with a lobbyist here and there. We had one lobbyist who had been convicted of a felony we didn't know about. This lobbyist created untold trouble for MAXIMUS. He overstepped his bounds and misrepresented the company. In his enthusiasm, he put too much pressure on the "powers that be," and it backfired on us. We lost a contract as an incumbent—unheard of before!

MAXIMUS needed to conduct more thorough background checks on the lobbyists who represented us. They are not all equal, and their reputations change over time. Overall, though, our experience with lobbyists was very good.

Politicians

The primary goal of a politician is to be reelected. Some are ideologues; some are pragmatic; some are loose cannons. Nevertheless, it seemed to me that all were interested in doing a good job. And with MAXIMUS administering some of their core programs, the politicians were interested in who we were and what we did to ensure their programs ran smoothly. We worked hard to help them understand that MAXIMUS had a long track record of delivering outstanding results at reasonable cost.

At times, I dealt directly with governors of large states to assure them personally that MAXIMUS was for real and would do a good job for them. MAXIMUS operated major government programs with contracts worth tens of millions and even hundreds of millions of dollars. The governors wanted to know who we were and that they could have confidence in us.

For a time, MAXIMUS had a small political action committee (MAXPAC), which contributed to various political campaigns. The money for the PAC came directly from donations by our employees. MAXPAC didn't provide MAXIMUS any political leverage because it gave to both the Republican and Democrat candidates in each election. However, as one political advisor told me, "You have to be a player." We could not sit on the sidelines. So we gave to both parties in accordance with the election laws. Administering a PAC was actually quite expensive.

Later, when we were a better-known contractor, MAXIMUS staff attended the National Governors Association conferences and other public administration conferences. I occasionally met privately with governors to discuss our work, including John Engler of Michigan, Tommy Thompson from Wisconsin (later Secretary of Health and Human Services), Jim Hodges of South Carolina, Janet Napolitano of Arizona (later Secretary of Homeland Security), Tom Ridge of Pennsylvania (first Secretary of Homeland Security), and many others. These people were all straight shooters.

My staff also met with George W. Bush when he was Governor of Texas; Grey Davis, Governor of California; John Rowland, Governor of Connecticut, and so on. We were important to these public executives as a firm since we could help them operate more effective social welfare programs. We could help their administrations look good (even if the latter two governors couldn't make themselves look good), at least in terms of the programs we were responsible for.

I remember one particular meeting with former Governor Thompson, then Secretary of the Department of Health and Human Services in Washington, DC. I went in to explain some of the new things we were doing that could help Health and Human Services programs across the United States. We often were an information source for state and federal department heads so they could do their jobs better. That's why they liked to talk to us—to find out what was going on elsewhere.

He asked me directly what I wanted—he was busy. I didn't have an answer—no one had ever asked me that before. I told him I just wanted to tell him what was going on. The meeting quickly ended. I should have asked him to endorse our privatization program to other governors, but I didn't. After that, I was always prepared to make a recommendation or ask for something when I met a powerful person.

Government Employee Unions

MAXIMUS was the enemy of government employee unions, at least in the United States. Recall the extensive problems we had with Service Employees International Union in Los Angeles County. Unions don't play fair—no doubt about it. For example, they maintained a website about MAXIMUS that was in large part false and totally misleading. The website published the worst news stories (that I suspect they planted) and gave a thoroughly inaccurate impression of our company. The union operatives worked hand in hand with the extreme left to poison the privatization well.

I tell the following story to show the extent of the union campaigns against MAXIMUS, as well as other companies privatizing government programs. I attended a privatization conference at Fordham University in New York City in the late 1990s. We found out about the conference only because I was invited to be a speaker on one of the panels. Otherwise, MAXIMUS would not have known about it.

The opening session was largely a union bashing of MAXIMUS, elaborating on what allegedly happened in our Wisconsin W-2 (Wisconsin Works) privatization project. This is explained later in Chapter 26 – Dealing with Disaster. I sat there, hardly believing what was being said in this huge amphitheater lecture hall with hundreds of attendees. I was amazed at the disinformation being spread. I must be naïve because I found it hard to believe what people are capable of doing.

After fifteen or twenty minutes, when the bashing was finished, I stood up where I was seated, high in the back of the hall, and announced in a loud voice to the entire audience that I was the Chief Executive Officer of MAXIMUS, and I would like to correct what had just been said. I asked the chair of the panel if I could do so and was granted permission.

I spoke for about five minutes and addressed the erroneous information, providing detailed facts on what actually happened in Wisconsin. The conference participants remained silent. I explained I would provide written documentation of MAXIMUS's performance to anyone who was interested. I also invited all participants to come to our offices in Milwaukee to see for themselves what was going on. Upon finishing, I received mild applause from the audience. In the hallway afterward, I was congratulated.

Later that afternoon, I was on a panel with two union members. One panelist was from the American Federation of State, County, and Municipal Employees and another from the Service Employees International Union. Of course, they had already prepared their speeches before they heard me in the opening session, and they went on to give their speeches, as prepared—MAXIMUS-bashing tirades. We were the target because MAXIMUS was the greatest *Privateer* of all. Yes, the title of the book originated at this conference.

The union representatives voiced a common theme in their presentations throughout the conference. They claimed privatization companies, in general, and MAXIMUS, in particular, were guilty of putting profits ahead of the interests of program recipients. After all, they reasoned, a company's duty was to its shareholders and not the people it was serving—the same old argument.

The two union representatives on my panel also alleged that MAXIMUS made many mistakes in processing cases, had lower performance ratings in terms of placing people in jobs, shortchanged recipients in eligibility determination, and was actually paid to move people off the rolls. I had to respond.

Fortunately, thanks to my father, I am a reasonably good spontaneous speaker—he taught me as a child to speak extemporaneously. I had also taken notes during union representatives' talks. I was allowed ten minutes for my speech. I decided to take the union reps head on and abandon my previously prepared notes. Here is what happened.

I waited a few seconds at the podium before I started speaking to make sure everyone was paying attention. I wanted the audience to be ready to hear what I had to say. I told the audience that a high percentage of MAXIMUS management staff had worked in government and had become disillusioned because of the limitations government imposed on what could be done. Our collective mission at MAXIMUS was to reform government from the private side since we all had been frustrated trying to reform government from the inside.

I commented we were not stupid people. Our staff knew the long-term interest of our shareholders was to put the recipients first and do an excellent job for our government clients. We knew we had detractors everywhere, like those before us now, who would take the slightest mistake on our part and blow it up beyond recognition.

I spoke that we very well understood MAXIMUS had to treat recipients better than the government did and, in fact, we did. I related that in Los

Angeles, for example, we had free refreshments for the moms and their kids who came into the GAIN centers. Some kids filled coffee filters up with cookies and took them home—which was fine with us. We paid for the refreshments out of "profit" since it was an unallowable cost.

I explained MAXIMUS had reception rooms rather than waiting rooms. We had tables with current magazines that applicants/recipients could browse. We timed how long they waited to see a caseworker and kept it under fifteen minutes. We had a satisfaction rating form that recipients could fill out and submit after every visit to our office. The average satisfaction rating across all five regions of Los Angeles was 99 percent. Hard to believe—but it was true.

I told them we always created a business-like setting for the recipients—not a dilapidated welfare office where they felt no one was concerned about them—but a place where they felt better about themselves. We also had a dress code our employees followed.

MAXIMUS took pains to spend more time than the government would to ensure a case was truly ineligible before denying benefits. The worst thing we could do was deny benefits to a recipient who truly deserved them. Therefore, in our processing procedures, we allowed one extra appeal, one more than the government permitted in its policies and procedures. We bent over backward to make sure our decisions were accurate and that we had the highest accuracy in eligibility determination that had ever been previously achieved.

In terms of finding people jobs, we outperformed our government counterparts in every project we had. Sometimes counties would have one region of the program administered by county government workers and another region administered by private contractors. This way the county administrators could compare the differences. *We were always better.*

I told them MAXIMUS was not better because we were smarter, but because we had more flexibility to hire and promote good people and to let go of nonperformers. We were better because we could set goals and pay bonuses to those who achieved them. And we were better because we had the freedom to innovate and do things government could not do.

I concluded by summing up that private sector had many advantages over the government in managing social welfare programs. I am not saying all private contractors were responsible—but MAXIMUS certainly was. And the union's criticisms were just plain wrong.

During the question-and-answer period afterward, several people stood up in the audience and said how glad they were I was present at the conference because they were getting the totally wrong impression about privatization.

Personally, as I have repeatedly said, I can't think of a good reason to have unions in government. Government is a benign employer, and the employees have elected representatives able to protect their interests. Nonetheless, government unions prevail—and they are very, very political. That's why unions still flourish in government.

To show the power of unions, consider the fate of the Los Angeles GAIN contract. After five years, when our contract was up for renewal, the composition of the Los Angeles Board of Supervisors had changed from three Republicans and two Democrats to two Republicans and three Democrats.

During the renewal hearings, the Department of Public Social Services (DPSS) repeatedly recommended to the Board of Supervisors that the MAXIMUS contract be extended for another five years. The department financial analysts showed MAXIMUS was much more cost-effective than they were, a tough pill to swallow. They pointed out that MAXIMUS's performance on the past contract had been closely monitored and had met or exceeded all contract specifications.

The hearings stretched over several weeks. In the end, Supervisor Yvonne Brathwaite Burke, Gloria Molina, and Edmund Edleman voted to give the jobs to the union and terminate the MAXIMUS contract. Talk about being disillusioned! Talk about what's wrong with politics! I can remember Jack Svahn and me sitting there wondering how it could have happened. We wandered around for the next couple of hours in a daze.

But we had broken the barrier with Los Angeles GAIN, and many other states and counties saw what had happened. Our work in privatization had just begun. In fact, it wasn't long before we were back in Los Angeles operating a welfare-to-work program in one region of Los Angeles County, competing with and soundly outperforming the government workers, amazingly many of our former employees.

Outperforming our former employees now in government—what does that tell you? It shows the private sector can motivate the same people better, and have them produce at a consistently higher level than the public sector can.

A Novel Approach to Privatization

After the Los Angeles GAIN experience, I approached the unions to try to find a way we could work together to improve government programs. Their members could benefit from our ability not only to match government salaries, but also to pay productivity bonuses. "If you can't beat them, join them."

Andy Stearn was president of the Service Employees International Union (SEIU) at the time; he is now retired. I met with him in his Washington, DC office to discuss a strategy whereby the unions would not block privatization, where working together we could be more efficient and produce better results for government.

He could see the handwriting on the wall. Even though the SEIU had successfully blocked privatization in many counties and states, government needed to become more efficient, and privatization was the answer. The battle still goes on today.

I suggested to Andy that the SEIU and MAXIMUS really had the same goals for employees. We both wanted employees to have good salaries and benefits; we both wanted them to have a fair adjudication process for their grievances; we both didn't want any sexual or racial discrimination; and we both wanted the employees to be able to advance according to their ability and not by a set of rigid rules. He agreed.

I proposed MAXIMUS join forces with the SEIU and allow them to manage our Human Resources Department on any project as a subcontractor. The SEIU could manage the grievance process, help set the competitive salary and fringe-benefit structure during contract bidding; oversee the hiring and termination of employees; and collect the union dues. The only string attached was they could not strike us on a particular project after a contract was signed.

He agreed to give it a try in Los Angeles County. I found him to be a fair-minded, far-sighted person. I liked him. We held several conference calls with representatives from SEIU Locals 660, 434, and 535, the local Los Angeles chapters, to try to arrive at a solution. My top staff even went out to meet with the union representatives and try to work with them.

In the end, the local Los Angeles unions would have none of it. They had the final say and soundly rejected our joint proposal. Both Andy and I were pretty surprised and disappointed, and we did not try again.

Still now, the unions and privatization contractors are at odds. Instead of replacing government employees in existing government programs, the contractors, including MAXIMUS, often win contracts to operate *new* government programs. That seems to be the politically-correct decision on how to deal with unions and privatization.

The Media

MAXIMUS needed a public relations department to deal with the media. We were in continual contact with the media, with press releases, responses to media questions, and the like.

The media were always a problem for us. Clearly, the fourth estate is a necessary part of our democratic society. Through their investigative journalism, they uncover corruption in government and in the private sector. I am 100 percent in support of this.

But how much damage do they do? And who controls them? In statistics, there is the concept of false positives and false negatives. A false positive occurred in our case when the media claimed to have found corruption at MAXIMUS when, in fact, there was no corruption. The positive allegation of corruption was false.

This damage occurred repeatedly concerning MAXIMUS. I can say with a clear conscience that MAXIMUS never engaged in any corrupt activity, at least while I was CEO. Corruption was repeatedly alleged by the media, but never proven. So the false positive rate for MAXIMUS was 100 percent. That's a bit high and counterproductive. It's "crying wolf" all the time, and it caused us a lot of problems.

On the other hand, how many times did the media investigate corruption and miss it? I would bet after my experience, the false negative rate approached 0 percent. The media always seemed to err on the side of sensationalism.

Our system of government promotes this huge, scavenging media machinery that accuses with impunity. It may be the only way we can guarantee a healthy democracy, but it comes with a high price. MAXIMUS spent a lot of money defending itself against false accusations. Unfortunately, even though we were innocent, we were hurt by the media.

The *Today Show* and Jane Pauley

After MAXIMUS won the Los Angeles GAIN program, I was invited to go on the *Today Show* with Jane Pauley to talk about privatization. NBC was very interested in us because Los Angeles GAIN was the first large-scale privatization of welfare reform in the nation. It was quite exciting. The *Today Show* paid for my travel and hotel room in New York City. Their studios are at Rockefeller Center.

Before the show, I went to the makeup artists, and they patted my face down with powder—a first. I was taken to the set, and watched Bryant Gumbel and Elizabeth Vargas. When my turn came, I sat facing Jane Pauley—a stunning woman.

When the camera light went on, she started asking me questions I had not been given ahead of time, and I answered as best I could. She asked how it was going? I told her we were receiving an overwhelmingly positive response from the people on welfare participating in the program. I actually had a letter from a welfare recipient who sent us $1 in the mail for the program. I read from some of our satisfaction survey results.

Then they switched to a live picture in Los Angeles with an individual from Catholic Charities. She also asked him how the program was going, and he said, "Not well at all." He went on to say how contracting out with a for-profit firm was a mistake and that our clients were not satisfied. Again, I was dumbfounded.

Catholic Charities had bid against MAXIMUS and lost the contract. This person from Catholic Charities had never been to any one of our five offices, for sure, because he would have seen the overwhelmingly positive response to the program. So I said to Jane Pauley live and on camera, "He is wrong—I don't know what else to say or where he got his information, but he is dead wrong."

Then there followed a commercial break, and she looked at me, not knowing what to do. I told her again off camera the person was wrong. After the break, we talked a bit longer, and the interview was over. She told me at least now we were on the "national agenda."

Fortunately, the Los Angeles Board of Supervisors felt I had done the best I could do under the circumstances. The lesson I learned again was never to underestimate our competitors. They can do anything at any time.

Business Week

Business Week also wanted to do a story on MAXIMUS since we were becoming pretty well known throughout the country. For some reason, the magazine was especially interested in a small contract we had in New Jersey. As I recall, we had the job of clearing the rolls of fraudulent claimants on the Supplemental Security Income (SSI) program, basically a disability program for the aged, blind, and disabled who are poor.

This was a one-of-a-kind contract for us. In other states, our job was to help recipients become eligible for SSI, so they would leave state-funded programs and move to federally-funded programs. The article was about how private firms could be tough on recipients who commit fraud and that private firms had a financial incentive to uncover such activities.

The *Business Week* photographer came to MAXIMUS headquarters in Virginia for a photo shoot. He asked me to lean forward from behind my desk with my fists down like a menacing CEO. I said to him, "I'm not going to do that." We're not enforcers for the government. We manage its programs. We help people. I pointed out our logo, "Helping Government Serve the People."

Well, he didn't know what to do, so we took some pictures outside the building. He eventually got some shots with which he was satisfied. Later, he called back to tell me the editor was really upset that I would not cooperate on the photo shoot. Again, the media had a preconception of what they wanted to communicate and tried to use me as their poster child.

In England, the media is much more partisan than in the United States. However, despite the claims, I believe the media is also extremely partisan in our country.

Newsweek

Don't underestimate the reach of the media, either. One week, *Newsweek* ran a short article on MAXIMUS that included my picture. I remember going through O'Hare Airport a couple of days later. Five or six people came up to me while I was changing planes and commented they knew me from somewhere but didn't know where. Did I remember them? I didn't. I went on to my departure gate puzzled. I finally figured it out—they had seen my picture in *Newsweek*. Oh!

In general, the media presented special challenges, but we had professional staff who knew how to work with them. The media is a fact of life we learned to live with.

On to the next chapter where life really got interesting.

CHAPTER 26

DEALING WITH DISASTER

I hardly know where to begin. It seems I was always dealing with disaster in one form or another. MAXIMUS was an honest company. We were a competent company, but it seemed from my perspective, we were always in trouble with somebody.

When the unions weren't making up stories about us, our competitors and the media were. When they weren't, aggressive prosecutors wanted nothing less than to land a for-profit company for graft and corruption. We were investigated almost every year by one organization or another. As I've said, MAXIMUS was never indicted, much less convicted, for any wrongdoing while I was CEO.

What follows are some nightmare stories MAXIMUS went through and somehow came out stronger on the other side. Someone called it "character building."

Mississippi Child Support

MAXIMUS won a major contract to operate the Mississippi Child Support Enforcement Program statewide. This was a major leap for child support enforcement privatization—an entire state! At the time,

MAXIMUS was responsible for enough child support cases to be the eighth largest program in the country. This new contract would put us way over the top.

The privatization contract was the idea of Republican Governor Kirk Fordice, a businessman who believed government should be more effective and efficient. His Human Services Director, Gregg Phillips, was solidly behind the governor.

Unfortunately, the legislature was largely Democratic and vigorously opposed the governor. In addition, the unions were involved. You wouldn't guess government unions were strong in Mississippi, but they were. When we brought our startup team to Jackson, we were warned to stay away from the windows in the hotel. There was a threat of snipers! We were being threatened! Gregg Phillip's wife was run off the road as a message to everyone. This union bullying was getting personal. Our opponents were warning us, and in Mississippi, you had better listen.

Regardless of the threats, we pressed forward. Again, we could not shy away from a major opportunity because there was a survival risk, literally. We started by taking over the Jackson and Vicksburg Child Support Enforcement Programs. The battle continued whether to allow MAXIMUS to privatize the rest of the state.

We opened the new offices, and did an excellent job. We absorbed the existing, unionized government workers and trained them in the MAXIMUS way. We provided our new staff with computers and training by experienced managers. We gave them goals and rewards for achieving the goals. They loved it, and child-support collections soared skyward.

After some six months, a Legislative Audit Committee visited our offices while I happened to be there working with our employees. The Audit Committee told me and other MAXIMUS management to leave the building while they interviewed our staff. The committee stayed in the building for a couple of hours meeting with all our employees. After they left, I assembled our staff and asked what happened?

The staff told me the committee wanted to know what it was like to work for MAXIMUS. They told the committee that they were much happier working for MAXIMUS than for the government. The committee pointedly asked one female employee whether she wanted to go back to the government. She asked them, "Would you go back to black and white TV?" Clearly, we did right by our employees.

One committee member asked another employee if I was a Democrat or a Republican. She said I was both. "He's a Democrat because he likes to help people, and he's a Republican because he makes money doing it." Never thought of it that way.

Nonetheless, the battle went on since the legislature had to approve the governor's budget each year. Each year we were in danger of losing our contract. One of the unstated problems was that many men in the legislature owed child support. The last thing they wanted was an aggressive private company forcing them to pay. We had lists printed of legislators who owed child support and made sure we did nothing beyond the ordinary to collect child support from them.

Nevertheless, the cascade of lies about MAXIMUS persisted. We tried to work with the press to counter the lies, but the press loved the confrontation between the governor, MAXIMUS, and the legislature. We were continually in the *Clarion Ledger*, the Jackson daily newspaper. During budget hearings, MAXIMUS was the prime topic of debate. We had stories in the paper on a daily basis, and there were no less than six political cartoons on the editorial page of MAXIMUS fighting with the legislature.

The governor wanted to fight back. Gregg Phillips, the Human Services Program Director, instructed us to hire political activists to help generate more public support for privatization. We hired lobbyists and campaign professionals to organize call-ins to the central switchboard of the state Capitol. The calls proclaimed the benefits of MAXIMUS and overloaded the switchboard for days. We hired professionals who brought in demonstrators by the busload in the middle of the day to protest in front of the Capitol.

We bought TV ads and flooded the airways with videos of the advantages of privatization with real stories. We did everything we were told to do by our state project officer. It was fun, but to no avail. The legislature was ultimately successful since it controlled the budget.

When Democrat Ronnie Musgrove was elected governor, the project was returned to the government unions, and the performance of the program sagged dramatically. Amazingly, no one cared. Today Mississippi privatizes only the legal components of the program.

Sometimes in privatization—maybe very often—the good guys lose.

West Virginia

Another major shock to MAXIMUS occurred in West Virginia in the early 1990s. We hired a free-lance consultant by the name of Kenneth Roberts to market child welfare systems for us in the Southeastern United States. He applied for the job; we reviewed his resume; and we interviewed him in our Virginia offices. He seemed like a decent fellow with the right qualifications, so we hired him.

He lived in Charleston, West Virginia, and promised to visit other states in his multistate area to advise us of plans by states to procure child-welfare systems. We paid him monthly to be part of our intelligence network. This was a typical deal in our business.

Sure enough, after about six months, an opportunity arose to bid on a child welfare system. It happened to be in West Virginia. Roberts sent us a draft RFP on which to comment. States sometimes issued a draft RFP to receive private industry input for their procurements. The potential bidders would ask questions and make suggestions, and the state would revise the RFP based on the input. MAXIMUS commented on the RFP and sent our comments back through Roberts.

States usually hold bidders' conferences immediately after the revised RFP is released to clarify any further ambiguities. When the bidders' conference was announced, we decided to send one of our full-time employees to attend. To our surprise, Roberts was leading the bidders' conference! Normally a government official runs the bidders' conference. When we confronted Roberts afterward, he said he did it as a favor to his former government client, who was sick and could not attend.

Nonetheless, we were suspicious, and we had our attorney in Charleston bring Roberts into his office and grill him extensively. After a couple of hours, Roberts admitted he was the government employee responsible for the procurement. Wow!

We consulted further with our attorney, and on his recommendation, sent a letter to the Secretary of the Department in West Virginia responsible for child welfare. We laid out our story of how we had hired Kenneth Roberts in good faith and only the day before found out he was actually a government employee. We wanted to report him for disciplinary action by the Department.

In the same letter, we asked if MAXIMUS could still bid on the contract. In a conversation with our attorney, we were told by the Department to go ahead and submit a bid. So we did.

Within a week after the bid was submitted, we found out the FBI was investigating MAXIMUS for bribing a government official. We were incredulous! The *Charleston Gazette* carried the story. One of our competitors, a division of Lockheed Martin, copied the story and sent it to every Child Support Director in the United States. This is the same company we later sued for tortious interference on another contract. Nevertheless, Lockheed's actions were perfectly legal since the story was in the public record.

What made matters worse was Kenneth Roberts swore in a plea bargain arrangement with the US Attorney that MAXIMUS staff knew all along he worked for the government. The US Attorney was interested in a big fish—MAXIMUS—not a small fish—Roberts. So the FBI came after us with guns blazing, well, almost blazing.

I traveled to Charleston to vet and then hire the law firm of Jackson & Kelly. They assigned a former US Attorney, Warren Upton, working for them to defend us. We thoroughly explained what happened in a seventy-page rebuttal, and fortunately, were able to attach relevant documents to back up our story. We also sent the seventy-page rebuttal to every Child Support Director in the United States and so remained in good stead with them.

The case dragged on for months and then a year, with endless interrogatories and questioning by the FBI. We ultimately agreed to testify before a grand jury without guarantee of immunity—very unusual—but we had to assert our innocence.

MAXIMUS was eventually cleared by the FBI. Kenneth Roberts went to jail for six months. Much later, we received a letter from our attorney explaining he had been notified "the United States Attorney's Office for the Southern District of West Virginia had closed its investigative file on Maximus, Inc."

In the end, we spent over $1 million in legal fees in our defense and expended hundreds of person hours cooperating with the investigation. Interestingly, this case never went away—the unions always used it to show the evils of a company like MAXIMUS. They didn't care about the facts.

So what did we learn from this experience? I am sad to say this, but I am sorry we reported Roberts. *We should have terminated his employment, not bid on the West Virginia contract, and gone away silently—no harm done.* By reporting him, we brought the house down on ourselves.

Sacramento, California

As told in the Prologue, the California Senate subpoenaed me to appear in Sacramento before the Senate Committee on Budget and Fiscal Review on May 31, 1989. I was to answer its questions about the Los Angeles GAIN contract. I was told later I was the first person subpoenaed by the California Senate in over ten years. The contract for the first privatization of social welfare programs was on the line.

As you read, the gallery was there for a public execution, which did not occur. Instead, the audience all heard how MAXIMUS was indeed qualified to win the contract and carry out the assignment of managing the GAIN Program. Nonetheless, the hearing was harrowing and made a permanent impression on me.

At the end of the hearing, the Senator and I were relieving ourselves in the men's room. I mentioned that this was the second pissing contest of the day, and he laughed. We bonded that day in some mysterious way.

Within a month, Senator Greene came to our Figueroa Office in Los Angeles. There, I suggested he randomly select a MAXIMUS case manager and ask anything he wanted. The case manager he selected was Akbar Piloti, who I did not know at the time. Senator Greene also talked to some recipients, and over the course of an hour, observed what was going on.

After he was done, he posed for a picture with Eddy Tanaka, head of the Department of Public Social Services, Gill Fernandez, our Figueroa Office Director, and me.

Akbar Piloti, a refugee from Afghanistan, later rose to become a Group President of MAXIMUS, in charge of thousands of people. He is still at MAXIMUS today. Akbar's rise demonstrates how we could rapidly promote capable people in the private sector and take them as far as they could go. *This could never have happened in government.*

Connecticut Child Care

The character of a company is not revealed by its behavior when all is going well, but rather by what it does when all hell is breaking loose. DVM

The State of Connecticut issued an RFP in early 1997 to centralize the management of its Child Care Program statewide. The program had been operating on a regional basis by state employees. As a result, the central office did not have much visibility or control over what was going on in the hinterlands. This RFP called for a privatization contract, where private sector workers performed case management and financial payment activities.

Apparently, a large number of fraudulent claims from child care providers were being paid since there was no centralized controls. Child care program costs had jumped in Connecticut from $44 million to $72 million in just two years. The state had to do something.

In the RFP, the state estimated that the winning contractor would receive 5,000 calls a week on a toll-free hotline and process 2,000 forms a month. We analyzed the workload and proposed a staff of sixty-two persons to do the job. MAXIMUS won the competition for the contract.

We had six months to develop the automated system for the project. The system would handle the processing of child care applications and the payment of the providers who had given the care. Since this was the first time any such activity had ever been centralized or privatized, there was much work to do. But MAXIMUS was undaunted.

Unfortunately, we had trouble developing the system. We lost some of the programming work two weeks before going live in September 1997. The system was not backed up, despite our policy to do so. This failure caused a massive flurry of activity as we tried to catch up. Recall the six stages of system development?

MAXIMUS was about a week behind with the system when the program went live in one "big bang." We transitioned from a regional operation to a statewide operation all at once. Anyone who has worked in such transitions knows that they are all hugely problematic.

My wedding date had been set well in advance for November 1, 1997, about a month and a half after the start of the project. Fortunately—or unfortunately—Donna and I took off to New Zealand for a three-week honeymoon. I knew MAXIMUS was having problems in the project, but I had no idea how severe they were.

Donna and I arrived in Los Angeles the day before Thanksgiving and checked into our Bel-Air hotel room at nine p.m. I turned on the TV and saw MAXIMUS on CNN Headline News under attack for completely mismanaging the Connecticut Child Care Program. Talk about a shock! I immediately made reservations to go to Hartford and made phone calls to my top people.

The day after I arrived in Hartford, a story appeared on the front page of the *Hartford Courant*—"CEO Leaves Honeymoon Boudoir to Rescue Project." Well, I didn't know what to say…"Anything for the project?"

The problems MAXIMUS was having were not limited to being behind in developing the system. Instead of receiving 5,000 calls a week as stated in the RFP, we were receiving 18,000 calls a week! Because our current staff couldn't handle the call volume, the problem became exponentially worse. People who could not get through on the first call, dialed again and again, clogging the lines even more—like a panic for the exits. Nobody got through.

As a result, child care providers weren't being paid; welfare recipients who had been hired by employers around the state had to quit their jobs to take care of their children and were forced back on welfare. It was a terrible mess! The *Hartford Courant*, the *New York Times,* and state politicians were blasting MAXIMUS daily. Protesters demonstrated outside our office. It was mayhem, and we were losing lots of money.

And to top that off, recipients were coming directly to our offices for help. Our offices were not designed with a reception room for recipients; we were supposed to be a central-processing facility. The office was crammed with people and with babies crying in the halls. I still remember seeing a little boy in our office peeing against the wall because he couldn't find the bathroom.

I immediately began hiring more staff and adding major expansions to the phone system. I also rented more office space—thankfully, it was available—and bought more computers, desks, and other equipment. The staff went from 62 to over 190 in two months—this all before we were able to bring the program under control. The Department issued a press release in the middle of December citing considerable progress by MAXIMUS. We didn't solve the problem until January. Of course, we were $3.2 million in the hole by then.

I knew not to ask the state for more money during the crisis, even if it was not all our fault. After all, the state had significantly underestimated the workload. We didn't object at first when the state refused to pay us—even for the workload specified in the contract. MAXIMUS received no payments at all for three months!

My strategy was to fix the problem at any cost, and then when the program was under control, try to negotiate a fair payment for MAXIMUS. *I had no leverage with the Department while the program was broken.*

When I finally met with the state project officer and asked for more money, she said no. She said the problem was caused by MAXIMUS since we should have anticipated the workload. I said we relied on the RFP; we had no experience with the Connecticut Child Care program. She wasn't listening.

In a subsequent private meeting, she told me, "In politics, perception is reality, and the perception is that MAXIMUS caused the problem." She said MAXIMUS was not going to receive any additional money to administer the program. I was speechless—for about two seconds. Then I told her, "Valerie, *in business, money is reality.* And if you don't pay us, we will give you back the program to run yourselves." This was the rare situation in which we had to stand up for our rights.

There followed some very intense and heated negotiations. I met with the Department Secretary and the Assistant Attorney General of the State. I told them they had to pay us for the extra work, and they refused. The Assistant Attorney General told me we had a contract, and he was going to enforce it. I told him there was no contract because they breached it when they didn't pay us. I did this on advice of counsel, by the way.

I said at the meeting, "We are turning the lights out at five p.m. and shutting down." We wanted to be paid for all the extra staff required to operate the program properly. I pulled an envelope from my suit breast pocket and told them this letter notifies you of your breach of contract and of our departure. It was five minutes to five p.m. When the Assistant

Attorney General saw the letter, he realized I wasn't bluffing—and I wasn't. They agreed to split the additional costs with MAXIMUS.

Unfortunately, we never got back on a good footing with the department, despite our heroic efforts and losses to ensure their program was well managed. They chose another company to run the program after our contract term ended. Incidentally, the other company didn't last very long.

The lessons were—negotiate from strength—and a bad experience will always come back to haunt you, regardless of outcome. I am pleased to report we went on to manage other state Child Care Programs successfully elsewhere. *However, when you have a showdown at high noon with a client, you lose, no matter how right you are.*

New York City

In 2000, MAXIMUS was caught in a bitter political crossfire in New York City that was almost our undoing. Again, we experienced the vulnerable position a for-profit company has managing a government welfare program.

Rudy Giuliani was a great mayor. He wanted to break the hold of non-profit organizations on the welfare-to-work program contracts in the city since the organizations were not very effective. He decided to put the contracts out for competitive bid. This intent was well advertised in advance. Since MAXIMUS was one of the prominent welfare-to-work companies in the United States, we, of course, were interested.

We called on the NYC Human Resources Administration, the welfare department where we had successfully provided consulting services earlier in our history. We asked to have a marketing meeting with some of their top people to find out what their thinking was and to give them ours. This practice was common for all firms.

We logged into their visitors register and met with some top officials for about a half hour. Most government officials meet with private contractors, so they could maintain interest in their programs and collect ideas on how to be innovative. The nonprofit organizations were always meeting inside the Human Resources Administration building since they had contracts with the Department.

Several months later, the RFP came out, and we bid on it. Well—good or bad—MAXIMUS won $104 million in contracts that the nonprofits lost. We were very happy. Then pandemonium struck!

The nonprofits complained stridently and bitterly to the city politicians, and the politicians started investigations. Politics in New York City is unbelievable, worse than Los Angeles. This was during the time when Rudy Giuliani was planning to run for the US Senate against Hillary Clinton. He was also a political enemy of the city's Democratic Controller, Alan G. Hevesi.

To gain political leverage against the mayor, Hevesi claimed there was corruption involved in awarding MAXIMUS the contracts. All manner of wild accusations were thrown around about how we had unfair access to the Human Resources Administration staff. This accusation was completely false; as I mentioned, the nonprofit organizations even had offices in the Department! Regardless, the nonprofits kept fueling the bonfires.

Then, of all things, it turned out in Wisconsin that MAXIMUS had hired the father of Jason Turner, the head of the Human Resources Administration. I checked into the rumor, and it was true—we needed a person to work on our prison release program in Wisconsin, and this man was recommended. He was the only qualified person our people could find. We were paying him about $25,000 per year.

Then the heat really got intense. The *Village Voice* went berserk; the *New York Times* started investigating, and there were articles on MAXIMUS every other day. I asked to meet with the editorial board of the *New York Times*, but was denied. I talked to its reporters at length, trying to explain our side of the story. We were guilty in their minds—when in fact, we were not guilty.

Inspired by Yogi Berra, I commented to one *New York Times* reporter that "MAXIMUS may have made some mistakes, but we didn't do anything wrong." It fell on deaf ears.

Hevesi was continually saying what a bad company MAXIMUS was. We never told him we were a key subcontractor working on his City Financial Management System (as the result of an acquisition). We never brought up that MAXIMUS Fleet Software was used for maintaining all the vehicles in the NYPD, NYFD, and the Sanitation Department. Nor did we mention MAXIMUS was managing the New York City Medicaid Managed Care program. We were a major contractor supporting the city, but we couldn't say anything.

In a strange twist to the story, one of our employees was a good friend of Hevesi's wife. Our employee related to one of my managers that she had been invited to dinner at their home and mentioned she was working for MAXIMUS. When Hevesi heard this, he reportedly told her, "MAXIMUS was not really a bad company; it was all politics." The story is hearsay, but I believed it.

To Giuliani's credit, he supported Jason Turner and the MAXIMUS contract 100 percent. He even wrote about the confrontation in his book, *Leadership*, published two years later. There was a court battle between Giuliani and Hevesi over who was authorized to register the MAXIMUS contract, which eventually went to the New York Appellate Court. Giuliani won. MAXIMUS was eventually allowed to work on the contract.

We were investigated by the Inspector General of the federal Department of Health and Human Services, the US Attorney for the Southern District of New York, and the New York City Inspector General. We were on the hot seat, to be sure. Everything that had happened in West Virginia came out in the newspapers, and we were allegedly guilty again.

I hired a team of crisis management consultants to help us with the problem. At one point, we thought MAXIMUS would be on *60 Minutes* with Mike Wallace; that's how far the media had exaggerated the situation. The crisis management consulting firm staged mock interviews with me, with one of them playing the role of Mike Wallace.

The videotapes surprised me. I looked very defensive, and therefore, very guilty. I was trying to set the record straight, yet I didn't seem credible. I was too serious. Instead, they taught me to be much more conversational. "Come on, Mike—you know this is political." "It's obvious we got caught in the crossfire between Clinton and Giuliani running for the Senate."Also, "We're a for-profit company in the welfare business—we're a great foil to use against the Mayor," etc.

Anyway, the battle went on and on. MAXIMUS was initially barred from bidding on additional contracts in New York City, pending outcome of the investigations. Moreover, we had much explaining to do to our other government clients. The MAXIMUS contract was ultimately terminated early for convenience by the Bloomberg administration because of the continuing controversy.

Here is a quote from the *New York Times* some nineteen months later that sums up the outcome.

> The substance of the cover-up charge by Mr. Hevesi yesterday returns to a 19-month-old argument between Mr. Giuliani and the comptroller over a $104 million

contract that the Giuliani administration wanted to give to a Virginia-based company to help welfare recipients find jobs.

Early last year, Mr. Hevesi accused Jason A. Turner, commissioner of the Human Resources Administration, of breaking city rules by showing favoritism to Maximus Inc., the bidder on the welfare-to-work contract. Mr. Hevesi initially blocked the contract, but the mayor sued and a state appellate court ultimately sided with the mayor, concluding that there was no evidence of corruption.

No evidence of corruption! Why were millions of dollars spent investigating us? Why were we denied a $104 million contract?

What did we learn? There is nothing you can do about politics. It goes with the territory. So we had to make sure MAXIMUS was squeaky clean because we would inevitably be investigated with a microscope—and then with a proctoscope.

Wisconsin W-2 Program

Even when the politicians leave you alone, the media and the unions go after you. The media doesn't like "thumb sucker" stories—do-good kind of things. They love scandals and corruption to report on—and the bigger the person or company, the more they feed on it. And the unions—well, I have covered them before.

MAXIMUS won a major watershed contract in Milwaukee to manage its Wisconsin Works program (W-2) in a portion of the city. This was an effort by the state to privatize the program since it had been operated so poorly by city government employees.

The rationale for having a private contractor manage the program was that the private contractor could be held accountable for meeting goals and could be fired and replaced if the goals were not met. Moreover, the private contractor could be paid based on reasonable costs—and any costs deemed excess, disallowed. This gave the state much more control over the private contractor than over the city employees. Sound familiar?

We met with the state at the beginning of the contract. They encouraged us repeatedly to "think outside of the box." Be innovative—do things the government can't do. We loved to hear that—that is exactly what MAXIMUS was about; that is what the private sector was about. So we did.

We held an off-site meeting at a hotel outside Milwaukee with some of our top welfare-to-work people across the country and came up with several great ideas. One was to bring in a successful African-American (Melba Moore, a Broadway singer who had reportedly once been on welfare in Milwaukee) and have her give motivational talks to welfare recipients.

We paid to bring her in from New York City. She performed a brief concert for the recipients, which showcased Melba's talents, and then gave her motivational talk. The recipients loved it. We also enjoyed rave reviews from our state contract handlers.

To further motivate recipients, we cut out paper stars for each welfare recipient finding a job and hand printed their first names on the stars. We then hung the stars along the ceiling where other recipients were receiving job training. We felt it would be great encouragement for the others to see how many of their peers had actually found jobs.

Milwaukee is a very liberal town, and the media must have hated for-profit companies. Incidentally—we took this job at no profit, and I think MAXIMUS still operates the program at no profit.

Anyway, one day the *Milwaukee Journal Sentinel* prints a page one headline: "MAXIMUS Goes Fishing on Tax Payer Money." The state had performed an audit of our expenses and noted we had bought fishing line without providing any justification. We bought the fishing line from a petty cash account and, therefore, had not recorded its purpose. The paper interpreted that we had bought the line for fishing gear and charged it to the state. Instead, the fishing line was used to hang the stars on the ceiling of our offices.

The state had no financial procedures manual to explain how MAXIMUS or any of the other privatization contractors were to account for their expenses. We did not justify petty cash expenses for the federal government, so we naturally thought we didn't have to justify petty cash expenses for Wisconsin. Wrong!

Even though we provided justifications later to the state, the media wasn't interested. Moreover, the unions and the investigative journalists knew nothing about government accounting—or at least they acted as if they knew nothing. MAXIMUS was extensively criticized for marketing expenses, which, subject to certain restrictions, are allowable expenses in reimbursing for company overhead in all government contracts, regardless of level. There are no restrictions on how our profits can be spent.

That article was like blood in the water. The *Milwaukee Business Journal* became involved—why I don't know—I thought it was pro-business. News reports came out that MAXIMUS had gone on vacation (the hotel) at taxpayers' expense and had entertainment brought in (Melba Moore) to entertain its staff at taxpayers' expense. The pounding went on. The state people, who knew what we had done with their blessing, did not come to our rescue. Nor did we point a finger at them in our defense.

The unions weighed in as well. Here's a short excerpt from just one article—this one was in the January-February, 2002, *Journal of Poverty*

Law and Policy. The article, entitled "Wisconsin Works – for Private Contractors, That Is," was written by Karyn Rotker (a staff attorney for the ACLU of Wisconsin Foundation), and Jane Ahlstrom and Fran Bernstein (both employed by the American Federation of State, County, and Municipal Employees).

This article, and many others like it, was written by the unions opposing privatization. The article was completely misleading. Here is one quote:

> To date, the state has not fined any agency for failure to serve a client. To the contrary, Maximus, which admitted that it misspent millions of tax dollars, received not a "three strikes" sanction but a renewed multimillion-dollar contract. As its "sanction," the state only required Maximus to repay the amount of the disallowed expenditures and to make a restitution of an additional $500,000 out of the agency's $4.4 million profit.

These statements are totally irresponsible, but they are not atypical of the unions.

MAXIMUS never admitted it misspent millions of tax dollars, because we didn't. We were not required to make restitution of $500,000; we did it voluntarily to show good faith. And we did not make $4.4 million in profits; we bid the contract at no profit.

I know because I was personally involved in this contract and made all the major decisions. In fact, this was the first and last time we bid a contract at no profit. Because the W-2 contract was so prestigious, we knew it would help us win many other contracts, which it did.

The telling statement in the quote, by the way, is that the state renewed our contract; in fact, the state later expanded it.

MAXIMUS management staff were also called before Wisconsin state legislative committees and berated in public: "How could you dare violate the public's trust? You must be ashamed of yourselves." They proclaimed MAXIMUS had handed out free golf balls at the National Governors Conference held in Wisconsin that year, as if it were a high crime. The legislators didn't understand government accounting either.

Moreover, we also had one particularly articulate detractor, an investigative journalist by the name of Jason DeParle. I spent at least three hours with him one afternoon explaining all about MAXIMUS and our Milwaukee project. He didn't hear a word I said. He later wrote articles and a book about welfare reform and continually castigated MAXIMUS. He even claimed our case managers were on crack cocaine among other charges. The extent of his distortions goes unmatched in our history. He reminded me of Michael Moore of documentary fame.

We definitely had start-up problems on this contract, but Jason took them to the extreme. We required longer than customary to indoctrinate the staff into our culture and to understand the communities in which we operated. We were slow in achieving the results we were striving for, but we ultimately became the top performer in Milwaukee. As proof, as I mentioned, when the state decided to consolidate regions in Milwaukee, they awarded MAXIMUS an additional region. I should have sued Jason for slander. He was particularly invidious. In my opinion, there are many journalists who wear the cloak of truth when in fact they are distorting the truth for their own gain.

It was all media, union, and political theater. We were automatically guilty before we could tell our side of the story—no one wanted to hear it anyway.

The lesson—as a for-profit company managing a welfare program—expect to get beaten up unfairly. Oh—and make sure you provide written justification for all your petty cash expenses!

MAXIMUS Compliance Program

Because of all these investigations and other problems, we had to initiate our own compliance program. So we hired an ex-FBI agent, Dennis Hoffman, to lead our compliance efforts. Dennis and his staff were dispatched every time we heard something that might indicate a problem. *We provided a toll-free, anonymous hotline to our staff to call in any suspected problem areas.*

We received a number of calls—the vast majority complaining about a supervisor the employee caller did not like. I remember one call that uncovered a problem in our California project to inform Medicaid recipients of their rights. This was a program where we sent people out to all the counties in the state to hold meetings with recipients. One of our workers was accepting money to allow recipients to skip the meetings. She was quickly fired.

In another case in New Jersey in 2002, eight of our employees were indicted for fraudulently enrolling themselves in the state's health insurance plan for children and families, even though they were not eligible. Since they entered the data into the computer for other eligible families, they decided to enter themselves as well. MAXIMUS, as a company, was not guilty, but we then had to start screening all the social security numbers of recipients receiving benefits against all our employee social security numbers to make sure this didn't happen again.

When you have five thousand people working for you, there is bound to be trouble. A city of five thousand has a police department to insure compliance with the law. We needed our own "police department," as well.

I am sorry to say there were other lesser nightmare stories that will go untold. But you can see MAXIMUS ran the gauntlet on its rise to prominence. That's why, in hindsight, the growth seems to have occurred at impossible odds. How could we have been one of the fastest growing public companies in America when all this was going on? I don't know.

As I said in the beginning of this book, MAXIMUS was founded to reform government, not make a lot of money. Our detractors would have you believe MAXIMUS was not successful in reforming government. As I relayed earlier, the irony is that our unintended spectacular financial success proved we were helping government overcome its limitations. This happened despite all the obstacles thrown in our way.

For twenty-nine years, I had a cartoon under my desk blotter that kept things in perspective. The scene showed seven businessmen in suits around a conference table, with a picture window overlooking a lawn with large trees. The caption said, "We could streamline the organization, or step up our advertising, or issue new stock. But since it's such a lovely day, why don't we just go out of business?" So if it really became too much to bear, I could always quit. But it never did.

CHAPTER 27

LAWSUITS AD INFINITUM

I f this were not enough, we also had problems with a continual barrage of lawsuits. Lawsuits come in all shapes and sizes. The best idea is to avoid litigation altogether. Several thousand years ago, Sun Tzu said the best battles are those that are won without being fought. The larger and more profitable companies are targets for lawsuits. Unfortunately, we gained much experience working with attorneys as MAXIMUS grew. I'll describe a few examples in this chapter and draw some lessons learned from them.

Promised Bonuses

The first lawsuit we had in the very early days of MAXIMUS was a simple one about a bonus allegedly promised an employee. The employee asserted he was not paid a $25,000 bonus promised to him, and so he sued MAXIMUS.

We had not been sued before, so this was a new experience. Rather than pay him off, I decided we would go to court and contest the claim, even if it cost more than the bonus. We would learn something.

MAXIMUS had not promised him a bonus. There may possibly have been some speculation about a bonus if a sale was made, but no promise.

The employee said a vice president promised him the bonus, which I approved. Our policy manual clearly stated that only the CEO could approve a bonus, so the employee had to claim I had.

His attorney put me on the stand. He started grilling me about the bonus policy and how it worked. He then asked me directly how I was so sure I had not approved the bonus to his client. A mistake.

I paused and said, "Because it would have been bigger than my bonus." Well, the jury took immediate notice and understood this was a bogus claim. End of lawsuit. The jury ruled for MAXIMUS.

Racketeering

MAXIMUS won a child support project in Arizona to reconcile child support payments like the one in Billerica, Massachusetts. This project is also the same type we had earlier in Tennessee.

Since considerable training is required to perform financial reconciliation work, we offered our staff in Massachusetts the opportunity to move to Arizona on a similar project. Many accepted our offer, and the Arizona project progressed nicely.

When the project started winding down, though, we realized we would have to let staff go. There was no additional financial reconciliation work in sight. Apparently, sixteen of the staff got together and went to an attorney. They claimed they were due an "end of project" bonus that MAXIMUS allegedly had promised them. Moreover, they claimed the same thing had happened to them in Massachusetts. They were promised an "end of project" bonus that had never been given.

Because this allegedly happened in two different states, the employee's attorney sued MAXIMUS under the Racketeer Influenced and Corrupt Organization (RICO) statutes. There was a key loophole in the RICO statute that allowed the suit. The loophole was closed by legislation one week after the suit was filed against MAXIMUS. However, we had just missed the cutoff.

We researched all our training presentations, staff briefings, and Human Resources manuals for both projects, and there was no mention of an "end of project" bonus. We never had an "end of project" bonus, and there was no record of one anywhere.

Moreover, in their depositions, the plaintiffs did not agree on the amount of the bonus they were promised, nor when they were promised to receive the bonus. We had a very strong case, but because we were threatened with racketeering, I felt it was better to settle with the plaintiffs, and not take any risks. After all, MAXIMUS was a government contractor, and if we had been convicted of racketeering—even if innocent—we would have lost the ability to bid on future contracts, an unacceptable outcome. We settled—I thought it was worth it.

The opposing attorney, John Charland, took his share of the settlement and, I suppose, used it to recruit more MAXIMUS staff in Arizona. He apparently convinced them he could settle again for more money. In addition, he asked for the names of all our staff in Massachusetts, so he could contact them, as well. And he filed for a class-action suit to cover all MAXIMUS employees he could not find, which made the problem significantly larger than the one I had originally settled.

Fortunately, the loophole in the RICO statute was closed, so it was a civil matter now, not criminal. That changed the whole picture. We could lose a civil case and not have it affect our other business. I told our attorney— Jeff Messing—that he had an unlimited budget to win the case. I didn't care if it cost $1 million in legal fees. MAXIMUS was not going to be extorted again because it would lead to even more extortions. We fought the case for two more years, going through many appeals and all manner of motions. Our opponent was smart and tenacious.

I am pleased to report in the end, MAXIMUS was exonerated, and the plaintiffs were deemed to have filed a frivolous lawsuit. We won a judgment against the plaintiffs! We garnished the plaintiffs' wages, even though many had left MAXIMUS. I made sure everyone in the company knew MAXIMUS was not an easy mark and would fight each frivolous suit to the maximum extent possible. John Charland learned a lesson, as well.

And I did fight every lawsuit that was egregious against us. But I continued to settle other smaller suits where it would have cost more to defend. During my term, MAXIMUS never lost a lawsuit filed against us, though we did settle many.

Securities Fraud

Having read this far, you know problems are always lurking nearby. I am telling the following story because it provided so many lessons and revelations, at least for me. And perhaps you will learn something useful too.

Right after going public, MAXIMUS found itself in a civil lawsuit for securities fraud by a former vice president. Ray Ruddy and I were named in the suit personally, so we were similarly charged. The vice president had resigned from the company some ten months before we went public. He claimed we deliberately hid from him our intent to go public. If he had known, he said he would have stayed at MAXIMUS and sold his stock at a much higher price. He claimed, therefore, we were guilty of securities fraud. At the time he resigned, we had no plans to go public. That decision wasn't even before me until well after he was gone. Nevertheless, he sued for $16 million.

I was amazed at how his attorney distorted reality, at least how I perceived it. It seemed the name of the game was to establish a theory—consistent with the provable facts—that supports your case—whether or not you believe the theory. In a civil case, you need only the preponderance of evidence—not evidence beyond a reasonable doubt, so the burden of proof is lower to make your case.

To make a long story short, our MAXIMUS attorneys recommended we stage several mock trials with different juries to predict how a jury would vote in an actual trial. We hired a company that did this as a business. We used one attorney to present our case, and another attorney to present our opponent's case, as we thought it would be presented.

Behind one-way mirrors, I watched the three different juries deliberate. It was fascinating! Members of one jury said I (Mastran) was a crook and typical of big business. Members in another jury room said the vice president was just grabbing for money and was a sore loser for leaving the company before the "big payday." Others said both sides were guilty. We could hear the questions they asked themselves and debated behind closed doors. Many of the questions stemmed from information they were not given in the attorney presentations. I was amazed at what members of the juries came up with.

The major lesson I learned was that in the absence of information, people substitute their own information based on their biases. If they were part of management in their current jobs, they tended to supply missing information that sided with management in the trial. If they were workers in their current job, they supplied the missing information to side with the vice president—a victim of a big corporation. Some people were neither on the side of big business or labor and tended to rely only on the facts presented.

We went through each jury deliberation and noted where people had substituted their biases for information not provided. *We then prepared to make sure the missing information would be provided during a real trial.*

At the conclusion of the mock trials, one jury voted for us, one jury voted for the vice president, and one jury was hung.

In the end, we settled. I was told that if the jury awarded the plaintiff even one dollar for his trouble, we would be guilty of securities fraud. It wasn't worth the chance.

Sexual Harassment/Hostile Workplace

As the size of MAXIMUS increased, we brought on more and more staff. Despite our training programs, we were sued by disgruntled employees who felt they had been subject to racial discrimination, sexual harassment, or a hostile workplace. As I covered earlier in the book, some of these claims were just the result of mistakes by management.

I mention a couple of the suits to show how ridiculous they can be. In a project in Sacramento, California, our staff were preparing for a visit by the state project officer. As mentioned earlier, we had a strict dress code that required a tie for all male employees.

The female project manager went around inspecting the attire of each employee. She saw one male employee with his tie askew, and she reached up and straightened it for him. Later, a sexual harassment suit was filed against MAXIMUS–not by the person whose tie was straightened, but by another male worker who said he suffered third party sexual harassment by observing it. Give me a break! When we told him we were going to fight him in court, he dropped the suit.

In our project in Milwaukee, we had a female worker who sued us for a hostile workplace. She complained she experienced migraine headaches because of florescent lights. We moved her to a private office and replaced the florescent lights with incandescent lights. She then complained she had to walk to the copy machine that again exposed her to florescent lights. When we refused to put the copy machine in her office, we were sued. We moved the copy machine next to her office, and she finally relented.

For a period of time, we had an average of thirty such lawsuits against us. As the company experienced more of these lawsuits, we established more and more policies and training programs to head off the more frivolous. In particular, we developed the Employee Rights Policy I covered earlier, and displayed it in every office. When the employees and their supervisors saw they had basic rights, the number of lawsuits started going down, and finally, we had no lawsuits for some time.

I have not included some of the more spectacular lawsuits against MAXIMUS to avoid any problems with unintended disclosures. Suffice it to say, our Harvard-educated, General Counsel, Dave Francis, was a very busy person, so you had best find a very good one. Thankfully, we did.

The best advice to our staff was to avoid lawsuits altogether. Emphasize training programs and implement policies and procedures to protect the company.

Virginia Supreme Court

Once in a while, we encountered a situation so egregious that we filed our own lawsuit. MAXIMUS competed with a division of Lockheed Martin for a Virginia child support program in Fairfax County, Virginia, where we were based. After an intense competition, the state notified MAXIMUS that we had been selected by the evaluation committee for award.

Lockheed immediately protested the selection, saying MAXIMUS had illegally influenced two members of the evaluation committee. The state then awarded the contract to Lockheed without informing us. When we found out the reason the contract had been awarded to Lockheed, we sued Lockheed for tortious interference. Lockheed caused us to lose the contract through false information. We had not influenced any members of the evaluation committee, and Lockheed staff knew it. There was nothing we could do to the state.

So the trial was held and witnesses clearly testified that Lockheed had falsely accused MAXIMUS. To our amazement, the trial judge dismissed the case in the middle of the trial in favor of Lockheed, saying we had not proved "malice." The judge said malice was required in tortious interference cases. Perhaps this occurred because Lockheed hired former Virginia Governor Mills Godwin, Jr. to represent it at the trial.

This ruling was so outrageous that we appealed to the Virginia Supreme Court. After a great deal of time, money, and effort, MAXIMUS was vindicated by the Supreme Court, which ruled the Circuit Court trial judge was in error. Malice was not required. MAXIMUS had helped establish case law in Virginia on tortious interference. To quote the court,

> Thus, to establish a prima facie cause of action in this case, Maximus was required to show that: (1) it had a contract expectancy; (2) Lockheed knew of the expectancy; (3) Lockheed intentionally interfered with the expectancy; (4) Lockheed used improper means or methods to interfere with the expectancy; and (5) Maximus suffered a loss as a result of Lockheed's disruption of the contract expectancy. *Maximus was not required to show malice or any other egregious conduct.* [Emphasis added]

So again, we went to trial to prove Lockheed committed tortious interference. In the end, we won nothing because the same trial judge reheard the case and again found for Lockheed for a different reason. The state stayed with Lockheed despite the ruling. We decided to throw in the towel. We lost the contract, the lawsuit, and a lot of money on legal fees. Recall, this was a lawsuit we initiated.

Even the US Supreme Court has judges with different ideological leanings, as do the lower courts. We experienced the same problem in New York City when the lower court judge ruled for the Democrats. The ruling was so outrageous it was appealed by Mayor Giuliani and won at the appellate level.

Sometimes it takes considerable effort to receive justice from the system. The lesson for us was, *Don't fight the system unless we are willing to go all the way to the end.*

CHAPTER 28

GOING PUBLIC

Some readers may be interested in the process of going public. MAXIMUS went public during the period when some of the disasters and lawsuits described in the last two chapters were going on.

Who Owned the Stock?

MAXIMUS was incorporated as a Subchapter S corporation to avoid double taxation. I was the majority stockholder, Ray Ruddy owned about 33 percent of the stock, and the rest of the staff owned 15 percent. Our stock was internally valued at "book value" or the liquidation value of the company. If granted the option, an employee could buy the stock at book value and then sell it back at book value when he or she left the company. Only employees could own stock. The employees' profit was the increase in book value between the time the stock was bought and when it was sold.

As mentioned before, we never took money out of MAXIMUS prior to going public other than our regular salaries and bonuses. The retained earnings truly reflected the value added during the period the stock was held by the stockholder. We did take money out to pay someone who left the company, but the money was his or hers already. It was a good system.

Courted by General Electric

In the summer of 1996, we received inquiries from General Electric that they might be interested in MAXIMUS. The negative media attention we were receiving did not bother them. GE owned a subsidiary company, Financial Guarantee Insurance Company (FGIC), which insured state, county, and municipal bonds. FGIC believed MAXIMUS could help state and local governments avoid defaulting on their bonds. We could operate programs for these governments, thereby making them more efficient and able to pay interest on their bonds. GE also saw how quickly MAXIMUS was growing and needed acquisitions to keep themselves growing—Jack Welch's style, you know.

It is amazing how intensely potential acquirers and investment bankers court owners of successful companies. They swarm you and fill your head with millions of dollars. This put visions of sugarplums into the heads of many of the key shareholders of MAXIMUS, who were also the key employees. It was always going on.

I didn't want to sell MAXIMUS because I didn't want to give up control. I was having too much fun running the company, despite our tribulations. I believed we had a lot more room to grow—we had just started privatizing government. There was no good reason to sell, and I couldn't imagine working for someone else. However, I felt an obligation to Ray Ruddy and the other shareholders to help them receive the true value for their stock. They wanted to sell MAXIMUS to the highest bidder.

As a result, I took the train to New York City with Ray Ruddy and met with the FGIC people. They seemed pleasant enough, but they did not understand our business in the slightest. We were naturally curious about how much they would offer, so we let the scenario play out. The more they learned about MAXIMUS, the more they were interested in buying us. Two of their financial analysts came to California in October to talk to me while I was working on a large contract. We had an undefined offer on the table of over $100 million, which ultimately went to $150 million.

Thinking about the offer nearly drove me crazy—I kept trying to do the right thing, but I really did not want to sell. My people were pressing me to sell, and the process dragged out for several months. Top people at GE called me and explained all the advantages of having GE behind MAXIMUS. In the end, I told them, "No thank you."

Instead, I asked Ray Ruddy to check out the investment bankers—let's see how they valued the company. If we went public, at least I would not be reporting to anyone else—we would still be in control. We met with Peter Pond and Brian Weber from Donaldson, Lufkin, and Jenrette (DLJ) at a restaurant in Tysons Corner, Virginia. They told us MAXIMUS was worth over $200 million.

The investment bankers saw the MAXIMUS story tied closely to the new federal legislation to overhaul welfare—The Personal Responsibility and Work Opportunity Reconciliation Act of 1996. Recall this legislation, commonly referred to as the Welfare Reform Act, allowed government to contract with private companies in the TANF Program. Since MAXIMUS's success in privatizing the Los Angeles GAIN program helped provide the impetus for this legislation, MAXIMUS would be a prime beneficiary.

DLJ's assessment made the decision to go public easier for us. I decided we should do so in December, 1996. A lot of preparatory work would be required.

Red Herring

Ray and I went to New York City to DLJ's offices on Park Avenue and began working on the Red Herring. The Red Herring is a document submitted by a company to the Securities and Exchange Commission (SEC) in order to have an Initial Public Offering (IPO). This is when the public buys your stock for the first time.

The Red Herring explains the company's basic business; the potential risks associated with that business; and the company's growth strategies, all with appropriate caveats. Past financials of the company are also included. The Red Herring is intended as a document that fairly and objectively informs prospective investors about the company.

We took a couple of months to assemble the document, working with accountants, attorneys, and bankers. I recall this process cost several hundred thousand dollars.

Investment bankers have a "sell side" and a "buy side." The sell side underwrites securities and raises money for companies like MAXIMUS. The buy side works with pension funds and other investors who buy these securities. There is often a "Chinese Wall" between the two sides. The "Chinese Wall" is an imaginary barrier that prevents one side of the business from talking to or learning about what the other side is doing.

We worked with analysts and people on the sell side to develop a slide-show presentation. We practiced presenting this to DLJ employees, who constructively criticized our performance. Once this process was completed, we went on a road show to meet with prospective investors.

The Road Show

The Road Show was a very tight schedule of meetings with mutual fund and hedge fund managers over an eight-day period. Meetings with these managers lasted for an hour or two. Lunches and dinners were sometimes scheduled, where Ray Ruddy and I met with five to twenty investors at a time. The drill was to give the slide show presentation and be open for questions. Sometimes we were forced to give an abbreviated presentation when the portfolio manager asked questions right away. It was a challenging and fun experience.

Ray and I traveled by private jet (leased for $25,000 a day) to reach all potential investors in the United States in the limited time allotted. I objected to the cost, but the bankers said it was worth it. Because of all the personal attention and private dinners, I gained ten pounds in that short time—my all-time high weight.

At the same time, PF Chang, Ralph Lauren, and Xoom were also going public, and we ran into them occasionally. We didn't have any polo shirts to give out, however.

In all, Ray and I gave fifty-five presentations throughout the United States and Europe. I had given the same presentation so many times I had it memorized. At the last presentation, in front of the Dreyfus Fund in New York City, something strange happened. I could hear myself speaking the words, and I could feel my mouth move, but I wasn't there. I was having an out-of-body experience. Very eerie! However, the presentation was a hit.

The road show experience was both exhilarating and harrowing. We wouldn't know whether or not particular managers would buy the stock. We could not discern their true level of interest. Ultimately, though, forty-eight of the fifty-five funds bought MAXIMUS stock. We were over-subscribed by a factor of three, or there were buy orders for three times the number of shares of stock we had for sale. The DLJ staff congratulated us on our performance.

Road Show Stories

Many interesting stories developed during the road show. The potential buyers vigorously challenged me and questioned my veracity. This was just part of the process. Here are a couple of the give-and-takes for illustrative purposes.

One noted fund manager in Los Angeles grilled me for about two hours in front of twenty of his staff. It was actually fun—like a sword fight—him thrusting and me parrying. I liked him, and I felt he was really getting good information by being so aggressive—he was smart and very fast. He must have liked the "give and take," as well, or he would not have let the discussion go on for so long. Finally, at the end, he asked me to give him one reason why he might not buy the stock. Clearly, in fun, I answered, "You're stupid." Everyone laughed. He liked the answer and signed up for 200,000 shares.

In another encounter in the Midwest, a fund manager kept asking me which of two MAXIMUS businesses—consulting or government operations—would I give up, if I had to give up one? I kept telling him that they were synergistic. The consulting business was a higher profit margin, lower revenue business; the government operations business (privatization) was a lower profit margin, higher revenue business. They fed off one another. Consulting recommended privatization, which taught us how to run the government program more efficiently. We could then consult with this added knowledge. Consulting also provided the additional cash flow needed for privatization.

Nonetheless, he kept pressing me. Finally, I told him his question reminded me of a story—I thought it was in the Bible—about an ass that was confronted by two equally high stacks of hay. In dithering between the two stacks, trying to decide which one to eat first, the ass starved to death. That seemed to satisfy him.

The point is you had to know your business and be honest. If you didn't or weren't, the portfolio managers would figure it out.

New York Stock Exchange Listing

We originally thought MAXIMUS would be listed on the NASDAQ, where the majority of new public companies are listed. However, the New York Stock Exchange called DLJ, and said they wanted MAXIMUS on their exchange. We were delighted because the NYSE had more history and seemed more prestigious.

MAXIMUS went public on Friday, June 13, 1997, under the symbol MMS. My father, my son, David, and soon-to-be wife, Donna, traveled with me to New York, the epicenter of world capitalism. We first had breakfast at the Exchange and then walked to the floor for the opening. It was a wonderful experience. MAXIMUS opened at seventeen and a quarter; I have the original chit used in the transaction.

In the fifteen years since going public, I am proud to say MAXIMUS stock never traded below its opening price. Although the price seemed to go in a sine wave for the longest time, despite our exponential growth, it worked its way upward. As of this writing, MMS trades over $57 a share and pays a dividend. The company stock has split two for one, so it's over $114 in old price terms.

Quarterly Analyst Calls

Every quarter, MAXIMUS was required to issue a financial statement. The company was literally under the microscope again, but from a different constituency. We scheduled conference calls every quarter, corresponding to the release of our earnings statements. My CFO would comment about the financial health of the company, and I would comment more on the business side. I made notes, naturally, to organize my thoughts.

I quickly found out the analysts overreacted to almost everything I said. They were skeptical, even though I was being as honest as I could be. If I indicated we were having a slight problem in New Jersey on a project, it would come across as an impending implosion of the company. The analysts seemed to magnify everything by tenfold or more. The stock would drop during and after the conference call, and everyone groaned.

I learned to write down my comments in advance and run them by my top people. By doing this, I received several different interpretations on what I was trying to say. It's amazing how ambiguous the English language can be. I often had to revise the comments until they were crystal clear and almost impossible to misinterpret.

Question-and-Answer Period

Then there was the question-and-answer period, which could not be scripted. We tried to anticipate the questions and develop scripts for the answers. However, we could never anticipate all the questions. Fortunately, I was a hands-on CEO and had a detailed knowledge of all our operations. For the most part, my CFO and I were able to answer analysts' questions and satisfy them.

I was often surprised at how the analysts focused on financial ratios and margins that I never bothered to track in managing MAXIMUS. They had financial models to keep updated, so they could forecast our earnings. I always wondered how they could forecast our earnings so far in the future, when we couldn't forecast a few quarters out.

There was one analyst, Bernie Picchi, at Lehman Brothers, who closely followed MAXIMUS. One time during a period of bad publicity, Bernie called me and said, as a courtesy, he was letting me know he was downgrading our stock. This meant he was moving it from a Buy to Neutral rating. We had experienced a good run up in stock price—we were about

$38 a share at the time. I said, "Bernie, it's fine with me. Go ahead and downgrade it."

He was astonished. He said no CEO whose stock he covered had ever agreed with a downgrade. I said I was just being honest, and he said he appreciated it. What good is it to have your stock overvalued in the market? Seems to me it only brings bigger problems. Later, I found out Bernie occasionally told this story when he gave speeches about being a stock analyst.

Financial Press

Contrary to the commercial media, the financial press was always good to MAXIMUS—a welcome change! I was interviewed in a friendly way by Maria Bartiromo on CNBC. She asked me why we were beating the likes of Lockheed Martin, MAXIMUS being a smaller company. I explained we were simply cheaper, with a lower overhead rate, and we had much more program expertise. I remember how hard it was to look directly into the camera lens without glancing off to the side.

The *Wall Street Transcript* also interviewed me. We had a large article in the publication. I was videotaped by Bloomberg's business arm for its private clients. In addition, the *Value Line Investment Survey* loved MAXIMUS.

The five financial analysts who covered us always spent a great deal of time on their reports—some as long as twenty pages—and did a fair job reporting on MAXIMUS. The financial press, however, was far more objective than commercial media. Their readership wanted hard news, not scandals.

The Ultimate Insider

I had "played" the stock market since high school. Even at West Point, I had a group of cadets investing in the market on my advice. It was great fun. I remember in the mid-1960s when the total volume traded on the NYSE was seven million shares. What a difference today!

For my master's thesis at Stanford in 1966, I wrote a paper on using subjective probability (Bayesian Statistics) to invest in the stock market. I received an A on the paper, and the professor encouraged me to continue expanding the concepts. I knew a lot about stocks and investing.

For ethical reasons, I never traded MAXIMUS for my own account while I was CEO, or since retirement. However, I was intensely interested in how the company was valued in the market since we had buyback programs, which I administered. Here is what I learned about stock prices.

I was the ultimate insider—I knew more about MAXIMUS than anyone on the planet. Over time, I realized the major influence on our stock price was the market as a whole. We were included in the Russell 2000 Index and the S&P SmallCap 600 Index. As these indices went up and down, so did MMS stock. *I also realized the price of MAXIMUS stock was uncorrelated with what was going on in the company.*

I remember when a particular analyst recommended that MAXIMUS stock be shorted (or sold first and bought back later) because it was allegedly going down to $12 per share. That person's assessment was totally wrong, but we couldn't say anything. She had no idea what she was writing about. Yet, obviously, it put pressure on the stock. That is another reason stocks go up and down—stock analysts.

The week-to-week and month-to-month trends in our stock price seemed to have nothing to do with the prospects for MAXIMUS. Stocks are driven ultimately by demand—and so it was the retail buyer and the mutual and hedge fund's immediate desire to put on or take off risk that drove the price of MAXIMUS stock up or down.

Working with the Board of Directors

By going public, we needed a Board of Directors. MAXIMUS attracted an excellent Board. All members were very accomplished people. The outside Directors when I was CEO included the following people:

- Four-Time Governor of Illinois—Jim Thomson

- EVP of $3 Billon Federal-Mogul—Paul Lederer

- CEO of Watson Wyatt Human Resources Consulting Firm— John Haley

- Secretary of US Veterans Administration—Jesse Brown (now deceased)

- Investment Banker/Venture Capitalist—Peter Pond

- Technology Consultant—Marilyn Seymann

- Mayor of Denver, Colorado—Wellington Webb.

With such a distinguished Board, I was not deprived of strong opinions or ready decision-makers.

After going public, I understood the Board was my boss, and I knew I had to take direction from them. I also knew they didn't believe I recognized that. I was not the majority owner of MAXIMUS anymore and was no longer entitled to make unilateral decisions on the direction of the company.

The Board had much to learn about our business and for about five years was not very active in the day-to-day operations of MAXIMUS.

When the Sarbanes-Oxley Act of 2002 came along, they felt more directly responsible for the company and began taking a more active role.

I was close to retirement, and the Board rightly felt the need for succession planning. Toward the end of my tenure, they created the position of Chief Operating Officer under me. Their choice, Lynn Davenport, Ray Ruddy's associate from Touche Ross, was given more and more responsibility. When, for all intents and purposes, Lynn no longer reported to me on day-to-day matters, I felt it was time to go. And so I did.

What I learned is the Board of Directors is very political—after all, most were politicians. Each member had been very successful in his or her individual careers, so naturally they thought they could run MAXIMUS as well as I could. After a couple of years after I left, they did, with a few big bumps along the way.

In hindsight, if I had wanted to retain control of MAXIMUS, I should not have recruited such a prominent board. And I should not have relinquished the Chairmanship. It was a good idea in those days to separate the position of CEO and Chairman—so we did. But truly, I wanted to retire. I'd seen and done a lot, and I needed to spend more time with my family and friends. I also wanted to pursue my new interest in music. Now I can do both—half of my time for each. Oops—I sneak golf in, as well!

PART VII:
CONCLUSIONS

Finally, it's time to close the book. These two chapters provide a glimpse at the future of privatization and then explain how government can rely on the private sector.

CHAPTER 29

FINAL THOUGHTS

By now, you should understand what I was trying to accomplish in this book. I wanted to show the limitations of government in administering social welfare entitlement programs. I also wanted to use the story of MAXIMUS to demonstrate the freedom and flexibility the private sector has to innovate, adapt, and solve problems much more readily than the government. In the process, I also hoped to explain how MAXIMUS became extremely successful as a business in reforming government. Finally, I wanted to show how difficult reforming government can be and why.

In this chapter, I present some final thoughts on what more privatization can do in social welfare entitlement programs.

Extend Privatization of TANF to Medicaid and Food Stamps

Despite all the progress that has been made, the vast majority of state and local governments still use government employees to determine eligibility for TANF, Medicaid, and Food Stamps. The principal reason is the interpretation of the law that prevents private contractors from determining eligibility for Food Stamps and Medicaid, even though they can determine eligibility for TANF and SCHIP—it makes no sense.

Determining eligibility for all three programs at once is the most cost-effective alternative.

Not only can hundreds of millions of dollars be saved, but also the recipients will be far better served, and the eligibility workers will experience much greater job satisfaction.

Reduce the Power of Government Employee Unions

Government employee unions are bankrupting state and local governments. Were it not for the unions, more government programs would have been privatized long ago. One option is to make union employees compete with the private sector in geographic regions of the state, county, or city and replace them if they are not performing. This will either improve their performance or deplete their ranks.

Another option is to privatize the programs and require the private contractor to absorb the employees as either union or nonunion workers. This worked well for MAXIMUS in Tennessee, Mississippi, and British Columbia. Again, there can be dramatic improvements in government performance.

Reexamine Recipient Fraud and Abuse

I have not discussed fraud and abuse in social welfare entitlement programs—yet it exists. I believe the extent of fraud and abuse is, at times, overstated in the media—much like everything is overstated by the media. At the same time, the problem often is understated by politicians—much like many problems are understated by politicians in office.

In entitlement programs for the poor and disadvantaged, there are many technical criteria for eligibility. If any of these technical criteria are not met, the case is deemed to be in error or fraudulent. Half the time it's the state or local government that makes the mistake and the other half, the recipient.

When it's the recipient's fault, the cause is often confusion over eligibility requirements. These mistakes occur largely due to language barriers or the technical nature of the requirement. However, in many cases the recipient is truly being fraudulent. And in many of those cases, the amount of real fraud is so small that many government officials don't think it's worth pursuing.

I have heard some government officials say that social welfare programs do not pay enough anyway, so why worry about fraud and abuse? What is the problem with having people who are ineligible receiving government benefits? The argument goes that they mostly are poor anyway and can use the money for shelter, food, or clothing or receive health care they otherwise wouldn't receive. There may be some merit to their arguments.

So I don't think much more effort than is currently expended is needed to contain recipient fraud and abuse, except perhaps in the disability programs. Though, anecdotally, there may be some egregious cases, overall there isn't much real money to be saved.

Agency error is another problem. Agencies deem families eligible who are not eligible and deny eligibility to families who are eligible. Agencies also make mistakes on the amount of the entitlement, especially when there is earned and unearned income in the case. Agency errors need to be better managed, and the private sector can help, especially when contracts have penalties for not doing so. While not much real money will be saved, program integrity will be restored, and recipients will be better served.

Focus on Provider Fraud and Abuse

Much more serious than recipient fraud and abuse is provider fraud and abuse. This abuse occurs mainly in health care programs but also in child care and to some extent in the Food Stamp Program. Government seemingly does not make economic decisions in controlling provider fraud and abuse. In most instances, the government doesn't do nearly enough to control it. The reason is these decisions are not driven by economics, but by political forces.

According to the federal Centers for Medicare and Medicaid Services (CMS), Medicaid fraud and abuse, alone, is costing Americans $30 billion every year. Recall that Medicaid is the program for the poor. And this fraud and abuse is coming largely from health care providers who fraudulently bill Medicaid for services never provided.

Medicare is the larger health care program for the elderly. I could find no estimates for the cost of fraud and abuse in Medicare—a telling result by itself. Fraud and abuse in Medicare probably costs significantly more than in Medicaid. The federal government does not spend nearly enough to control fraud and abuse cost effectively in either program. Spending more could result in significant savings.

The private sector could be employed much more extensively to root out provider fraud and abuse in Medicaid and Medicare. Much more needs to be done, and tens of billions could be saved.

I mentioned the Child Care Program in Connecticut saw huge increases in child care costs, though minuscule compared to Medicare and Medicaid. Welfare recipients were being paid to watch other welfare recipient's children, but the system was being abused. The potential for fraud was extreme. MAXIMUS helped reduce the fraud in that program significantly.

I might add that paying a child care subsidy on behalf of someone with a job is far better than paying a welfare check to someone staying at home. In the best of all social welfare scenarios, the child care program costs will go up as the welfare program costs go down.

At any rate, provider fraud and abuse is a major problem, and government should hire the private sector to go after it and save the government real money.

Use the Private Sector to Means-Test Medicare and Social Security

According to government forecasts, both Medicare and Social Security are ultimately going bankrupt if nothing is done. There is an increasing awareness that these programs should be means-tested—that is people with higher incomes or higher net worth should pay higher premiums. If this is done, then means-testing will take a considerable amount of labor to ensure the new eligibility rules are properly administered.

The choices are as follows:

- Create an expanded, unionized federal bureaucracy in the IRS or somewhere else to conduct the means-testing of all beneficiaries,

- Delegate this responsibility to the states, as has been traditionally done with means-tested programs, or

- Contract out this responsibility to the private sector.

I believe the third choice is the far more cost-effective way to go and can be done through the states if desired. The states can be given authority to contract out the work.

So there is much room for improvement in government entitlement programs where the private sector can help. In Appendix A, I lay out a simplified scheme for reorganizing government agencies administering these social welfare entitlement programs.

President's Principles

Finally, I wish to conclude with the leadership program we initiated in MAXIMUS a couple of years before I retired. As you know by now, we had some twenty-one division and group presidents. They had to be motivated and capable of ensuring MAXIMUS remained true to its mission and its culture.

I worked with our senior staff to develop a number of leadership principles for our Executive Development Program. We designed these principles to guide these leaders so they would carry on the tradition of MAXIMUS—improving our ability to help people in need. The principles supplemented our mission statement and tenets of our corporate culture. They were designed for the future Presidents of MAXIMUS. I had them printed and embedded in an acrylic stand for each executive's desk. Below are the Ten Principles for MAXIMUS Presidents.

- **Be a Leader** – Take charge of your operation; set the example; point the way; accept accountability for results.

- **Know Your Business Model** – Understand what business you are in and the major factors influencing revenues and profits.

- **Manage Your Forecast** – Make sure your financial forecast comes true—don't just hope it does. This will help you forecast better because you know it represents a commitment.

- **Demand Performance** – You must set high standards of performance for your people—demand it. Make sure you let your non-performers go.

- **Communicate Continually** – Stay in touch with your staff and your superiors. *Management is a contact sport.*

- **Develop Your People** – Your job is to strengthen the staff in the organization and their values.

- **Provide Value to Your Clients** – Your job is to provide value to the government to justify our profit.

- **Ensure Quality** – You personally are responsible for every deliverable to the government. Make sure they are of the highest quality.

- **Fix Your Mistakes Quickly** – Admit and fix your mistakes quickly. Tell the client what is going on and what you are doing about it.

- **Be Honest** – Be honest with your staff, your clients, and yourself. If you don't know the truth, you cannot deal with reality effectively.

I was taking every opportunity to give our staff guidance on how to do their jobs. I was trying to enhance the presidents' capability to carry out our mission of "Helping Government Serve the People," then and into the future.

CHAPTER 30

A VALUED PARTNER

In closing this book, I would like to provide an excerpt from our 2002 Annual Report that shows how the private sector can be a valued partner to government. I knew we were a company the government could rely on, and this statement is the proof. Here is the excerpt.

September 11…One Story

When the hijacked planes crashed into the World Trade Center on the morning of September 11th, MAXIMUS employees were already at work in their offices only a few blocks away from the disaster site. Dan Walsky, our project manager at the New York State Department of Health's enrollment program, immediately began the critical task of trying to keep his staff calm and safe from harm. The MAXIMUS staff watched in disbelief as the sky outside their windows disappeared behind a black cloud of smoke, dust, and debris. Fortunately, everyone from MAXIMUS was safely evacuated from the area.

Dan stayed at the MAXIMUS office and spent the next day preparing to transfer the project's large and complex call center operation to a satellite office in Brooklyn. With MAXIMUS Corporate Office support, Dan and his staff were able to expeditiously move the necessary phone lines, computers, and other equipment to this site. Meanwhile, project staff continued to provide integral program services from home, using their laptops to access MAXIMUS systems.

Determined to do their part in restoring a sense of normalcy in New York City, MAXIMUS employees navigated multiple transportation disruptions, and in some cases, walked for miles in order to report back to work.

Within 48 hours after the disaster, the project was once again moving full-steam ahead. By September 13, MAXIMUS had relocated its entire New York State Medicaid Enrollment team to the new site, and astonishingly, continued to provide the same high-performance, high-quality service delivery as they had before September 11. MAXIMUS is a company that government can truly rely on—even in the worst of times.

MAXIMUS – "Helping Government Serve the People."

I had accomplished much of what I set out to do. My hope is that what I learned along the way can be used by others to make sure people in need are well served.

So that's the story of MAXIMUS and me. Being a Privateer wasn't so bad after all.

Appendix A

GOVERNMENT OF THE FUTURE

In this appendix, I summarize information for government administrators on how to improve their programs.

New Organizational Structure

There are many organizational components common to state and local government agencies administering social welfare entitlement programs. In the future, I believe these government agencies could be organized as follows.

> **Program Administrators** – These staff would be responsible for the administration of the agency, just as they are now. The Secretary of the Agency, Public Relations, Legislative Liaison, Human Relations, Accounting, and Systems staff (which could be privatized) are needed.

> **Department Program Managers/Policy Makers** – These staff would be responsible for setting the standards for the various programs and developing and evaluating policies governing the programs. As well, they would interpret

federal or state policy and implement it as agency policy. They would help set the requirements for the work to be done by the private sector. Setting agency policy should not be privatized because it can be discretionary.

Contract Officers – These agency staff would be responsible for constructing the contracts, managing the competitive procurement process, and approving contract payments. They would work with the administrator and policy makers to determine the scope of work required from the private companies.

Contract Monitors – These staff would be the quality control personnel who assist the Contracting Officers to make sure the contractor is performing properly. They can also evaluate contractor bids to select the companies they will be working with.

Contractors – These are the qualified firms that would be working for the agency. Each agency should have a stable of contractors to perform the ministerial duties required in the agency programs. High performance goals should be enforced, with penalties for failing to meet those goals. Contractors who don't perform should be replaced.

There may be other government workers required in the agency based on the specific agency mission. Any discretionary functions need to be performed by government employees—all ministerial duties, to the extent possible, should be privatized.

An agency organized as described above will be far more efficient than the traditional organization. Government has to change, and the organization above is what the change should look like.

Good Privatization Contracts

Assuming the agency wants to hire private companies to perform ministerial duties, how can that desire translate into well-structured contracts? Here are the elements of a good contract for both the government and the private sector.

>   **Definable Risk** – One of the jobs of government is to take on risks that cannot be well defined, risks the private sector cannot assume at reasonable costs. For example, no private contractor can assume the risks of paying benefits when the number of beneficiaries on the rolls can significantly increase based on the state of the economy.

>   At one time, the idea of an IMO (Income Maintenance Organization) was floated, whereby the private contractor would guarantee income levels for a caseload. This was a variant of an HMO (Health Maintenance Organization), in which health care companies guarantee health services. But many of the families had either earned and unearned income, and if that income ceased, the private company could not replace it. So any contract being contemplated for privatization has to have definable risks so the prospective contractors can calculate responsible bids.

>   **Non-Discretionary or Ministerial Duties** – Contractors should not be hired when discretionary duties are involved. Eligibility determination is not a discretionary duty. Any task that can be set down as a series of policies and procedures to be followed is acceptable to contract out since it represents a ministerial duty. Yes, a worker can smile if he or she wants, or be pleasant, but that is not considered discretionary. Workers can also make

mistakes—that is not considered discretionary either. Most functions in government that do not involve policymaking or law enforcement are non-discretionary.

Competitive Procurement – Make sure companies compete for the contract. This will require them to submit new ideas on how the work can be done more efficiently at lower cost. By having competitors, the government has an alternative firm to go to in the unlikely event the selected firm fails and has to be terminated.

Government needs to maintain its options. In some states and counties, different contractors are selected to manage the social welfare program in different regions of the state or county. This is an excellent policy since the alternative firms are right there and already signed up.

Reputable Companies Only – Make sure the qualifications are spelled out clearly so only reputable and well-financed companies bid on the contract. Sometimes this is hard to determine, but the company needs the financial resources to fix problems when they occur, because they will occur. If the task is so new that there are no experienced companies, require a large performance bond so only those companies confident in their capability to do the job will bid.

The best-qualified companies will have employees who have worked in the program before and understand it from a hands-on perspective. Having former government employees on the staff is a good sign the company knows what it is doing. While cost is a significant factor in determining the winner, the cost has to be reasonable to do the job. Firms that underbid the scope of work are only creating more trouble for themselves and the government.

Clear Contract Objectives – The contract has to have clear objectives in line with agency objectives. The contractor is an extension of the government and, therefore, should have the same objectives. The objectives should be accompanied with performance standards. In the aforementioned California Healthy Families contract, MAXIMUS had 295 performance standards to meet each month. These standards were good for the agency and us. However, the performance standards have to be attainable and sustainable.

Active Monitoring of Contract – As mentioned earlier, all major privatization contracts need to be monitored. The performance standards are the basis of monitoring, but there can be other monitoring, as well. We have had teams of four to eight monitors visiting our offices regularly, looking at case records, talking to recipients, and auditing our systems. Interestingly, these agencies never monitored themselves so assiduously. That's OK. We're here to be monitored. As I have said elsewhere, the more MAXIMUS was monitored, the better we were.

Payment Based on Performance – To the extent there are desired recipient-related outcomes, the contractor should be paid on outcomes. In some contracts, placing welfare recipients into jobs was the outcome, and MAXIMUS was paid for each recipient placed. A corollary to this is to penalize performance for not meeting performance standards. There should be a schedule for how much the contractor loses by missing a performance standard. Of course, these terms need to be negotiated up front, or the government will cause itself unnecessary expense.

Follow these guidelines, and the agency will have a successful privatization contract.

APPENDIX B

MAXIMUS TIMELINE

1975	October	MAXIMUS Founded
1984		New York City Error Reduction Project
1984		Ray Ruddy Joins MAXIMUS
1987	October	Los Angeles GAIN Contract Won
1989	May	Senator Greene Hearing in Sacramento
1989	October	Massachusetts CSE Financial Reconciliation
1991	May	Arizona CSE Financial Reconciliation
1992	June	*Newsweek* Article
1992	June	Privatization of CSE in Davidson County, Tennessee
1993		Tennessee CSE Financial Reconciliation

1993		Arizona Lawsuit
1995		Nebraska Enrollment Broker Privatization
1995		Mississippi CSE Privatization
1996		Social Security Administration Drug Program
1997	January	California Health Care Options Privatization
1997	June	MAXIMUS Goes Public
1997	July	Michigan Enrollment Broker Privatization
1997	July	Texas Enrollment Broker Privatization
1997	September	Wisconsin W-2 Privatization
1998		New York City Enrollment Broker Privatization
1998	March	*Time Magazine* Article
1999	May	Fordham University Conference on Privatization
2000	January	New York City Welfare to Work Privatization
2003	April	California Healthy Families Privatization
2004	August	British Columbia Health Services Privatization

APPENDIX C

SCOPE OF MAXIMUS CONTRACTING

Most people don't have the slightest idea of what goes on in government, or for that matter, the extent government relies on private companies for help. We used to say MAXIMUS was the "shadow government."

Here is a sampling of what MAXIMUS did for the federal, state, and local governments. Recall we had contracts in all fifty states, forty-nine of the largest cities, and twenty-seven of the largest counties in the United States—some 3,000 contracts ongoing at one time. Try to imagine the scope of what all the other companies did, as well.

Before I start the overview, though, I'll mention that MAXIMUS did have several small contracts in the early years with commercial companies such as McDonald's, Master Card, Hospital Corporation of America, and Abbott Labs. The stories are very interesting, but not really representative for this book.

We also worked for some nonprofits—Blue Cross/Blue Shield Plans, Joint Commission for Accreditation of Hospitals, and Cornell Medical College, among others. Some of the companies we acquired also had commercial contracts, but we did not develop that business after we acquired the companies. The vast, vast majority of MAXIMUS work was with the government, and I tried to keep it that way, given our mission statement.

Federal Contracting

Initially, MAXIMUS accepted business anywhere we could find it. The number of contracts in social welfare programs was limited at that time, so we supplemented our work with other government work. In what follows, I describe *a few, representative contracts* we performed in the following federal agencies.

Department of Defense – Here are a few selected MAXIMUS contracts with the Department of Defense. For the Assistant Secretary of Defense for Health Affairs, we helped develop the specifications for the CHAMPUS Information System, the program that provides health care for retired military and dependents. We studied the Army Veterinary Corps, as explained earlier in the book. We also conceived of and helped develop the National Disaster Medical System (NDMS), which is an interagency agreement, linking Department of Defense, Veterans Administration, and Public Health Service hospitals, as well as private hospitals, into a single network. The NDMS is activated in times of war or national emergency when the military hospitals alone are overwhelmed. For the US Army, MAXIMUS was responsible for several years for assessing the reliability of all Army nuclear weapons systems and performed a number of other contracts for the military.

US Veterans Administration – We worked on numerous contracts with the VA, including one to develop specifications for its automated systems across all its departments. We interviewed veterans across the United States to see if they were satisfied with the services being provided. We had a $1 million task order contract by which the VA could tap us for any special studies it needed. We also developed a smart card for veterans and tested it in several cities.

Department of Agriculture – MAXIMUS worked for the Food and Nutrition Service on the Food Stamp program. We developed a program for corrective action for states whose Food Stamp error rate was too high. We also did major consulting work on the Electronics Benefit Transfer program for Food Stamps.

Health Resources and Services Administration – For many years, MAXIMUS was the preferred contractor for studies involving organ donation. We worked with many of the organizations around the country to facilitate the program.

Social Security Administration – This is an independent agency for which MAXIMUS did a considerable amount of work. We developed the Cost Effectiveness Measure System for its Disability Determination Service. We worked on its Five Year Systems Development Plan. We also operate even today the Ticket to Work program, which helps people on the disability rolls to find jobs.

Centers for Medicare and Medicaid Services – This agency is one of the largest in the Department of Health and Human Services. MAXIMUS currently operates the appeals process for all Americans denied Medicare benefits. We helped develop the Medicaid Quality Control Program. We performed many studies for the agency and managed the large state Medicaid Managed Care and SCHIP programs funded by the agency.

Administration for Children and Families – MAXIMUS performed a great many studies for this agency, to include studies of eligibility workers, training for suicide hotline workers, and others. As you know, we also helped the federal government develop the Integrated Quality Control System—a bureaucratic landmark! The Federal Office of Child Support Enforcement was within this agency, and we conducted studies on how to prioritize cases for processing to maximize child support collections, among others. We privatized many Child Support Enforcement Programs around the country.

National Institutes of Health – MAXIMUS performed a number of contracts with various institutes of the National Institutes of Health. In one early study, we established new means of estimating the number of alcoholics in the United States. We also installed computer systems in the institute that works on AIDS research.

USAID – For the US Agency for International Development, MAXIMUS had a large contract to develop and install a comprehensive hospital and clinic information system for 30 million people in Egypt. We developed the system in Arabic and installed it in eighteen hospitals and two hundred clinics throughout the country.

State Contracting

All fifty states contract out for help. The amount of contracting is extensive. MAXIMUS specialized in contracting with different state governments. We worked in every state, so I will not list them and what we did for them.

Every state's procurement processes was different. We had to learn how each state did business, what its standard contracts were like, and how sophisticated it was in the procurement process.

General Consulting – MAXIMUS was expert in helping states reduce their error rates in their social welfare programs. This was important because the federal government threatened to penalize the states financially if the error rate was too high. We also helped with all manner of studies for states, counties, and cities, from finding qualified candidates to fill key positions in government to evaluating various programs.

Advanced Planning Documents – If a state wanted federal money to help build its massive automated systems for welfare, Medicaid, child welfare, child support enforcement, and the like, it needed approval from the federal government. The Advanced Planning Document (APD) was the plan the responsible federal agency would review to see if the system complied with federal requirements. MAXIMUS was an expert in this area and wrote the APDs for more than half the states. We could do this because we understood the programs better than other companies did.

Revenue Maximization – This business found federal money for states they did not know they were entitled to. We worked in Pennsylvania, Tennessee, Florida, Connecticut, Nebraska, Maine, Illinois, and many other states to find them money. This business was very profitable since we worked on a contingency basis.

Systems Development – MAXIMUS also developed a number of state-wide systems for states. We developed child care systems for Maryland and Georgia. We developed initial child support systems in Tennessee. We developed Medicaid Managed Care systems in Utah, California, Michigan, Texas, New York, and many others.

Privatization Services – States also privatized many of their functions. We privatized child support enforcement, welfare-to-work, Medicaid Managed Care, child care financial management, and other programs. These are discussed more extensively in the book proper since this area represented the explosive growth of MAXIMUS. We also won a four-year contract in 1999 called Arizona Works to administer the TANF program while the Arizona Department of Economic Security managed Food Stamps and Medicaid. This was one of the early projects after PRWORA.

County/City Contracting

Counties and Cities also contract out extensively. California is a county-administered state. That means many of the programs are contracted out county by county. Los Angeles County contracted out our first major privatization contract. The Medicaid program was administered at the state level, and we won state contracts to administer that program. When we acquired companies, they tended to do local government work. We sought these companies out to complement our state government work. Here is a small sample of the other contracts MAXIMUS had at the local level.

General Consulting – As an example, we had a major project to work with New York City to reduce its welfare error rate from around 8 percent to under 4 percent. We helped the Human Resources Administration implement an eighty-person quality control unit and provided an automated system for the quality control reviewers to record their findings. We also provided renewed policies and procedures for the welfare workers to minimize the chance of errors. New York City then had the lowest error rate of any of the remaining fifty-seven counties in New York State.

Cost Allocation – We had contracts in over two thousand counties to provide various services. One of the more popular was cost-allocation services so governments could conduct their accounting properly. This contract was similar to revenue maximization, but it focused more on accounting practices.

Fleet Management Software – MAXIMUS was the foremost fleet management software company in the world. Our software managed police department, fire department, and sanitation department fleets for all the major cities, as well as several mass-transit systems in the United States. The software is also in use by the Royal Mail in England.

Court Systems – We had court systems that were installed in over 150 courts around the United States. We won the contract to automate all the courts in Massachusetts during my tenure. We automated civil and criminal courts, traffic and family courts, bankruptcy courts and others.

Schools Systems – We developed a student information system for grades K–12 called SchoolMAX. This system was installed throughout the country, including the Unified Los Angeles County Public Schools.

ERP Systems – These systems are fully automated human resource and accounting systems. We implement the PeopleSoft version of the Enterprise Resource Planning systems. The software was later bought out by Oracle. We installed major systems in Oklahoma, North Dakota, the BART system in San Francisco, and other places.

MAXIMUS had a full range of consulting, privatization, and systems services for government. Check out maximus.com for the latest.

APPENDIX D

MAXIMUS PEOPLE WHO HELPED ME

I want to stress very strongly I had immense help in the growth of MAXIMUS. Many others played an integral and significant part in this story. The persons who have survived in my memory over the years are listed below. They are listed in the time period I recall they joined MAXIMUS. Those who contributed the most know who they are, so I will not try to identify them—an impossible task to be sure.

Almost everyone was a friend. Thanks to them all.

Early Years

Stephen Stollmack, Peter Mathews, Evelyn Schoppet, Nan Conver, Donna Muldoon Schirf, Alice Meana, Bob White, Bob Muzzio, Colleen Bryan, Shelley Mastran, Dean Conley, Kellei Lamborne, Margaret Jones, Howard Miller

Early 1980s

Bill Benton, Pam Tomlinson, Joan Miller, Pete Thacker, Elyse Kaye, Richard Keiser, Mike Mahoney, Charlie McKay, Linda Look, Pat Mellen, Phyllis Elliott, Irene Bocella, Janet Boodro, Pauline Charpentier, Leslie Graham, Heather

Nelson, Neil Ritchie, Betsy Small, Mark Spahn, Sid Nethery, Carole Nethery, Nina Perkins, Laura Pluto, John Hobden, Fred Gustafson

Mid- to Late 1980s

Ray Ruddy, Dora Alvez, John Lau, Gene DeLucia, Jack Svahn, Jim Wingman, Patty Perry, Linda Deimeke, Regina Fatiani, Ellen Grayson Barnes, Christine Lindley, Russ Meekins, Christie Oakley, Bob Fallon, Debbie Chassman, Akbar Piloti, Cheryl Fury, Gil Fernandez, Carol Roberto, Catherine Tracey, Bob Sarno, Abe Thomas, Liza Albright, Holly Payne, Walter Huelsman, Phil Richardson, John Proctor, John Hager

Early 1990s

Alan Richey, Ed Hilz, Lynn Davenport, Mike Truby, Jim Valliere, Bill Dineen, Al Wong, Dave Hogan, Bob Johnson, Jeannie Wilson, Bob Wright, Joyce Barnes, Sue Pepin, Larry Townsend Melissa Pappas, Jennifer Lockwood, Kevin Dorney, Art Nerret, Ilene Baylinson, Martha Tolson, Janice Lane, Joe Perry

Mid- to Late 1990s

John Boyer, Rachael Rowland, Tom McGraw, Mary Satterfield, Katie Conrad, David Francis, Jan Ruff, Bob Britton, Dave Heaney, Dwayne Brown, Tom Grissen, Barry Hammersley, Dennis Hoffman, Michael Sullivan, John Anzivino, Russ Beliveau, Viann Hardy, Paul Mack, Drew Hoffman, Gary Gumbert, Kari Dingman, Mark Erard, Gary DeLuca, Lisa Miles, Susan Norris, Glen Truglio, David Richardson, Dick Lacombe, Bob Melia, Dick Bradley, Stephanie Crawford, Suzanne Biskin, Alyce Bodoff, Al Wong, Tom Curran, Laurie Oliveri, Judye Yellon, Carrie Lorenger, Dave Casey, Nick Figurelli, Susan McCann, Susan LaFever, Jerry Stepaniak, Margaret Martins, Kathryn Lowell

Early 2000s

Jim Paulits, Dave Crawford, George Casey, Charles Gray, Rich Montoni, Gary Glickman, Gene Costa, David Nichols, Tatia Wagner, Margaret Carrera, Michael Hobday, David Walker, Kathleen McWilliams, Buzz Randall, Mike Humm, Todd House, Phil Geiger, Tom Stack, Randy Riefel, Tom Barr, Randy Fritz, Kit Letchworth, Dan Walsky, Tom Carrato, Brian Pollick, Susan Lerner, Mark Epstein, Lou Chappui, Mark Erad, Chris Zitzow, Pete Digre, Don Brown

Host of Others in Support Roles

Joe Mastran, Dawn Moffett, Keven Kvasnicka, Patti Stinson, Susan Boren, Yvette McMannis, Calvin Johnson, Diane Parcel, Rodney Wilkins, Kweko Biney, Rose Leon, Bob Burkhart, Constance Knight, Rhea Tatlinger, John Tatlinger, Joyce Keller, George Halfpap, Robin Bielier, Dan Barrett, Jan Mastran, Joan Stodgel, Nicole Stodgel, Marlow Barkley, Cheri McCormick, Margaret Snyder, Dawn Boots, Marlowe Barkley, Antonette Fraizer, Jeff Rowles, Julie McCormick, Mary Barrett, Valerie Simpson, Gwen Apperson, Yuchin Song, Antoinette Frasier, Peter Baylinson, Evan Baylinson

Outside Board of Directors

Jim Thompson, Jesse Brown, Peter Pond, Marilyn Seymann, John Haley, Wellington Webb, Paul Lederer

Best Clients

John Martinelli, Eddy Tanaka, Bill Delehy, Alan Friedberg, California Healthy Families Project Officer, Greg Phillips, Lou Iannuzelli, Stan Frerking, Joe Murphy, Dorothy Lakritz

Made in the USA
Charleston, SC
30 November 2012